Slavery in the North

Slavery in the North

Forgetting History and Recovering Memory

Marc Howard Ross

PENN

UNIVERSITY OF PENNSYLVANIA PRESS

PHILADELPHIA

Published by
University of Pennsylvania Press
Philadelphia, Pennsylvania 19104-4112
www.upenn.edu/pennpress

Printed in the United States of America
on acid-free paper

10 9 8 7 6 5 4 3 2 1

Library of Congress Cataloging-in-Publication Data

Names: Ross, Marc Howard, author.
Title: Slavery in the North : forgetting history and recovering memory / Marc
    Howard Ross.
Description: 1st edition. | Philadelphia : University of Pennsylvania Press,
    [2018] | Includes bibliographical references and index.
Identifiers: LCCN 2018016677 | ISBN 978–0-8122–5038–1 (hardcover : alk. paper)
Subjects: LCSH: Slavery—Northeastern States—History. | Slavery—Northeastern
    States—Historiography. | Collective memory—United States. | Public
    history—United States. | Historic sites—Political aspects—Northeastern States.
Classification: LCC E441. R797 2018 | DDC 306.3/620974—dc23
LC record available at https://lccn.loc.gov/2018016677

For our wonderful grandchildren
Katherine, Thomas, Natalie, Noah, Wyatt, Max, and Leo
who all care deeply about social justice

Whites stand on history's mountain and Blacks stand in history's hollow. Until we overcome unequal history, we cannot overcome unequal opportunity.
—Lyndon Baines Johnson, Austin, Texas, December 1972

Contents

Illustrations

Preface

Although the focus of this book—enslavement in the North—is a new subject for me, the ways that I have approached it grew out of my own previous work. Much of my research and writing has focused on intense, difficult-to-resolve ethnic and racial conflicts, especially in situations of what I call cultural contestation. In these conflicts, questions of identity and identity denial are central, while the material interests at stake are often far less significant. Winning or losing in these conflicts revolves around group recognition, acknowledgment, and inclusion or exclusion. Examples of these conflicts are minority language disputes such as those in Spain and Canada and contention over the meaning and use of the Confederate battle flag in the United States. In these conflicts, the goal is not so much material gain as it is symbolic recognition of group worth and inclusion in a society's narratives, ritual expressions, and enactments, and its public and commemorative landscape.

An intense conflict of this sort, in fact, occurred only a few miles from my home. On the mall in Independence National Historical Park in Philadelphia there was controversy over how to mark and recount the story of the house in which George Washington lived between 1790 and 1797 while he was president and to which he brought nine enslaved Africans. When this story first became public in 2002, there was extensive local news coverage, and African American groups and professional historians mobilized to demand that the full story be told. But the devil is in the details, and differences developed over what the story was, how it should be told, and what it meant for the city and for the park created in the early Cold War years to celebrate freedom and liberty, not to deal with the country's sordid and complicated experience of slavery. How could competing goals be met?

I followed the story keenly for several years, and in 2010 I interviewed Michael Coard, the founder and leader of Avenging the Ancestors Coalition

(ATAC), the most important civic group that mobilized to demand a meaningful memorial on the site. Upon learning that I was doing research for a book, he suggested that I attend ATAC's monthly meetings to learn about their efforts. I took him up on his offer, and for the past seven years I have gone to about half of ATAC's monthly meetings and a higher proportion of their rallies and special events. At first, I went as an observer wanting to learn more about their work and what was happening at the President's House/Slavery Memorial site after it officially opened in December 2010. As I continued to attend ATAC meetings and events, I felt more like a participant and supporter.

Their monthly meetings at Zion Baptist Church in North Philadelphia generally draw between thirty and seventy-five people. New members are at every meeting I have attended, and some people attend and speak more regularly than others. There is always a formal agenda, and speakers need to sign up ahead of time. The group is older, rather than younger, and men and women attend in more or less equal numbers. Their orientation is militant, Afrocentric, and nonviolent. I often wear ATAC buttons at meetings and on some occasions I have described myself to others as an ATAC member because I identified with ATAC's main goals and respected what they are trying to accomplish. Initially, I was concerned about how a white person who attended their meetings regularly would be viewed. What I discovered was that while some people were initially curious about why I was there, all were friendly and welcoming and seemed to view my regular presence as support.

I must thank the group for helping me learn about and understand not only their views but also the deep emotions about the past and current situation in the city and country. Attending ATAC meetings and events gave me a much richer understanding of these deep emotions that some African Americans feel regarding the lack of widespread recognition and acknowledgment of enslavement in the North and its connection to present-day lack of opportunity and bias at work and by police. I also learned the importance of the ancestors and the need to honor them in appropriate ways, such as in the libation ceremonies that open all their meetings and ceremonies. The ancestors are not references to people who are from people's immediate families, but rather a collective reference to the many enslaved people of African origin brought to North America since 1619 and their descendants. There are many allusions to the suffering they underwent, their struggles to survive, and the various forms of resistance to enslavement they demonstrated. What I often heard was anger that few people with power in society take their concerns seriously and that they continue to suffer the indignities of second-class citizenship. At the same time, they are committed to using all the tools available to them—the courts, elections, public protests, the media, and economic actions—to publicize their demands and to make it hard for those in authority to ignore them.

As my project developed into an interest in the North more generally, I traveled to a number of sites of slavery in the region and read about others in books and articles that I discuss in various places in this book. Rhode Island is particularly interesting because of the way the small state is now explaining its role in the purchase and sale of enslaved people and the importance of the profits from the slave trade for development in Providence, Bristol, Newport, and other towns. Another Northern site that now effectively recounts its slave past dating back to the middle of the seventeenth century is the small city of Portsmouth, New Hampshire, which in 2015 inaugurated a memorial marking an African Burying Ground, part of which was hidden for years under an old city street. I also went to the former Confederate South—to Virginia, North Carolina, and South Carolina—to visit former plantations that once had large enslaved populations to learn how they recount their past today, what they tell visitors about the lives of the enslaved people who lived and toiled there, and how the narratives are similar to and different from those told in the North.

The process of putting the pieces together and connecting them was slow and challenging. This almost ten-year exploration took me to diverse places and meetings with many people who helped me refine my questions and answers. I read widely since there was so much that I never knew about slavery, collective memory, or forgetting. I visited many sites connected to slavery, attended public meetings and conferences, and I interviewed most of the main actors engaged in the decisions about the project at the President's House/ Slavery Memorial site in Independence National Historical Park. I mention all this because readers of a book may presume that the author knew where the research was leading right from the start. That's not how it works much of the time, however, and I have found that the detours along the way often add insight to the eventual outcome.

This examination of collective forgetting and memory recovery draws on my experience as a political psychologist focused on the role of culture in framing political conflicts and their management. I am not a historian by training and I did little original historical research as such. I have relied on the work of others for their careful and insightful study of what many people have previously viewed as an insignificant topic. My hope is that this work will add to the growing awareness and understanding of slavery's role in American history in the North as well as the South and to more fully understand its legacy for the present and future.

Throughout this book I generally use the terms *enslavement, enslaved*, or *enslaver* rather than *slavery, slave*, or *master*. Calling someone enslaved or writing about enslavement makes it clear that an enslaver is involved and locates agency in the process by which one person chooses to enslave another. The word *slavery* is used in the book's title as a more familiar term to readers than *enslavement*.

Introduction

For some time, I have been interested in how societies recount stories about themselves, their past, and who they are today. When I go somewhere for the first time—either within or outside the United States—I like to take a public tour or visit a national museum to try to learn the new place's self-reported narratives. Such accounts are not necessarily correct, but they often reveal what people in a particular place want visitors—as well as locals—to think about them. What matters about their histories? Who are the local heroes? What events are important? Who is included and excluded from these accounts?

My interest in collective remembering and forgetting led me to wonder, more specifically, about two questions that are central to this book: Why and how was the collective memory of almost 250 years of enslavement in the North forgotten so widely and for so long? And why and how has public awareness and a collective memory of Northern slavery been partially recovered in recent decades?

It is not that slavery wasn't practiced in the North, as these chapters will elaborate in greater detail. Slavery in the lands that became the United States is as old as the settlement of the colonies, and enslaved people existed in all of these colonies—North and South—starting with twenty Africans sold, bartered, or exchanged in Virginia in 1619.[1] The introduction of slavery is usually explained by the abundance of available land, the shortage of labor to work it, and the absence of moral objections to slavery as a practice. Slavery in the British colonies and later in the states of the northeastern region of the United States was far more widespread and pervasive than is commonly believed.

For most of a decade, I visited sites of slavery in the northeast and mid-Atlantic, read about them and many others, and wondered why I knew so little of this history of the place where I have lived my entire life. As if to encapsulate this story, when I had almost completed this book, I learned that some of the campus of Bryn Mawr College, where I taught political science from 1968 until 2014, was once part of the northernmost tobacco plantation in the eighteenth century, with twenty to twenty-five enslaved workers. In 1719 Richard Harrison, a Quaker and tobacco farmer in Maryland, acquired 695 acres that he named Harriton Plantation, in what is now Lower Merion Township, just outside Philadelphia. He and his son, also named Richard, raised tobacco there until the son's death in 1759. There were burials on Harriton Plantation, including at least two on the family's burying ground, thought to belong to enslaved people who worked in the house, and others in a separate burying ground nearby where enslaved field hands were buried. The house and land then passed to Harrison's daughter Hannah, and to her daughter Hannah, who married Charles Thomson who later became secretary of the Continental Congress.[2] Slavery probably ended there with their marriage, since Charles was a staunch abolitionist (Pusey 2015).

Bryn Mawr College opened in 1885, and the land that was once part of the Harriton Plantation was bequeathed to the college in the mid-twentieth century. Until the recent "Black at Bryn Mawr" project that started in 2014, I had never heard about any link between the college and slavery. "Black at Bryn Mawr" was a student project that documented the experience and treatment of Black people at the college.[3] The website the students built included a discussion of past practices at the school, including the racist beliefs of M. Carey Thomas, the college's president from 1894 to 1922, whose views have been increasingly acknowledged in recent decades (Horowitz 1994). Jessie Redman Fauset was the only African American undergraduate at Bryn Mawr during her long presidency, and soon after she entered in 1904, Thomas raised funds so this student could quickly transfer to Cornell. Enid Cook, who attended the school from 1927 to 1931, was its first African American graduate, and the decision to admit her was slow and controversial. During her years at Bryn Mawr she was not permitted to live in the residence halls, and there was no effort by the college to recruit other Black students, due to fear of a backlash from students and a loss of financial support. "Black at Bryn Mawr" also investigated the college's labor policies and working conditions for its all-Black staff of "maids and porters," many of whom were housed in small, cramped attic garrets in the college's dorms. The "Black at Bryn Mawr" project includes walking tours and workshops that highlight key discoveries from the students' archival research, in the hopes that it will help spread awareness of the college's forgotten history.

My interest in how Northerners collectively managed to forget about slavery outside the South originated, however, out of an emotionally intense conflict that began in Philadelphia in 2002, when the knowledge came to light that George Washington had brought eight (later discovered to be nine) enslaved Africans to his house from 1790 to 1797, when he was president and Philadelphia was the country's capital. The President's House, 1znwhich was torn down in 1832, stood only one block from Independence Hall and also served as the country's first executive office building. Its rear structures, where some of the enslaved worked and slept, were identified as the Slave Quarters. They abut the present entrance to the Liberty Bell Center, through which people pass to see the Liberty Bell. As Michael Coard, the leader of Avenging the Ancestors Coalition (ATAC) in Philadelphia, has said, "To get into the heaven of liberty, you literally have to cross the hell of slavery."

The story of Washington's enslaved workers in Philadelphia first broke with a detailed article in a small Pennsylvania history journal (Lawler 2002b), a radio interview with historian Gary Nash, and a front-page article in the Sunday *Philadelphia Inquirer*. For the next eight years, controversy raged over how to recognize or commemorate the story of slavery at this site (Chapters 4 and 5). As I watched it unfold and move toward a settlement (if not a resolution), I interviewed a large number of the participants and puzzled about why the story of slavery in Philadelphia, in particular, and in the North, more generally, was so unfamiliar to me and others who had grown up in Philadelphia, New York, Boston, and other cities and towns in the region.

My investigation soon expanded to consider how some of that forgotten history has been partially recovered in the past twenty-five years. It became a story about public history more broadly. People are now learning more about sites of enslavement in the region, the North's domination of the slave trade, and how its own white citizens profited from the economic, political, and social advantages that slavery and racial hierarchy have conferred on them, even long after legal slavery had ended. Slavery was not just a Southern problem, as Northerners, who have benefited from white privilege for generations, had been repeating for generations.

As a partial corrective, in this project I do not emphasize racial subjugation and prejudice in the South. Instead, I focus on where I have lived my entire life—the North—and ask why the history of enslavement seems to be a deep, dark secret and a taboo subject for inclusion in history and collective memory. Was I just absent from public school in New York City on the day this was taught? Why did I learn only recently that my elementary school, P.S. 26, was named after Rufus King, a New Yorker who signed the Declaration of Independence and was both a slaveholder and a member of the New York Manumission Society (Hodges 1999: 166–67)? Why and how did Northerners manage to "erase" almost all collective memories of something that persisted for almost 250 years and involved tens of thousands of people? Why are relatively recent rediscoveries of sites of enslavement in the North so surprising to many, including myself? How did the story of thousands of people "disappear" from public awareness? Why did the common narrative that slavery, racial segregation, and oppression were only Southern problems achieve its hegemonic status in the mid- to late twentieth century?

If the story of Northern slavery was, and is, largely unknown, it is not unknowable. There were enslaved people in all parts of New England where, except for Rhode Island, they constituted a relatively small percentage of the population. I discuss the nature of Northern enslavement in greater detail in Chapter 2. For now, it is important to note that agriculture in New England was not always easy or highly productive, which meant that shipping and trading became critical economic activities for the region's growth and development (Warren 2016). At that time, trade and commerce were much more readily conducted on water than land. Ships moved throughout the Atlantic world relatively easily in comparison with overland travel. As a result, merchants in the British colonies in the North bought and sold goods and people with Africa, Europe, the Southern colonies, and the Caribbean islands. New England was as fully implicated in the story of slavery in the North as the mid-Atlantic region but not quite in the same ways. Bailyn (2000: 254–55) argues:

It was slavery, nevertheless, that made the commercial economy of eighteenth-century New England possible and that drove it forward. As Barbara Solow and others have shown, the dynamic element in the region's economy was the profits from the Atlantic trade, and they rested almost entirely, directly or indirectly, on the flow of New England products to the slave plantations and the sugar and tobacco industries that they serviced. The export of fish, timber, agricultural products, and cattle and horses on which the New England merchants' profits mainly depended reached markets in the West Indies and secondarily in the plantation world of the mainland South. Without the sugar and tobacco industries, based on slave labor, and without the growth of the slave trade, there would not have been markets anywhere nearly sufficient to create the returns that made possible the purchase of European goods, the extended credit, and the leisured life that New Englanders enjoyed. Slavery was the ultimate source of the commercial economy of eighteenth-century New England. Only a few of New England's merchants actually engaged in the slave trade, but all of them profited by it, lived off it.

New Englanders were the colonial leaders in the slave trade as shipbuilders, shippers, and merchants who bought and sold enslaved Africans. During the eighteenth century, when the famous "triangle trade" flourished, they sent thousands of ships to Africa where they purchased local captives who were then transported across the Atlantic and sold in the Caribbean or Southern colonies and states. The ships returned home with a few captives, timber, molasses, and sugarcane to produce more rum to trade in Africa for slaves. The wealth from this trade financed the rise of many of the members of the country's early economic and social elite: its prestigious universities including Harvard, Yale, Brown, Princeton, and Columbia; and, soon after, the region's early factories that used slave-grown cotton to produce relatively inexpensive clothing for the enslaved workers and the tools they used on Southern plantations.

New Englanders' professions over the years that American slavery was a "Southern problem" were hardly accurate. They too profited greatly from it and across many generations. While nothing in New England—or any other parts of the North—looks like any tropes of slavery in films such as *Gone with the Wind*, today there are certainly places to see and hear accounts of enslavement dating back to the early decades of the seventeenth century.

Indeed, only recently has the reality of Northern slavery received any significant public recognition, despite its duration of nearly two and a half centuries and the tens of thousands of people involved. *New York Times* columnist Brent Staples questions why "Americans typically grow up believing that slavery was confined to the cotton fields of the South and that the North was always made up of free states." In New York, he notes, "the myth of the free North has been surprisingly durable. The truth is that New York was at one time a center of the slave trade. . . . By conveniently 'forgetting' slavery, Northerners have historically absolved themselves of complicity while heaping blame onto the shoulders of the plantation South" (Staples 2005).

Similarly, historian and journalist Douglas Harper (2003) recounts that in about 2000 he began researching Northern slavery during the course of his general Civil War research and noticed a dearth of online information about it: "At the time [in 2000], I kept running into people, most of them born and raised in 'free' states, who had no idea there ever were slaves in the North. And search engines on the Internet turned up nothing to indicate that blacks had been held in bondage in all thirteen of the original states. A Google search of, say, 'Northern slavery' or 'slavery in the North' would send you to pages about slavery in North Carolina in the 1850s, or northern Sudan today, or Northern attitudes about Southern slavery."[4] Within a few years, Harper built a website that offers useful, specific information about slavery in each of the Northern colonies, and the Northwest Territories that later formed Ohio, Illinois, Indiana, and Wisconsin, as well as diverse short essays on a variety of issues associated with Northern slavery. In his introduction, Harper (2003) writes:

> African slavery is so much the outstanding feature of the South, in the unthinking view of it that people often forget there had been slaves in all the old colonies. Slaves were auctioned openly in the Market House of Philadelphia; in the shadow of Congregational churches in Rhode Island; in Boston taverns and warehouses; and weekly, sometimes daily, in Merchant's Coffee House of New York. Such Northern heroes of the American Revolution as John Hancock

and Benjamin Franklin bought, sold, and owned black people. William Henry Seward, Lincoln's anti-slavery Secretary of State during the Civil War, born in 1801, grew up in Orange County, New York, in a slave-owning family and amid neighbors who owned slaves if they could afford them. The family of Abraham Lincoln himself, when it lived in Pennsylvania in colonial times, owned slaves. When the minutemen marched off to face the redcoats at Lexington in 1775, the wives, boys and old men they left behind in Framingham took up axes, clubs, and pitchforks and barred themselves in their homes because of a widespread, and widely credited, rumor that the local slaves planned to rise up and massacre the white inhabitants while the militia was away.[5]

Most historians writing about slavery in the North offer similar observations. In the preface to her book *For Adam's Sake*, Allegra di Bonaventura wrote that " 'forgetting' had been purposeful. New Englanders in the nineteenth century had studiously erased and omitted inconvenient and unsavory aspects of the region's collective past in favor of a more heroic and wholesome narrative of their own history" (2013: xv). And Adams and Pleck point out: "The news that slavery had been a vital part of New England life and economy began to reach the public in various formats. Special issues of journals, conferences, exhibits, and teacher workshops were devoted to exploring the role New England played in the slave trade and the region's *cultural amnesia* about the history of slavery, an amnesia which dates to the nineteenth century" (2010: 25; italics added).

At one level, however, slavery in the North was never really forgotten, at least not for a number of professional and lay historians who for decades variously researched and wrote about it, or for those families that quietly passed on stories of their own ancestors' slave-owning past. Town histories written in New England at the turn of the twentieth century told about enslaved and free Blacks who once had lived in them (e.g., Sheldon 1893, 1895, 1896; Earle 1898, 1900; Smith 1905, 1906).

While there are many fewer books and articles since the mid-twentieth century on slavery in the North than on Southern slavery, they do exist, although for a time most historians treated them as not very significant. Since the 1990s, as I describe later, there has been far more research and writing on this topic and some increased interest from the public more generally. Nonetheless, this topic suffers from widespread collective forgetting.

Collective memory has been the subject of a great deal of study in recent years, while the topic of collective forgetting has received far less attention. Yet both matter, and when we ask what is remembered, we are implicitly suggesting that there are also many events and people that are forgotten. This inquiry puts forgetting at the center of the study. Central to the argument, first introduced in Chapter 1, is that collective remembering and forgetting are different in important ways from the same processes on the individual level, primarily because individual and collective memories are stored in very different ways. I want to consider how and why forgetting took place in the case of Northern slavery rather than just asserting that it did. Chapter 2 addresses this directly, offering six ways to understand the disappearance of collective memories of Northern slavery. Just as significant as the dynamics of collective forgetting is how memories, once forgotten, are recovered, retained, and transmitted.

Before turning to that project, however, it is worth considering common but unpersuasive answers to the question, how did we collectively forget about Northern enslavement? Some suggest that Northern slavery took place so long ago that it is not relevant to whites or Blacks alive today. This is an explanation that I mention not because I think it has merit but because it is often raised. In part this is a variation on the "let's not dwell on the past" argument, which often is combined with the statement from many whites that they are descendants of people who first came to the country after slavery had ended so its existence has little to do with them. The topic of slavery remains a complicated one in the United States and is not easily discussed in many public settings. When whites proclaim that it took place so long ago that Blacks should "get over it," conversations end and anger rises. The demand for reparations—whether material or symbolic—for the descendants of the enslaved only heightens tensions, as do comments that African Americans need to pull themselves up by their bootstraps "the way my ancestors did."

But the history of slavery and the collective forgetting of the country's treatment of African Americans still matter today. Thomas Sugrue's story of the resistance to civil rights demands in the North in the immediate post-World War II era focuses on examples of Northern collective forgetting around its own more recent long-term and systematic racial discrimination

(Sugrue 2008). He explains how massive and violent opposition to housing and school integration throughout the region after the war persisted, despite the North's self-image as a place where equal opportunities for all prevailed. Soon enough, the story of Northerners' resistance to equal rights and opportunities was forgotten. The reality is that segregation in the North has increased over the past fifty years and so has the racial segregation of Northern big city school systems, as whites have either fled to majority-white suburbs or placed their children in private or parochial schools with few African American students if they could afford to do so. Economic factors have also played a role in access to opportunities. In 2013 the net worth of the average white household in the country was over $141,900, while the average for African Americans was just $11,000. By 2016 the wealth gap between Black and white families grew by 16 percent.[6] Why has the gap between African American and white poverty increased rather than declined in recent decades?[7]

The assumption that we should let the past be forgotten, however, does usefully provoke questions about what makes distant events meaningful in the present and keeps collective memories of them alive. An important part of the answers is that the needs of the present are crucial in shaping what we remember from the past and how we use it. When past events are connected to present problems and needs, they are relevant. As Douglas (1986: 69) points out, "When we look closely at the construction of past time, we find the process has very little to do with the past at all and everything to do with the present."

Another implausible explanation for this collective forgetting is that Northern slavery was insignificant statistically and economically. This argument has been made in a number of different ways, but none is consistent with the evidence. One belief is that there were not many enslaved Africans in the North when compared with the Southern colonies and then states. While this is correct for the most part, it is not a very helpful standard when we also learn that in the 1750s, about 10 percent of Rhode Island's population was enslaved, and that New York had the largest enslaved urban population in North America until 1750, when Charleston surpassed it (Berlin and Harris 2005a: 4). Numerically, many thousands of people were enslaved in the North.

A variation is to argue that the enslaved were treated far better in the North than in the South. Some elaborate that because the typical Northern slave owner possessed only one or two enslaved Africans, they were often seen almost as family members. In comparison with the large, Deep South cotton plantations of the mid-nineteenth century, that is likely to be the case. But other factors of control and domination make this argument questionable. Fitts (1996, 1998), for example, argues that spatial proximity not only provided intimacy but also served as a mechanism of social control and also emphasized social status differences between owners and enslaved in the North that were made abundantly clear in daily interactions.

Work for the enslaved was perhaps less arduous, since the Northern economy was more varied than that of the South. Growing seasons were shorter and because a higher proportion of the enslaved lived in towns and cities, they often practiced one or more skilled trades. At the same time, in the North the many ups and downs in the annual and longer-term economic cycles led to frequent sales of enslaved people, the separation of children from their mothers, and the "renting out" of enslaved persons, sometimes for short periods and sometimes for longer ones. As a result, the social world of the enslaved was unstable and the establishment of social relationships and families often difficult, especially in rural communities with very few other Blacks. Treatment by individual owners was not always kind—some regularly beat, raped, and threatened the enslaved with sales which would divide families. Colonial newspapers carried ads for runaway slaves in almost every edition, which suggests that despite the low chances of success, many enslaved people still preferred to try to escape. Most important, the enslaved were not free to live, work, and spend their free time as they chose.

Even when Northern slavery is recognized, the most generally held popular view of it, and one that many historians propagated for years, was that Northern slavery was insignificant economically and produced no real advantage to slaveholders. More recently this claim has been widely challenged. The labor of the enslaved in the North was central, not marginal, to the region's and the country's economic development. Detailed small community studies have reinforced this view (Melish 1998; di Bonaventura 2013; Baptist 2014; O'Toole 2016).

Lorenzo Greene first challenged this argument, pointing out the wide range of jobs that the enslaved performed and their significant contributions to building the economy: "Free labor was scarce and wages were high. . . . It was primarily to furnish laborers that Negro slaves were brought into New England. They were introduced to satisfy not a specific but a general need. To meet the demands of New England's diversified economy, the slave had to be more skilled and more versatile than the average plantation Negro accustomed to the routine cultivation of a single crop. . . . The impression, nevertheless, has prevailed that because of adverse geographic and economic conditions slave labor was of little value to New England masters" (Greene [1942] 1969: 100–101). Northern slavery in the seventeenth and eighteenth centuries was not tied to large-scale production. Yet Melish states that even small numbers mattered in colonial farms and towns: "I suggest not only that slaves' household labor had economic value per se but also that their performance of it released white males to engage in new professional, artisan, and entrepreneurial activities, thus increasing productivity and easing the transition from a household-based to a market economy" (Melish 1998: 8).

Another feature of the colonial economy in the North: the large farms, or plantations,[8] in the Narragansett region of eastern Rhode Island, in Connecticut, in the Hudson River Valley, and on eastern Long Island, where food was raised for sale in the Caribbean islands to feed the enslaved working on the sugar plantations (Farrow, Lang, and Frank 2005; Griswold 2013).

Melish (1998) agrees with Greene's argument concerning the centrality of slave labor as a motor of economic development and adds that New Englanders emphasized the narrative of a "free, white New England. In fact, a virtual amnesia about slavery in New England had a history almost as old as the history of local slavery itself" (Melish 1998: xiii).[9] She argues that the story of New England as the antithesis of the slave South emerged with the Constitutional Convention and the leap from the erasure of the *experience of slavery* to the illusion of the absence of *people of color* that soon followed. The new narrative then emphasized how free white labor built the nascent industrial economy of New England. It stressed the hardworking, independent yeoman farmer whose work spurred New England's growth and prosperity. This narrative was only occasionally challenged until recently.

In towns and cities, the enslaved labored as skilled craftsmen and a few women worked in the region's earliest industries. They provided significant labor as shipbuilders, dockworkers, sailors, tanners, coopers, iron founders, house builders, and the brute labor for public works projects. On small rural farms, even one or two additional people could double or triple the workforce during the planting and harvest seasons.

Most crucial to understanding slavery in the North, however, is its central role in the slave trade and the impact of this trade on the accumulation of capital and the subsequent economic development of the region. In fact, some suggest that in economic terms, slave trading was more important than the direct contributions by the work of enslaved people (Horton and Horton 1997: 5). Eighty percent of slaving voyages leaving North America sailed from Northern ports, and the earnings from this trade built the capital that financed the region's early industries, from rum distilleries to textile mills—including those that produced the clothing enslaved people in the South wore and the tools they used on cotton and other plantations. Slavery was also central to the rise of the early social and economic elites in the colonial period, a high proportion of whom were slave traders and slave owners, especially in cities such as Boston, Providence, New York, and Philadelphia.

The huge slave trade was lucrative and provided significant wealth that financed many of the early Northern factories that first produced rum and then textiles toward the end of the eighteenth and early nineteenth centuries. McManus points out that "the slave traffic quickly became one of the cornerstones of New England's commercial prosperity. It was the linchpin of the triangular trade linking New England, Africa, and the West Indies in a bond of economic interdependence. . . . Since it was rum that held this network together, a great distilling industry sprang up in New England to keep the trade going" (1973: 9). With the invention and spread of the cotton gin after 1800, mills were able to procure increasing amounts of cotton grown almost entirely by slave labor on Southern plantations. Northern industry produced ships used in the slave trade, which boosted the region's economy. The trade produced a wide range of jobs for shipbuilders, workers in rum factories, insurance companies, and sailors, a large proportion of whom were Black. This meant that slave labor was at the heart of Northern prosperity and development even after the gradual abolition of slavery in the region. Slave traders like James DeWolf bought and sold thousands of people, and even today his wealth, and the wealth those working for him accumulated, can be seen in the mansions and wharves of Bristol, Rhode Island (Johnson 2014).

The claim that slavery in the North was perhaps forgotten because it was not very important in comparison with its practice on Southern plantations is flawed on both moral and empirical grounds. Morally, even one enslaved person is one too many. Empirically, the numerical disparities between the regions were smaller during the colonial period than after the Revolution. New York, for example, had the largest enslaved population in the North, but throughout the eighteenth century it was always between five and ten times smaller than Virginia's and never more than two-thirds of Maryland's (Berlin 1998: 369–71). However, the comparison between Northern slavery in the seventeenth and eighteenth centuries prior to the American Revolution and the South in the nineteenth century is very different. After the invention of the cotton gin in 1793, the Louisiana Purchase a decade later, and the spread of large-scale plantation agriculture within a few decades into the Deep South, slavery became far more extensive than it had been in either region during the colonial period.

Perhaps the most pervasive and straightforward explanation for why Northern slavery disappeared from the country's collective memory focuses on Northern, and especially New England, narratives about history. Beginning in the first half of the nineteenth century, many white people regularly denied its importance and sometimes even its existence. This produced self-serving narratives of the region's moral superiority in having abolished slavery. The narratives often morphed into a claim that slavery in the North was nothing like its Southern counterpart and that the treatment of enslaved people in the North was far more benevolent. The emerging narrative stressed the hardworking, independent yeoman farmer and a moral system that was the antithesis of the slave South. An important consequence is that the story of enslaved and later free Blacks in the North was essentially dropped from the region's story of its development, a form of denial.[10]

Historian Lorenzo Greene, in his detailed 1942 study of New England slavery, wrote that it was generally believed that colonial Massachusetts was hostile to slavery. He quotes William H. Sumner, a soldier-historian from Massachusetts, who wrote in 1858, "slavery was repugnant to the Puritans and was regarded by them with abhorrence," which was certainly not the case (Greene [1942] 1969: 66). Greene also cites Senator Charles Sumner's 1854 statement on the Senate floor that there was no record of any person having been born into slavery in Massachusetts and denials from nineteenth-century historian John Gorham Palfrey and Massachusetts chief justice Francis Dana that slavery was ever legal in the state, despite the 1641 law that explicitly recognized slavery as legal (63).

This explanation is inadequate in many ways, not just because it gets the facts wrong but because the causal sequence is flawed for one reason:

it never addresses why these narratives developed and were apparently so powerful in New England and other parts of the North. To be really useful, a good explanation needs to address the motivations for the narrative's creation and its widespread acceptance. I would suggest at least two motivations. One is political and stresses the sectional politics of the nineteenth century that produced strong Northern and Southern competition over political and economic interests—ironically at the same time that many Northern and Southern economic and social elites actually shared common interests and cooperated throughout the antebellum period (Bailey 1998; Baptist 2014). Mobilization of white workers and farmers increasingly emphasized and demonstrated regional differences in cultures and interests, which made it easy for politicians to support narratives of Northern virtues and Southern vices. Second, the explanation has little to say about why these new narratives were so appealing to white Northerners that they were willing to forget their earlier participation in slavery.[11] This erasure of the memory of slavery from the Northern landscape certainly came, in part, from the shame and guilt that many white Northerners felt about their past practices.

Another facile explanation for the absence of the memory of enslavement in the North is that there is very little in the written records concerning slavery in the region. Few documents describe the daily lives, thoughts, and experiences of those enslaved in the North, but this is not the case across the board, particularly when we consider what the authors of more recent books have been able to document (e.g., Gerzina 2008; Adams and Pleck 2010; Stewart 2010; di Bonaventura 2013; Cranston and Dunay 2014; Hardesty 2016; O'Toole 2016; Dunbar 2017). We know a lot more—and are able to know even more—than this simple generalization suggests. Historians and archaeologists in the past seventy-five years have used a wide range of public records and artifacts to draw conclusions about the lives of those people who were enslaved and have found far more in Northern archives, diaries, and objects than many people once believed to exist.

There are records concerning sales and purchases of the enslaved, the kinds of work they did, court cases in which they were involved, and the practice of renting out enslaved people. In some cases, their births and deaths, the names of the children, and even their health records have been found. We know about the arrival of ships transporting enslaved people for sale, where many slave sales took place, and, often, prices paid for them. In many cases the enslaved were able to purchase their own freedom or that of their loved ones. Katherine Hayes (2013), whose archaeological and archival work discovered a great deal about the Sylvester Manor plantation on eastern Long Island, wrote that she found much more in town records than she had expected about enslaved and free Blacks, even though many local town and village histories written in the nineteenth and twentieth centuries regularly omitted any reference to them. At the same site, Mac Griswold (2013) went through the Sylvester family's archives and learned a good deal about how the enslaved there lived and toiled, going back to the mid-seventeenth century. This same kind of research is now taking place in other parts of the North as well.

For all the new material uncovered in recent years, records that would lend this history the texture of individual lives remain relatively scarce. Making slavery in the North interesting and compelling can be difficult, when it is hard to present it in an emotionally engaging manner that includes details about the lives of individual enslaved people, and some specifics about how they lived and worked, let alone what they felt and thought. There is precious little physical evidence such as buildings or objects from daily life. While some letters, diaries, and public and court records, including probate documents and wills associated with enslavement, exist, only a few offer the perspective of the enslaved themselves. Yet some historians have been able to use somewhat small pieces of evidence to provide insights into the daily lives of the enslaved.

Images can offer powerful ways to connect to history, but we have almost no pictures or drawings of individuals enslaved in the North. Museums and memorials that communicate details about historical events to the public depend on such tangible objects to attract visitors and to make narratives come alive. Compelling print or media presentations ideally contain stories that are both detailed and imageable to be powerful. In contrast to the North, the South has far more visible sites of slavery, stories about specific individuals and their lives, and objects that are linked to its antebellum slave history. The houses, plantations, written records, monuments, memorials, films, and books that focus on Southern slavery make it easier to present than its Northern counterpart.

Yet in the South, for decades, details available about life under slavery were frequently ignored in favor of a nostalgic image of plantation life, even where it was not difficult to document what actually took place and materials for doing so abounded. So, clearly, the presence or absence of artifacts alone does not account for the strength of collective memory or narrative. For many years, if these places and objects were presented at all, it was often an afterthought, resembling an idyllic *Gone with the Wind* portrayal, in which the enslaved were often referred to as servants and portrayed in stereotypical roles as obedient, happy, and well cared for.

More recently, however, attention to slavery on Southern house tours is increasing. Some slave sites offer explanations of antebellum life, with attention on the enslaved rather than exclusively on plantation owners and their lifestyle, as told through the plantation house and its objects and the gardens. Yet, far less is said in these places about how the enslaved lived, and generally their housing and household objects are not displayed prominently, if at all—mainly because most housing for the enslaved was torn down long ago and no one kept their personal items. Details about the enslaved's work were known but not talked about much in historical research or in visitor tours until recently for the most part (Eichstedt and Small 2002).

While "out of sight, out of mind" is an important dynamic, and one plausible explanation for the invisibility of Northern slavery, not all places, people, and events that are no longer visible are forgotten. Think of the power of partial relics or even narratives transmitted across many generations and their power for many religious groups. Winners in wars and revolutions do their best to remove visible traces of past regimes, but when even fragments remain, they can be the focus of great emotional intensity, as is the case with the Western Wall in Jerusalem's Old City, relics of ancient Christianity that are objects of veneration in Catholic churches worldwide, and sacred pilgrimage sites for almost all religious groups.[12]

In the 150 to 175 years since Northern slavery ended, many of its sites of slavery have changed significantly, as much by neglect and development as by intentional actions to remove an embarrassing past. The combination of the forces of economic growth and modernization, on the one hand, and the dominant, generally unstated, belief that traces of Northern slavery were not important enough to preserve either in the physical record or through accounts of past events certainly contributed to largescale forgetting. In addition, if and when later generations of whites talked or wrote about slavery in the North, it typically was explained as different, more benign, and on a much smaller scale than its Southern counterpart (e.g., Smith 1906, Greene [1942] 1969). Also, because slavery in the North was not characterized by large plantations and in most cases the enslaved lived under the same roof as their owners, it was easy for many people to refer to the enslaved as servants, rather than slaves, and some authors have used the term "family slavery" to differentiate it from circumstances on Southern plantations. This practice was reinforced in many parts of the North where upon gaining manumission, many of those once enslaved continued to work for their former owners, or new ones, as indentured servants for long terms, although their lives were hardly different under this new arrangement.

Memory recovery for individuals or communities is an uneven process. In some cases, it is rapid and limited. In others, it can be complex and occur over a long time. Two distinct features of memory recovery are clear. One involves the acquisition of evidence that provides information along with an understanding of its meaning. This can be as simple as documents that had been hidden or forgotten for many decades or as complicated as scattered objects or records that need to be pieced together to be understood so they can assist memory recovery. Technology can also play a role. DNA analysis confirmed that Thomas Jefferson was the father of Sally Hemings's children—something that is now included in tour-guide presentations at Monticello.

The second feature is a shift in beliefs about what is important so that what had previously been available is no longer ignored. An obvious example is the rise in awareness of the role that women and other minorities have played in history. Where school textbooks once paid little to no attention to the stories and achievements of people who were not white males, in more recent decades there has been a significant shift in how we think about the contributions of formerly ignored or forgotten people in local and national narratives. This is the case of enslavement in recent decades in the South as well as the North. In the past twenty-five years, there has clearly been a sharp rise in the academic and popular interest in slavery in both regions (Berlin 2004).

To consider only a few examples: archaeological work, such as the excavations at George Washington's Mount Vernon plantation, has contributed significantly to our knowledge of Black life during slavery (Schwarz 2001).[13] At Mount Vernon, part of the slave quarters tour shows visitors a reconstructed slave dwelling—one of the several places on Washington's multiple plantations where the enslaved lived. In 2016, an exhibit at Mount Vernon's visitor center offered detailed information about the lives of nineteen of the enslaved people the Washingtons owned.[14]

Even more detailed and impressive are the presentations of enslaved life at Monticello, Thomas Jefferson's plantation. Thanks to archaeologists there, visitors can now tour Mulberry Row, where white artisans, free Blacks, and the enslaved all worked. In addition, the archives at Monticello contain many more details about specific enslaved individuals than those at Mount Vernon. The Monticello website provides a great deal of material that describes life on the plantation and offers profiles of a number of workers (both the enslaved and free) who toiled there. Enslavement at Monticello is a central part of the tour, and the site's research on some of its enslaved people and their descendants—including dozens alive today—makes their tours very powerful. Sites of slavery in the Charleston, South Carolina, and the New Orleans area and elsewhere now offer tours that include stories of the lives of the enslaved as well.

In recent years, Northern museums have had a hard time obtaining artifacts to display for the public, since most were made out of materials that were not easy to preserve or valued. But this has not uniformly deterred them from telling the story. The New-York Historical Society's stunning 2005 exhibit "Slavery in New York," for example, had very few local material objects from the seventeenth and eighteenth centuries other than maps, drawings, and papers (or copies of them).[15] Notable exceptions were handmade items, such as a cradle and some chairs, crafted by enslaved people who were clearly expert woodworkers. These were supplemented by illustrations and text panels that described the enslavement, arrival in the colonies, slave revolts, white codes to control the enslaved, the Revolutionary period during which the British offered freedom to slaves who left their owners, the story of those who served in the nascent American army, the protracted battle for abolition in New York, the hard life for free Blacks in the city, and the severe discrimination to which they were subjected after achieving manumission. However, such materials often have less impact on visitors than actual objects from the time period, as are now shown at the visitor center of Lower Manhattan's African Burial Ground, which is described below.

The Smithsonian National Museum of African American History and Culture (NMAAHC) that opened on the National Mall in Washington in 2016 faced the daunting challenge of finding and obtaining appropriate objects for its exhibits on slavery from both the North and the South.[16] Many articles that would be of widespread interest are already in regional museums, even next door in the National Museum of American History, which understandably does not wish to provide all its materials on the history of African Americans to the new museum. Effectively, that would segregate the two collections into white and Black locations. An article in the *New York Times* about the museum's quest for artifacts highlighted the issues.

> The slavery exhibition is, in many ways, the most difficult part of the museum to fill with objects. Very few slave possessions survive, and many major documents relating to the era are already in other museums or private collections.
>
> [Richard] Rabinowitz, the co-curator of the exhibition, said that . . . the museum's display will try to convey a vivid sense of slave culture, from religion and music to what people ate and how they entertained themselves. "We're not only interested in the Missouri Compromise, we're not only interested in Harriet Tubman's escape, we're interested in how enslaved people lived day to day," he said. As an example, he explained how a simple iron pot, of the kind a slave woman might have used to cook rice for her family, could be the starting point for a discussion about food traditions brought over from Africa, the role of women in slave families and what life was like in a slave cabin. "You can imagine the rice pot sitting and cooking for most of the day," Mr. Rabinowitz said. "You have to try to evoke the quality of coming back and, even in the summertime, after a full day of work, it may be the last bits of twilight, and just having a chance to sit around that pot and to eat that food. Who's it been prepared by? What's said around that pot? You can really create a whole story around that." (Taylor 2011)

A major reason for this collective memory recovery is the radical shift in the study of history that began in the 1960s, when the social and cultural history of ordinary people, including minorities and women, began to be seen as a significant area for study alongside great wars and political leaders. In addition, the diversification of the scholars in the field that was once totally dominated by white males brought in new voices and new problems deemed worthy of inquiry. This emergence of "bottom-up" history led to new questions, methods, and theories that encouraged the collection of a wider range of evidence and a broadening of theoretical perspectives.

One consequence of these shifts was a sharp increase in research into the nitty-gritty details of American slavery and a perspective that moved the focus away from slaveholders exclusively to one that also focused on the lives of the enslaved. It has been accompanied by a sharp increase among African Americans as well as many others in recent decades—not just scholars—who have become more broadly interested in genealogy and family history. In most cases, African Americans cannot know their specific ancestors who were brought to this country. However, through DNA testing, many have learned more about the areas in Africa from which their ancestors originated. In addition, African Americans have shown a great interest in the history of their own communities and how they developed and changed over time. Family and kinship matter a great deal to African Americans, as they do to most Americans. African Americans often expressed the importance of kinship in terms of "the ancestors," a broad social definition of kin rather than a more limited genealogical one that most whites employ. This represents a broader and more generalized connectedness in the community rooted in a strong sense of group identity and a shared past. It is also what Rosenzweig and Thelen (1998) found in their large survey project that showed that African Americans identified more with their larger community and ancestors than whites.

Memory recovery involves digging up the past either literally or metaphorically. Alderman and Campbell (2008) use the term "symbolic excavation" to describe the use of objects and/or landscapes to recount narratives of slavery that were previously untold in museums, monuments and places where it had existed (2008: 339). They point out that "artifacts and material traces can be used as a political tool to facilitate the excavation and narration of the slave experience rather than simply hindering or deflecting critical discussions of slavery . . . both to reproduce and resist the marginalization of the enslaved signals a departure of traditional cultural and historical investigations which have tended to view and treat objects and relics as mere material evidence" (Alderman and Campbell 2008: 340).

Objects and landscapes, they argue, link us to the raw emotions of enslavement, especially when the presentations oblige visitors to closely approach or touch the objects themselves, as they do in the African Burial Ground National Monument Visitor Center in Lower Manhattan, the Slave Relic Museum in Walterboro, South Carolina, that recently closed, and the Lest We Forget Museum in Philadelphia.[17] Physical evidence adds a credibility

Figure 1. Slavery Memorial, created by Rodney Leon, African Burial Ground in Lower Manhattan. View from the street side where one enters the area.

that connects people across time and space in a way that narratives alone often cannot do.

At the same time, "excavated" objects and landscapes produce new details that are the building blocks for narratives—sometimes in the form of documents but, as in the case of the African Burial Ground, sometimes through physical remains that facilitate new or expanded narratives. The rediscovery of physical sites and objects is a powerful tool in memory recovery, providing people with a place to recount narratives about the past and objects—even fragments of objects—to link the past and present in emotionally meaningful ways. In addition, rediscovered sites can become important locations for the performance of rituals and ceremonies marking the past and connecting it to people alive in the present, as Zerubavel

(1995) explains in the case of the development of Israeli collective memories when Jews returned after a 1,900-year exile. All of these meanings are found in the story of New York's African Burial Ground and in the other stories of the memory recovery of Northern slavery discussed in later chapters.

Collective memory is not simply the sum of what individuals in a community have inside their heads. It is also what society stores in its narratives, ritual expressions and enactments, and displays in its public and commemorative landscape. Without these storage mechanisms, collective memories cannot survive, and what one generation experiences as important will fade from memories over time as succeeding generations die. This understanding of collective memory as embedded in the public, commemorative landscape is central to my analysis, and it is critical to understanding what a society remembers and what it forgets.

The almost accidental rediscovery of an eighteenth-century African Burial Ground in lower Manhattan in the early 1990s illustrates many important aspects of collective memory recovery (Figure 1). Before 1991 the site, in lower Manhattan a block from City Hall, was a parking lot and it is now a National Monument, a National Park Service (NPS) site, and the home of the first slavery memorial built on federal land. The story of this site contains a great deal of emotional power for many of the city's African Americans, despite the fact that no one has uncovered the names of the individuals buried there between the late seventeenth century and 1794, and no one has come forward to identify him- or herself as a direct descendant of someone buried there (Kilgannon 2003).[18] Michael Frazier, the NPS historian at the site, told me that the only enslaved people identified in New York by name in the records were found in the British *Book of Negroes* compiled during the American Revolution when the British controlled the city. Many of these people were then taken to live in freedom in Nova Scotia (personal interview, April 2017).

The first enslaved Africans in New York, then called New Amsterdam, arrived while the city was under Dutch rule in 1626. Many were owned by the Dutch East India Company and provided much of the labor that built the city's early infrastructure and performed at least a third of the physical labor in the city during the colonial period (Davis 2006: 128). Under the Dutch the enslaved could own land. The Dutch also established a system called "Half-Slavery," in which some Africans were not owned but had to provide work for the settlement when it was needed. Most important, while they were considered free, their children were not. The Dutch allowed Blacks to attend church and to learn to read and write (Ottley and Weatherby 1967: 11); they permitted church marriages for Blacks as well (Hodges 1999: 16). The Dutch also established large farms in the Hudson River Valley, Long Island, and New Jersey that used enslaved Africans' labor to provision the city more and more over time (White 1991).[19] After 1664, when the English seized the colony, the number of enslaved Africans increased, while their rights decreased. After failed slave revolts in 1712 and 1741, those supposedly involved were treated brutally, and restrictions on Blacks in the city were further tightened (Ottley and Weatherby 1967: 23–24 and 27–28; Lepore 2005a: 78–88, 2005b).

In New York, for most of the first half of the eighteenth century, enslaved Africans constituted about 15 percent of the colony's population but 21 percent of the city's, and by 1770 they numbered just under 20,000 (Lepore 2005b). White reports that in 1790 enslavement was highest in the outlying regions of New York—Richmond (Staten Island), Queens, and Kings (Brooklyn) counties: "about four out of every ten white households living within a ten to twelve mile radius of New York City owned slaves," and almost 60 percent of the households in Kings County had enslaved people (White 1995: 2). Strikingly, these rates were higher than those of any Southern state at the time (White 1995: 4).

In New York and elsewhere in colonial North America, neither enslaved nor free Black people could be buried within many towns or cities or with whites. Generally, their remains were placed in separate burying grounds outside the city walls or boundaries, or in separate sections of public burying grounds. In recent years, some of these long-forgotten sites have become a focus of discovery and attention for African Americans who feel that restoring them is an important way to honor the ancestors even if it is not possible to know their names or specific details about their lives. Visiting these sites today, many African Americans feel a strong emotional connection to their past and to their long-deceased ancestors who were brought to North America against their will as slaves (Wright and Hughes 1996, Galland 2007). Burying grounds are often crucial places for recovering memories in the absence of other forms of evidence (Chapter 7). This was certainly the case in New York, when in the early 1990s the General Services Administration (GSA) planned to build a new office tower in lower Manhattan not far from City Hall. Before proceeding, the GSA was required to conduct an archaeological excavation of the site to determine the possible impact of the proposed construction on the natural and cultural environment. An almost two-hundred-year-old map of the area showed a "Negros Buriel Ground" on the site, and further research revealed that it was established in the 1690s and closed in 1794 (Cantwell and Wall 2001: 280).

When the archaeological excavation began, the expectation was that little of value would be found, as the area had seen so much development and redevelopment since the Burial Ground was closed 190 years earlier. The low expectations were related to the widespread belief that while "the presence of the enslaved in colonial New York and its environs has always been known . . . it did not form part of the historical consciousness of the city's modern residents" (Cantwell and Wall 2001: 278). More important, no one realized at the start that the area the city originally designated for the burial ground outside its early walls was on low swampy land in a ravine (i.e., undesirable) and that several centuries ago the entire lower Broadway area was far hillier than it is today. Before major development in the nineteenth century, however, the hills were leveled and low-lying areas filled in so that the burials turned out to be eighteen to twenty-five feet below today's ground level and had not been disturbed by almost two centuries of building and rebuilding. An estimated 15,000 to 20,000 people are buried there. Bioarchaeologist Michael Blakey explained:

> The African Burial Ground was a municipal cemetery afforded [the Africans'] use, where they buried their loved ones carefully and with generosity. As examples, our research shows that the bodies were wrapped in linen shrouds with care and methodically positioned in well-built cedar or pine coffins. Women were sometimes buried in the same coffin as their newborn children, both having died at about the same time. In another telling example, a child was found buried with a solid silver ear-bob or pendant, an object of rare economic value for these impoverished people, which apparently had greater value to them as a gesture of care for the deceased child. . . . Although late nineteenth and twentieth century urban development periodically unearthed human skeletons with little apparent concern for sanctity, the African Burial Ground had, by then, largely faded from everyone's memory. (Blakey 1998: 53–54)

The dig began in the spring of 1991 and quickly produced significant controversy (Harris 2003; Berlin and Harris 2005b). Preliminary testing showed human remains in the area, and within a few months it was clear that the scope of the find exceeded any expectations. However, the GSA was worried about cost and schedule delays and immediately initiated a large-scale excavation, without developing any treatment or mitigation plans, contrary to standard archaeological practice (Katz 2006: 40). A few months later, they publicly announced that they had found human remains on the site and promised to treat them "with the utmost care and dignity." Soon the New York City Landmarks Preservation Commission and the Advisory Council on Historic Preservation recommended that before proceeding the archaeological team needed to develop a research plan and obtain input from the descendant community in the city.

Tension increased when it became clear that the GSA was not following the Memorandum of Agreement it had signed and wanted to expedite the dig by using the "coroner's method" involving shovels instead of the more careful standard archaeological tools and methods that take more time and are less likely to destroy buried remains. In addition, the GSA began concurrent building construction. Soon afterward a backhoe operator working in the wrong place on the site destroyed the integrity of at least twenty burials (Cantwell and Wall 2001; Harrington 1993). Finally, there were protests that the forensic team had wrapped some of the remains in newspapers and cardboard boxes and that they were not stored with proper environmental controls (Katz 2006: 43). African Americans in New York City held meetings, religious observances, vigils, and protests at the cemetery's edge (Blakey 1998: 54).

Community outrage grew in the following months. The GSA began meetings in which they were providing updates, but the descendant community was still not involved in any decision making, although they had been promised that they would be. Some people began to call for a halt to the dig to stop disturbing the ancestors. In addition, they wanted a memorial and exhibit, for the site to be proclaimed a national landmark, and a dignified reburial of those remains that had been removed already (Cantwell and Wall 2001: 284). Objections were voiced as well to the primarily white team, and demands were made that African Americans take the lead in interpreting the African materials that had been uncovered. By spring, amid the deteriorating situation, hearings on the situation at City Hall and a large community meeting in nearby Trinity Church were held. Protesters demanded an end to the excavation, arguing that the ancestors should be disturbed no more, and they viewed further excavation as sacrilege. They stressed that the remains were not scientific specimens but ancestors who deserved to rest in peace. One man, quoting an old spiritual, explained, " 'Some of them bones is my mother's bones, come together to rise and shine; some of them bones is my father's bones, and some of them bones is mine,' so there is a sense of very personal connection our community has to the African Burial Ground because this is about family" (*Slavery's Buried Past* 1996). " 'It was the considered judgment of virtually every African-American I knew that they shouldn't have been disturbed in the first place,' said Howard Dodson, director the Schomburg Center for Research in Black Culture" (Luo 2003). Many African Americans felt intensely that once again their needs and concerns were being ignored (LaRoche and Blakey 1997). Large numbers of people turned out for the public meetings to express their outrage and call for an end to the dig.

In June 1992, the city's Advisory Council on Historic Preservation rejected as inadequate the research design that was finally submitted, and soon a more experienced archaeological team, John Milner Associates of Pennsylvania, was hired. The descendant community continued to hold meetings and ceremonies. New York's African American mayor David Dinkins asked the GSA to end the excavation as the descendant community had demanded, but the local GSA head insisted that they were required to continue. The Congressional Black Caucus became involved, and Chicago Congressman Gus Savage, head of the subcommittee that oversaw GSA funding, held hearings in New York at which the GSA continued to insist that it would not suspend the excavation. Savage then demanded that the GSA show some respect and abruptly halted the hearing. He added, "Don't waste your time asking this subcommittee for anything else as long as I'm chairman, unless you can figure out a way to go around me! I am not going to be part of your disrespect" (Cantwell and Wall 2001: 287). Three days later the GSA agreed to halt the dig, modified the design of a four-story pavilion so as not to disturb the remains over which they had originally planned to build, and applied to have the site named a National Historic Landmark, a status that was granted the next year.

GSA then created an advisory panel that chose Michael Blakey's team of bioarchaeologists at Howard University to conduct the analysis of the remains, which were officially transferred to Blakey and his team in a moving public libation ceremony. Blakey had apparently convinced most of the protesters that the research on those already disinterred should continue and that his team's findings would significantly aid the public's understanding of

New York's slave past. They soon began their slow research on the remains of 419 enslaved and free Africans, half of whom were children under twelve, many of whom had died of malnutrition.[20]

Emotions ran high over the site and the discoveries on and about it,[21] which many in the local descendant community easily related to, viewing it as "part of the common heritage and group identity of African Americans who came together as a distinctive group in order to preserve and respect a plot of land that they consider *their* collective, sacred ground" (Blakey 1998: 54). Mayor Dinkins (1994) wrote: "Millions of Americans celebrate Ellis Island as the symbol of their communal identity in this land. Others celebrate Plymouth Rock. Until a few years ago, African-American New Yorkers had no site to call our own. There was no place which said, we were here, we contributed, we played a significant role in New York's history right from the beginning. . . . Now we—their descendants—have the symbol of our heritage embodied in lower Manhattan's African Burial Ground. The African Burial Ground is the irrefutable testimony to the contributions and suffering of our ancestors." In the same spirit in August 1995 a royal delegation of Ghanaian Chiefs visited the Howard University laboratory where the remains were at the time and poured libations at the burial ground as an act of apology and atonement on behalf of their ancestors' participation in the Atlantic slave trade (Blakey 1998: 55).

Meanwhile, Blakey's bioarchaeology team learned a great deal about the conditions under which these enslaved people had lived and died (Blakey 2001). DNA tests of forty individuals showed that the vast majority came from West Africa and were likely Asante, Benin, Tuareg, Ibo, Yoruba, or Senegambians. The archaeological work also uncovered a number of symbolic African artifacts, the most striking of which may be Akan,[22] including the Sankofa symbol[23] created with nails on the outside of one coffin (Blakey 2001: 411).

The research revealed that for these Africans in the eighteenth century early death was common; half of the population died in childhood, and nearly 40 percent of those children died as infants—all rates that were nearly twice those of the rates found among the English colonists (Blakey 1998: 56). Children often suffered from severe malnutrition and disease, and their bodies were highly stressed with defective bones and teeth. Among the adults were many cases showing severe stress from work and a good number showing severe malnutrition. The strains of load-bearing and other physical labor stressed the musculoskeletal systems of many to the margins of human capacity and often beyond it. As Blakey (1998: 56) wrote:

> Muscle attachments become enlarged when muscles undergo frequent strain. Most of the population of men and women have enlarged muscle attachments in the neck, arms, and legs. . . . The majority of both men and women from the African Burial Ground exhibit such effects of excessive strain, most frequently involving the muscles. . . . What is more, we often see fractures of the spine, including healed fractures of the first bone of the neck, that result from traumatic loads or force to the top of the head.

Young women had particularly high mortality that Blakey related to their importation directly from Africa (unlike most men, who were first "seasoned" in the Caribbean) and conditions in New York (Blakey 2001: 411).

In an effort to explain the linkage between the emotional depth expressed over the deaths more than two hundred years earlier to individuals whose names were unknown, Blakey proposed an answer very related to one developed throughout this book:

> The vivid contrasting of a human face of slavery with its dehumanizing conditions I believe accounts for much of the strong public feeling regarding this work [Blakey 1998], as it appears in six documentary films, hundreds of news articles, and scores of radio interviews. The power of the most primary of evidence of Northern slavery, the bones of the people themselves, has overturned the mythology of the free North according to introductory textbooks. (Blakey 2001: 414)

In 2003, after the research at Howard was completed, the remains were returned to New York for reinterment. They were placed in seven crypts in mahogany coffins made in Ghana for the occasion. Four of them—those of a man, a woman, a boy, and a girl—were carried in a cortege that traveled to New York from Washington through Baltimore, Wilmington, Delaware, Philadelphia, and Newark, New Jersey, and stopped at African American churches in each for memorial services en route. When the cortege arrived in New York, a ceremony was held at the site of an earlier slave market at South and Wall Streets, followed by a tour of the city's five boroughs before

Figure 2. Steps at the Rodney Leon memorial, leading to the lower area whose walls contain African sacred symbols.

reburial at the memorial (Luo 2003). Over 10,000 people attended the moving "Rites of Ancestral Return" ceremony, including a delegation of chiefs from West Africa. The mostly African American crowd expressed both joy at the events and sadness at the memories they evoked. At several points the speaker asked, "What do we want?" and the crowd roared back, "Reparations."

Upon completion, the site included the modified GSA building, Rodney Leon's striking African Burial Ground National Monument (Figure 2), which holds the reinterred remains of people who were originally buried there, and a National Park Service Visitor Center that presents the history of early slavery in New York under both the Dutch and English, photos of the excavation, objects used by the enslavers and the enslaved, and a description of enslavement as well as early slave revolts in the city (Figure 3).

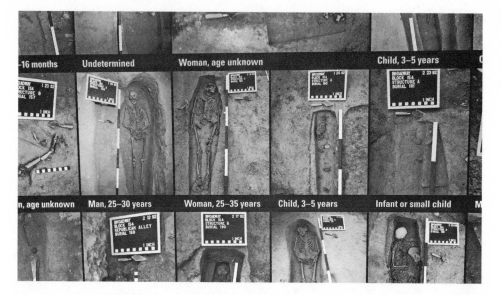

Figure 3. A panel from the African Burial Ground Visitor Center shows images of the remains of several people who were disinterred and later reinterred on the site.

A video shown in the auditorium and others viewable on small screens tell the story of slavery in early America and that of the African Burial Ground.

As a result of the publicity about the African Burial Ground, the narrative of slavery in New York became more visible than it had been in many decades, and a place that was associated with its practice provided a location where rituals to mark the city's slave past could be held. The New-York Historical Society opened its "Slavery in New York" exhibit in 2005 to great fanfare and public interest. This exhibit, along with the discoveries at the African Burial Ground, news that slave traders and owners were founders and funders of Brown, Yale, Harvard, and other major universities in the North, and revelations about the enslaved Africans in George Washington's President's House in Philadelphia, challenged the narrative of the irrelevance of Northern slavery. It encouraged people working in local communities in New England and the Middle States to explore their own local histories.

The story of New York's African Burial Ground presages and illustrates many of the themes that run throughout the following chapters and that are evident in controversies over other sites of enslaved life. These themes include long-forgotten past events, often sudden discoveries of sites or events that once were intimate parts of slavery in the North, mobilization of support for memorializing and remembering them, developing narratives about events that were associated with them, marking them in visibly distinct ways, and integrating their stories in various cultural ways. My focus is on the interplay between collective forgetting and recovering memories of enslavement in the North, especially as they involve the changing narratives, rituals, and visible displays on the public and commemorative landscape that serve as critical repositories for society's collective memories. The dynamics of popular participation and, more often than not, resistance to its demands play a crucial role as once lost stories of the past return to public awareness.

Chapter 1

Collective Memory

All history is retrospective. We're always looking at the past through the lens of later developments. How else could we see it? We see ourselves, as subjects, among those later developments.
    —Louis Menand, "The Elvic Oracle," *New Yorker*, November 16, 2015

It is tempting to think about collective memories simply as the sum of individual memories, but the two types are stored quite differently and have very different "life histories." Individual memories are idiosyncratic. They are socially rooted but are stored in individual brains through neurological processes that are still somewhat mysterious, though they have become better understood in recent years. When individuals die, their memories are lost forever unless these have been recorded or passed on to others. However, collective memories are stored entirely differently, and individuals and groups often access them for hundreds of years or more. They exist in narratives that are recounted to the young and old alike, in images created by artists, photographs, films and television shows, books, musical compositions, statues, monuments, memorials, museums, buildings, ritual events, former battlefields, and other sacred sites. In some cases, the memories stored are explicit in their messages, while others are more metaphorical and require interpretations that can, and do, shift over time. The messages found in these cultural expressions are not necessarily enduring, however, and they require active contemporary engagement, interpretation, and accessibility to remain emotionally meaningful, even when they are initially "set in stone" and intended to be eternal. Places associated with people and events both sacred and mundane are another crucial device for the preservation of collective memories (Connerton 1989; Nora 1989; Ross 2009a).

Historian Alon Confino defines collective memory as "a subjective experience of a social group that essentially sustains a relationship of power. Simply stated, it is who wants whom to remember what and why" (1997: 1393). Confino also points out that, "One of the significant contributions of memory studies has been to explore how the construction of the past, through a process of invention and appropriation, affected the relationship of power within society" (1997: 1393).[1] Collective memories are about emotionally salient events and persons in the past that have particular relevance to how a group understands itself and the challenges it faces in the present and future. These accounts are not simply trivial historical details about the past. They convey crucial social, political, and moral lessons that can be important resources in present struggles. This means that collective memories are, as Trouillot argues always incomplete (Trouillot 1995: 49–52). Blight makes a similar point when he says, "Collective memory should be seen as a set of practices and ideas embedded in a culture, which people learn to decode and convert into their identities" (2002).

Some authors interested in this topic focus on the difference between popular memory and history, the latter of which emphasizes facts, specific events, and truths (as positivists use the term), and an "objective" past that can be found in documents and other artifacts such as archaeological evidence.[2] People generally understand the past by situating it within their social framework and developing a more subjective understanding of it through popular narratives and accounts. They experience it through the eyes and minds of participants in the events and their descendants (Rosenzweig and Thelen 1998; Olick, Vinitzky-Seroussi, and Levy 2011). For others, however, the distinction is not so clear once they explore the constructed and selective use of historical "facts." Trouillot (1995: 3–8) questions the utility of the extreme positions of both the positivist and constructivist models, arguing: "Whereas the positivist view hides the tropes of power behind a naïve epistemology, the constructivist one denies the autonomy of the sociohistorical process. Taken to its logical end point, constructivism views the historical narrative as one fiction among others" (Trouillot 1995: 6).

Recent interest in collective memory extends back to Maurice Halbwachs and the Annales School in France in the mid- to late twentieth century. Their work focused on social history and memories and mentalities outside the purview of the official state histories of formal institutions, wars, and kings. These historians saw it as crucial to understand "the system of beliefs and collective representations, myths, and images with which people in the past understood and gave meaning to their world" (Confino 2011: 37). Young (1993: 6), citing Halbwachs, also argues "that both the reasons for memory and the forms memory takes are always socially mandated."

An oversimplified distinction between objective history and subjective popular memory also fails to recognize that both are built on particular narratives. These narratives include plausible explanations about the past, as found in culturally accessible locations such as archives, school texts, films, commemorative events, family stories, and emotionally significant sacred places, which are also the foundations for public history. For Confino, the distinction between history and memory is complicated because history, like memory, is socially and culturally constituted, even though "Historians create narratives about the past with the *intention* of telling truthful stories. The truth of their stories is never stable, for it is socially and culturally constructed, and their stories can never tell the whole truth about the past. . . . Yet memory and history converge, because historians have been the great priests of the nation-state, as well as other groups and identities, thus shaping their memory via history" (Confino 2011: 43).

Opinions differ as to the extent to which there needs to be consensus about content for a memory to truly qualify as "collective." We can certainly identify events, people, and groups in many societies about which many people have clear memories, either from direct experience or from learning about them from others. At the same time, because many people remember the exact same large-scale events and important individuals differently, there is invariably significant diversity in what exactly is remembered and the specific emotions associated with these memories.

Consider the strong beliefs and emotions in the collective memories of four events from American history: the founding of the United States, the Civil War, World War II, and the Vietnam War. The first two of these events are beyond the personal experiences of anyone alive today or their immediate ancestors, while the two twentieth-century wars are in the living memory of many Americans, either through their own experiences or through the accounts of family members and friends who lived through them.[3] There is wide consensus in how Americans think about the founding of the country in the late eighteenth century and in their understanding of World War II, but there are significant differences in both the content and emotions concerning the Civil War and Vietnam. For example, the specific memories of the American Civil War and the lessons drawn from it are strikingly divergent in the North and South and among whites and Blacks. In addition, the content and affect have changed over time for some people. Yet all four of these events are the object of collective memory, even though in two of the cases there is lower consensus around the content and emotions associated with them. The key point in terms of collective memory is that most Americans have knowledge and feelings about all four of these events, as opposed to the Mexican War, the Spanish-American War—or slavery in the North.

The same question about consensus arises when we study what people share in the same culture (Ross 2009b). They do not have identical beliefs or engage in the same behaviors, because there is invariably within-group diversity in any community (Norton 2004; Ross 2009b). Cultures are not membership groups such as labor unions or states that provide membership or identity cards that quickly signal whether someone is or is not included. By themselves, shared beliefs or actions do not tell us all we want to know about shared cultural identities. Hence, people may hold common views or engage in similar actions but consider themselves part of very different cultural traditions. Conversely, people who are part of the same culture may hold diverse views on many issues or engage in very different behaviors. Anthropologist Robert LeVine (1984), building on Clifford Geertz (1973), argues that culture is best understood as a shared system of meanings—what some describe as mutually intelligible schema or worldviews—rather than homogeneity of particular practices or specific beliefs. While there is significant within-culture variation in thoughts, feelings, and behaviors, what people share are common systems of meaning—understandings of the symbols and representations they communicate (LeVine 1984: 68).

Collective memories, like culture, are formed and persist through social interaction, as Halbwachs, the French sociologist, emphasized in his still influential analysis of collective memory (Halbwachs [1950] 1997). Halbwachs, Olick (1999: 335) points out, "reminds [us] that it is only individuals who remember, even if they do much of the remembering together. Group memberships provide the materials for memory and prod the individual into recalling particular events and forgetting others. Groups can even produce memories in individuals of events that they never 'experienced' in any direct sense."

Halbwachs underscores the importance of institutions, social frameworks, and specific practices—especially rituals and commemorative activities—that reinforce the acquisition, retention, and power of memories of certain past events and the forgetting of others (Middleton and Edwards 1990; Olick and Robbins 1998; Olick 1999; Fogu and Kansteiner 2006; Lebow 2006). As Young (1993: xi) points out, "If societies remember, it is only insofar as their institutions and rituals organize, shape, even inspire their constituents' memories."

What matters from the past shifts over time, not only because groups add new events and experiences to their collective memories but also because of changing ways they reinterpret and utilize the distant past in light of present challenges. Forgotten collective memories are sometimes recovered and remembered as contemporary interests and needs shift. For example, since the 1970s (and the television series *Roots* and the best-selling Alex Haley novel on which it was based) many African Americans became more interested in learning about their African ancestors. They traveled to "the motherland" and had DNA tests to learn the specific origins of their enslaved African ancestors. In some cases, this has quickened their interest in African history, dress, language, and cuisine. A growing number of festivals feature African themes and cultures in the United States, in both the North and South.

Olick, Vinitzky-Seroussi, and Levy (2011: 18) suggest that "it is impossible for individuals to remember in any coherent and persistent fashion outside of group contexts; these are necessary social frameworks of individual memory." "The invention of tradition" examines how the past and memories of it are constructed and revised over time, and in a variety of settings. This line of thought emphasizes that rituals are not produced spontaneously, any more than the memories associated with them (Hobsbawm and Ranger 1983; Ranger 1997). They remind us that important national (and other) holiday celebrations and festivals such as July 14 (Bastille Day in France) or July 12 (which marks the Battle of the Boyne for Protestants in Northern Ireland) were not widely celebrated until more than a century after the events they commemorate. They developed in the Third French Republic and among the Protestants in Northern Ireland, respectively, only when they served the needs of political and social groups in these societies. Similarly, memories surrounding important historical figures and places are rarely static and can readily and dramatically change as needs and conditions shift over time (Schwartz 1991, 1997, 2000).

We too easily read history backward. For example, the Liberty Bell in Philadelphia was not called by that name in July 1776, when it was rung to mark the public reading of the Declaration of Independence. Similarly, the Confederate Battle flag has acquired multiple meanings over time. Early after the Civil War it was viewed as a soldier's flag and often was displayed in cemeteries where Confederate soldiers were buried. Shortly after World War II, however, it was regularly displayed in more political contexts; first in 1948 by Strom Thurmond, then the governor of South Carolina, when he ran for president as a Dixiecrat, and his supporters wanted to demonstrate their strong opposition to integration (Coski 2005). This symbolic connection only intensified after the *Brown v. Board of Education* decision in 1954, when it became part of some state flags. The flag's political use has continued in many parts of the South for decades. It was not until the 2015 massacre in Charleston's Emanuel African Methodist Episcopal Church that many conservative white Southern politicians were willing to call the flag a racist symbol of slavery and agree to remove it from public displays, as happened on the South Carolina capitol grounds, followed by the removal of four prominent Confederate monuments in New Orleans in 2017.

Collective memories are socially constructed accounts that change in response to contemporary political events and social conditions. "Historians routinely warn against practices of inventing, reinventing, and reconstructing the past in the service of the present, but this is precisely what is encouraged—indeed celebrated—in the case of collective remembering" (Wertsch and Roediger 2008: 320). School textbooks in some regions of the United States, for example, have added more images and texts devoted to the experiences of African Americans. Today the civil rights movement gets significant coverage and its leaders are often discussed in detail. It's as if there was a sudden realization that their lives were part of American history and the experiences of white males were not the only ones who mattered in the country (Fitzgerald 1979). But in regions such as the South, the amount of coverage has changed more slowly.[4]

Of course, historians often alter or shift their narratives—either intentionally or unintentionally—since they are also products of particular cultural and political communities. Similarly, public history also changes over time. In the end, neither memories nor historical accounts are set in stone, despite the efforts of monument builders and others to create unchanging and inviolable legacies. At the same time, the assertion that the past can be constructed and reconstructed does not mean that all accounts are equally plausible, equally capable of initial acceptance or of persistence over time. There are some real limits to what can and cannot be effectively constructed at any point in time, because available materials are structured and finite, restraining social and individual choice as Schudson (1989) points out. As a result, once the past is enshrined in a particular way, it can be hard, but certainly not impossible, to alter. Changes to narratives must make sense to be acceptable (Blair, Dickinson, and Ott 2010: 14)

To understand how Americans think about the past, historians Rosenzweig and Thelen (1998) asked a national sample what the past means to them and posed questions about how they use it. The answers they received support Halbwachs's ideas about the role of social structure in shaping what people know about the past and how their memories of it are shaped. Their data emphasize the importance of personal—and especially family—networks in providing both cognitive and emotional accounts about the past that connect proximate memories to more distant ones. Rosenzweig and Thelen also found that group identities matter in filtering the past and how it is used. For example, Blacks are more likely than whites to refer to their ancestors collectively— not just the ones to whom they are directly related—and to see their own histories as a microcosm of the group experience.

In sum, they found that memories that matter are both cognitive and affective; there is variation in content within and between groups even when people share mutually intelligible frames and meanings to interpret events; for most of us, events and people who can be connected cognitively and emotionally to our own life experiences are the most significant ones; racial and ethnic identities sometimes play an important role in shaping particular memories; written histories and school textbooks are not as salient as accounts from family and friends; and personally experienced historical sites and museums are more important in developing collective memories than school texts and many media presentations, which are often seen as either distant or biased (Rosenzweig and Thelen 1998).

Collective memories are found in narratives groups tell about themselves, in social enactments and representations that occur in ceremonies and rituals, and in public and commemorative landscapes and the objects associated with them. In thinking about slavery in the North, it is clear that there is a dearth of all three, which can variously be viewed as a cause or a product of the absence of collective memories of slavery in the region. These kinds of narratives and social enactments tend to have a snowball effect. For example, since the early 1990s, more sites of slavery in the North have been rediscovered, followed by archaeological finds, museum exhibits, and television shows on the topic, and public awareness of Northern slavery has clearly risen.

Who shares collective memories and how are these groups defined? If we begin with a particular group of people—large or small—we can ask what memories are held in common. Or we can start with individuals and ask which memories they share with others. Which approach makes the most sense depends on the questions being asked (Confino 2011: 48). The first approach is most relevant if one is interested in the collective memories found in groups of family members or those in local communities, work groups, gender groups, age cohorts, or those in larger collectivities such as those defined around ethnic, racial, or national identities. Using this approach would reveal that all human groups, of whatever size and composition, have certain collective memories with which a large proportion of its members are familiar, in part because they share cultural frames and systems of meaning. Memories of important people and prominent events such as some elections, assassinations, traumatic natural and human-made disasters, and wars are widely shared. Acts of bravery and heroism and sporting and entertainment events are also remembered by large numbers of people in the same generation or country, although in many cases these memories are ephemeral and not enduring. At the same time, there is internal diversity among people in large collectivities, such as religious, ethnic, or national groups, that produces variation in the content and the affect surrounding their shared collective memories and in the intensity with which they are held. An event such as the O. J. Simpson trial produced very different reactions from Blacks and whites when the verdict was announced. Whites were generally furious that he was not convicted, since most believed he had murdered his wife, while many Blacks were glad he was acquitted, because it showed that the jury rejected a racist, lying policeman's testimony even if they believed Simpson was guilty of the murder.[5] Reactions to political candidates and events often differ across religious and racial lines. But this does not mean that people in the different groups are not part of the same culture; instead, it means that the specific beliefs differ and reflect the diversity found within any large group.

   In contrast, starting with individuals, rather than with a group, will show that no one shares *all* his or her memories with other people, and even those that are shared are not all shared with the same people. We live in multiple social worlds and participate in multiple social networks. An initial reaction might be that if the memories are not all the same within a group, then they are not part of a collectivity. A more nuanced reflection would be that with all collective memories there are some parts for which there is widespread agreement in content and associated emotions, while there are other parts about which there are differences in emphasis and even outright disagreement. For some people studying collective memories, this poses a crucial methodological conundrum. However, this is the messy reality of social life. The diversity of social networks in any community makes identification of collective memories difficult, but this does not mean that they are not worth understanding.

In thinking about the nature of groups that share collective memories, the fact that people have multiple identities has important consequences. The size of any group and the extent to which it is nested inside larger identity groups are also relevant. An excellent illustration of nesting, in which smaller diverse groups can also share larger identities, is illustrated in W. Lloyd Warner's 1959 study of Memorial Day commemorations in Yankee City (Newburyport, Massachusetts) in the 1930s. Warner describes distinct phases of the commemorations that begin with separate activities for distinct religious communities in the city, scores of rituals in cemeteries, churches, and associations, and finally a citywide parade and ceremony, in which all the diverse groups participate. A different pattern looks more like a Venn diagram, in which there are zones of uniqueness and zones of commonality among different identities. For example, Rosenzweig and Thelen's exploration of Americans' sense of the past shows that while there are shared memories across white, Black, and Native Americans, there were also distinct differences between the groups in terms of which memories are more important to each one (Rosenzweig and Thelen 1998: chap. 6).

There is always diversity in the extent to which particular collective memories are shared and the size of the sharing community. As the Warner example of Memorial Day illustrates, a Venn diagram is often appropriate to map (at least conceptually) what is widely shared and what is more unique to each smaller group in the city. It is fair to suggest that in virtually no case are the same memories universally held. In the United States, ethnic and racial groups certainly share some memories, such as those involving wars, major disasters, and major political figures, while surveys reveal between-group differences in their content and affect. For example, certain holidays are more or less universal and others are recognized and celebrated by only some members of some groups. Even in cases where the holidays are more or less universal, such as Memorial Day or New Year's Day, celebration and commemoration of them vary widely.

Some rituals and holidays are quite specific to single groups. Religious holidays easily come to mind, but they are not the only ones. Other examples include ethnic occasions such as Columbus Day, which is a public holiday in some cities and states that historically had a large Italian population,[6] St. Patrick's Day, which is marked in cities with a sizable Irish population (and those who like to drink green beer), and Mardi Gras, which is celebrated in New Orleans; and ethnic festivals such as Chinese New Year and Cinco de Mayo. A number of Southern states celebrate Robert E. Lee Day, often in conjunction with Martin Luther King Jr. Day. Juneteenth has been celebrated since 1865, almost exclusively by African Americans, to mark the end of slavery on June 19, 1865. In 1980, Texas was the first state to establish it as a state holiday as Kachun recounts in telling the story of the holiday's evolution (Kachun 2011).[7]

Collective memories are developed, retained, and transmitted over time through a few generic mechanisms. There is widespread agreement that social and individual remembering (and forgetting) are tightly connected, as Halbwachs first argued; and that social dynamics are central to understanding the salience and accessibility of collective memories for individuals. Both are crucial to understanding the content and structure of collective memories and their relevance for social and political life.[8]

Collective memories are socially constructed, and as such they are continually reconstructed as social and political conditions change. At some times the process is more explicit than at others. Zerubavel's (1995) argument about the development of Israeli collective memory is very relevant. She asks how Zionists in the early to mid-twentieth century coming to Israel from a wide range of countries, sharing no single language, and seeing themselves as the descendants of the members of a state that had disappeared over 1,900 years earlier, built a collective memory to form the foundation for a national narrative. She shows how past defeats are commemorated as heroic events, and become the basis for "holiday celebrations, festivals, monuments, songs, stories, plays and educational texts" (Zerubavel 1995: 5). Her analysis explains how this occurred and is constituted as a shared collective memory of the nation that had not existed for centuries. The effort at memory construction is strikingly explicit in this example and, at the same time, seamlessly successful. It is an excellent example of how the present needs of the state (Israel) drove the development of an intense and powerful collective memory of shared past experiences. In her analysis of collective memory reconstruction, she integrates and emphasizes the role of narratives, ritual expressions and enactments, and sacred visible places on the public landscape.

Collective memory development, retention, and transmission have wide-ranging social sources. The most obvious one is the influence of the small face-to-face worlds in which people live. The substantial literature on socialization has documented for decades now the importance of family, school, peer group, and work settings in collective memory.[9] Importantly, in addition to the cognitive and affective learning that occurs in these social contexts, people also learn "theories" about the world,[10] including beliefs about the groups in it and how one should behave in particular situations.[11] For example, Americans learn about race and the social meaning of racial differences early in life and in a variety of social settings. Whites and Blacks each learn stories about the past that are significantly different in many ways that influence their collective memories.

Direct and indirect personal experiences are a crucial way that memories are created, retained, and communicated.[12] For example, Rosenzweig and Thelen (1998) find that learning about an event, such as World War II or the civil rights movement, through an older family member or friend is a powerful transmission channel. Their data show that these sources are trusted more highly than history books or the media. They also argue that the emotional connections to people with whom one is close render their accounts more emotionally powerful than those of strangers. We should not be surprised to learn this, for it is how traditional cultures have transmitted important information for generations. As Confino (2011: 41) argues, social power is central to understanding collective memory, and "the study of memory explores how a social group, be it a family, a class, or a nation, constructs a past through a process of invention and appropriation, and what it means to the relationship of power within society. Differently expressed, the historian of memory considers who wants whom to remember what and why, and how memory is produced, received and rejected." The development, retention, and transmission of collective memories are facilitated through shared narratives, ritual expressions and enactments, and visible public and commemorative landscapes, each of which can serve as social *aides mémoires* that strengthen collective memories while heightening their emotional salience (Ross 2007, 2009a).[13] Each involves social processes that connect individuals to the social worlds in which they live and work and reinforce the social nature of collective memories.

Narratives are explanations for events, large and small, in the form of short, commonsense stories. They are communicated through a wide range of expressions and enactments that may be mundane or special—activities, religious practices, music, films, theater, paintings, language use, books, statues, museum presentations, memorials, public monuments, clothing, or flag displays that symbolically connect the past and present (Ross 2007: chap. 3). Crucially, narratives are infused with strong emotions that communicate far more than historical details. Acquired through social learning, they involve "the assimilation by an individual of narratives or *scripts* about himself and his exchanges with other people" (Winter and Sivan 1999: 11). Scripts matter at two levels. First, through rehearsal, individuals and societies increase the access and recall of memories when narratives are retold in public. Narratives meet many needs, and people are especially likely to rely upon them when they are disoriented and struggling to make sense of events in situations of high uncertainty and stress. In this way narratives become bridges across time and space, drawing on shared identities and memories (Volkan 1988; Ross 2007).

What is particularly significant is not the historical truth or falsity of narratives about the past, but their emotional relevance to people in the present. When narratives evoke identities, they connect people who share the identity in both the present and the past. Ancestors and contemporary descendants are connected in ways that emphasize empathy and sharing across time and space. In the American context, this linkage is especially powerful for African Americans and Native Americans (Rosenzweig and Thelen 1998). In the United States, most white and Black narratives about themselves and each other are quite explicit and often highly charged emotionally. There is very little sharing of these narratives across racial lines, although on some topics each may have a pretty clear idea about what the other is saying and thinking, while on others, their speculation is off-base. In addition, there often is much suspicion and distrust in many of the narratives that each tells about the other.

Rituals are social enactments and behaviors whose central elements and the contexts in which they occur are emotionally meaningful. Rituals and social enactments can take many forms, ranging from small family gatherings to community festivals and society-wide holidays. They can mark historical or present-day events, and recent experiences. Large rituals can communicate key parts of a group's self-understood identity and history. They are a powerful way to create and strengthen narratives and the collective memories they invoke within a social group. While rituals are experienced as timeless and unchanging, this is often not the case. Rather, rituals are regularly invented, modified, and reinvented over time to address present fears and needs (Hobsbawm and Ranger 1983; Connerton 1989).[14] Rituals not only invoke aggregated individual memories—they are also about "emergent conceptions of the past crystallized into symbolic structures" (Schwartz 2000: 8). Participation in activities such as festivals and commemorative ceremonies is important in Connerton's analysis of memory, and he emphasizes that rites are not merely expressive, formal, or limited in their effect to ritual occasions (1989: 44); he adds that rituals commemorate continuity and in so doing shape communal memory (1989: 48), connecting people across time and space and promoting a sense of shared fate. In a similar vein, Schwartz points out that commemoration mobilizes symbols to awaken ideas and feelings about the past. It means remembering together (Schwartz 2000: 9).[15] Connerton emphasizes that "ritual is not only an alternative way of expressing certain beliefs, but that certain ideas can be expressed only in ritual" (1989: 54).

A society's visible public and commemorative landscapes communicate and frame social and political messages using places and objects imbued with emotional significance that express a society's core values and honor its heroes using images, objects, and other expressive representations (Nora 1989; Cosgrove 1998). A good way to think of the public landscape is the buildings, statues, and other objects that are found in places accessible to the public, while commemorative sites are a subclass that mark people and events of particular emotional significance to a society's or group's collective past. "One's memory, like one's most intimate dreams, originates from the symbols, landscape, and past that are shared by a given society . . . embedded in a specific cultural, social, and political context" (Confino 2011: 41). Some sites are sacred, even nonreligious ones. Sacred landscapes frame social and political messages and communicate power and belonging through how they represent inclusion and exclusion, demonstrate hierarchy, and portray dominant and subordinate groups in particular ways. They can create and transmit collective memories as well as change them over time.

Physical sites matter because of what once took place on them, the events or people that are associated with them, and the objects they contain.

Blair, Dickinson, and Ott argue that place often organizes memory and can serve as a memory prompt (2010: 1, 24). Rosenzweig and Thelen note that the trustworthiness of historical sites and objects partly grows from the visitor's sense that they are experiencing the past "almost as it had originally been experienced" (1998: 106). Physical links to narratives associated with sites are crucial to maintaining and strengthening the emotional significance of the memories they embody. Religious communities certainly recognize this, and all of the world's great religions have sacred sites that connect followers to each other through pilgrimages to or rituals that take place at the sites. Armstrong (1996: 175–93), writing about Jerusalem's history, argues that for over three centuries Christians were not particularly interested in specific historical sites such as those where Jesus had been, nor were they focused on relics—physical objects that were associated with significant people and events in the past. This changed after Constantine converted to Christianity in the fourth century, when his mother Helena went to Jerusalem, visited many sites historically associated with Jesus's life, and "discovered" the True Cross. Its pieces became relics that were quickly dispersed to many Christian churches throughout the West, linking people thousands of miles away to the Holy Land and its key events.

Physical sites and objects can represent group identity when rituals take place on or with them, enhancing a narrative's emotional significance. Yet Crane (1997: 138) reminds us that "collective memory ultimately is located not in sites but in individuals. All narratives, all sites, all texts remain objects until they are 'read' or referred to by individuals thinking historically." Her most important point is that individual agency renders historical sites emotionally relevant.[16] Examples of this connection abound in holidays and rituals built on uniting people across time and space. They invite us to consider important and consequential questions: Who is present and who is absent in public representations? What are the qualities of those people and objects portrayed in them? Who controls the representations and to what extent are they contested? How is hierarchy portrayed and what qualities are associated with particular positions within a society's hierarchy? Who and what are missing and why are they absent?

Exclusion and inclusion in a society are powerfully expressed through the restriction or expansion of a society's narratives, its ritual expressions and enactments, and its visible, public, and commemorative landscapes. Exclusion of groups of people from the narratives of key events from the past, participation in important ritual events, and the public landscape is an obvious denial of belonging—a form of distancing and forgetting. Obviously this has been the case with race in the United States, since the colonial period. Pictures and stories about the country's founding leaders, heroes, and most important figures were for many generations invariably white and male. Somehow Blacks, Native Americans, and other minority males and almost all females were not deemed worthy of inclusion. This was normalized for many and until recently only a small minority ever publicly objected.

More inclusive narratives, rituals, and public landscapes can powerfully communicate shared connections and a common stake in society. Inclusion can render the previously unseen visible, give voice to those once voiceless, and publicly identify what was previously invisible. Inclusion offers powerful messages that can reshape relations among those who once fought bitterly, offering acceptance and legitimation that both reflects and promotes changes in intergroup relationships. Through inclusion, groups can more easily develop a partially shared identity that helps mourn past losses and expresses hopes and aspirations for a shared future.

Effective inclusion in narratives, rituals, and visible, public, and commemorative landscapes is perhaps usefully thought about in terms of social participation. Participation in social and political activities can heighten memory creation and retention for individuals and groups. Verba (1961) found strong support for what he termed the participation hypothesis, the idea that once people engage in a behavior they are more likely to be emotionally invested in it. Such experiences are then more likely to be remembered, in part to justify the energy and resources that the individual or group invested in an action in the first place. In politics, the participation mechanism often operates by getting people to take small steps—attending a meeting, signing a petition, donating a small amount of money—which makes them more committed to a cause and willing to invest more time and energy in actions on its behalf. Of course, this is the reverse of the widespread belief, at least in Western culture, that to get people to do (or remember) something they first need to be persuaded that it is important.

The relevance of the participation hypothesis for understanding collective memory dynamics is that active engagement in ceremonies and ritual events where group narratives are recounted and significant symbols are publicly invoked or displayed often heightens both awareness and retention of collective memories. These events can take many different forms and can involve large or small groups of people.

While Verba focused on direct participation, it is useful to also consider the impact of indirect participation through the media and its effect on the development, retention, and transmission of collective memory. Media messages can seem powerful, but this hardly means that whatever appears in the media is automatically remembered accurately. Too often it is assumed that the content of media presentations, either in the form of news stories or as entertainment, is automatically and uncritically accepted by listeners or viewers. Research over many decades, however, shows that the connection between the message sent and the message retained is often weak or nonexistent, even when the message is repeated many times.[17] When a message is at odds with strong, previously held beliefs or not connected to one's present needs, a media message is easier to dismiss. To be retained, media messages require not just reception but social processing and interpretation as well. To be communicated and remembered, messages must resonate with viewers or listeners when they are processed and reinforced through interaction with others in their social worlds. Finally, contestation among messages often arises from the diverse memories associated with different social contexts, resulting in a "comingling of reception, representation and contestation" (Confino 1997: 1399).

Not all media messages are equally relevant, and only some create powerful memories for people that heighten the likelihood of their long-term retention. Prominent among these are unexpected, traumatic ones in which the media images are retained and transmitted across generations. Dayan and Katz (1992) emphasize the commemorative aspects of some media events and how they communicate a yearning for togetherness and fusion that are especially relevant in emotionally intense situations. Live media coverage of historical events, often occasions of state or tragedies, can transfix a nation or the world, and collectively experiencing them in small groups of family and friends then reinforces their emotional strength and shared perception of reality (Dayan and Katz 1992: 177).

Collective memories matter because they connect people in a society and can facilitate collective action. Consider the case of the 9/11 attacks on New York and Washington. Within a few hours, they were described as sneak attacks similar to Pearl Harbor in 1941, easily prompting most people to believe that such an attack warranted a military response. The fact that in 1941 a major country had initiated the attack and in 2001 the attack came from a terrorist group and not a state was not seen as significant. Hence, when the Bush administration announced it would launch an attack on Afghanistan, the American public had already been prepared to overwhelmingly support the idea.[18]

At the same time, collective memories, even when they are deeply felt, do not explain group mobilization in any simple, automatic way. Rather, the emotions and beliefs contained in the memories need to be transformed into plausible actions—a process that concretizes the connections between the memories about the past and what might be done in the present and future. Any good explanation would also need to consider opportunity structures and resources that promote or inhibit action for the group as well. Weak groups facing strong opponents are much less likely to act forcefully than the reverse. Collective memories are not always forever. Some last longer than others and some are forgotten relatively quickly. Sometimes we are puzzled about what is retained and what is not. Like remembering, the reasons for forgetting are neither automatic nor always obvious.

For a long time, collective memories in the North about slavery were virtually nonexistent—virtually, but not entirely. Some African Americans and whites were aware of enslavement in the North although as time passed it appears that their numbers diminished, until recovery of the memories began in the 1990s. In terms of the development of collective memory, perhaps the earliest historical work is William C. Nell's 1855 book *The Colored Patriots of the American Revolution* ([1855] 1968). Nell, who worked with both William Lloyd Garrison and Frederick Douglass, traveled to twenty states where he conducted interviews with Blacks who had served in the Revolutionary War and the War of 1812. He visited cemeteries to examine gravestones and consulted local records to write about those who fought in these wars, as well as distinguished Black patriots such as poets Phillis Wheatley and James Whitfield. Nell was instrumental in getting the state of Massachusetts to place a large monument on the Boston Common, dedicated to Crispus Attucks, the Black soldier who was the first person killed in the Boston Massacre, and to restore the celebration of the day Attucks died as a state holiday. The volume is filled with accounts of dozens of individuals and their achievements as well as commentary on salient political issues concerning the treatment of Blacks just five years before the start of the Civil War.

For the most part, however, even when historians wrote about or mentioned slavery in the North, it was typically overshadowed by what took place in the South and frequently dismissed by many as an insignificant sideshow. In addition, because Northern slavery was rarely associated with specific places in the public landscape, there were few narratives about it that received much, if any, attention, and it was absent from school and college history courses. Finally, while there certainly were African Americans who knew about its existence, it was not something that generated any significant interest from most Blacks and whites.

Memories of it have been hard to sustain, and it seems worthwhile to ask why this is so. The brief answer I propose here, and which the following chapters will explore, is that crucial prerequisites for collective memory retention were missing: there were not many notable narratives transmitted across generations, there were almost no ritual enactments or expressions, and there was an almost total absence of public and commemorative landscapes or objects associated with Northern slavery.[19] Without any of these, collective memories of Northern slavery grew weaker and weaker until they virtually disappeared, except for pockets of amateur and professional historians. Each of these elements might have fostered a growth in the others, but none were sufficiently strong to do so.

Chapter 2

Surveying Enslavement in the North

Slavery has long been identified in the national consciousness as a Southern institution. The time to bury the myth is long overdue. Slavery is a story about America, all of America.

—Anne Farrow, Joel Lang, and Jenifer Frank,
Complicity: How the North Promoted, Prolonged and Profited from Slavery

Even if slavery in the North is not remembered or known, it was and is knowable. Slavery in the Northern colonies and states lasted well over two hundred years and involved tens of thousands of enslaved people, slave owners, and traders. Ironically, white Southerners—specifically, Confederate enthusiasts and white supremacists—are among those with the most awareness of Northern slavery, and they regularly publicize its story.[1] Their goal, of course, is self-exculpatory: "Don't criticize us when you guys did the same thing." Despite their efforts over the years, however, there has only been a modest increase in Northern knowledge about what took place in the region, and what has been internalized is hardly due to neo-Confederate efforts.

The colonies that became the United States in 1776 had a population of only about 2.5 million people, of whom about 20 percent or half a million were enslaved. About half of the enslaved people lived in Virginia, Maryland, and Delaware, another 10 to 12 percent in the North, and the remainder farther South. New York had the greatest number of enslaved people and the highest percentage in the North, followed by New Jersey, while the territories that became the states of Vermont, New Hampshire, and Maine had the smallest total populations and the lowest percentage of enslaved people. The greatest number of enslaved people in New England was in Connecticut, while Rhode Island had the highest percentage. The numbers are quite different if we look, for example, at their distribution across social classes or consider the proportion of households with at least one enslaved person. For example, middle- and upper-class households, particularly in the larger cities such as Boston, New York, and Philadelphia, were the most likely to be slaveholders, and at times during the colonial period 50 percent of their households included enslaved people. Enslavement was also much more likely in the households in which the head was a member of certain professions. For example, based on his analysis of estate inventories, Main reported that in Connecticut, "by 1774, half of all the ministers, lawyers, and public officials owned slaves, and a third of all the doctors" (Harper 2003, citing various numbers reported by Main [1985]).

Table 1 provides estimates of the size of the enslaved population in each Northern colony and state from the peak period in the mid-eighteenth century until the country's first census in 1790. While these numbers are probably a fair guide to the size of the enslaved population in the region, they should not be seen as absolutely accurate for several reasons. First, during the colonial period, censuses were conducted at different times and more or less often by the individual colonies and localities. Second, Mc-Manus (1973: 199) warns that "colonial census returns generally used the words *Negroes, blacks, and slaves* interchangeably. Thus, the occasional inclusion of freedmen tends to overestimate somewhat the actual number of bondsmen. On the other hand, in colonies where slaves were taxed as polls or personality, the masters were likely to underreport their holdings. All figures are therefore approximate, providing estimates of population trends rather than precise counts."

Enslaved people were brought to New York beginning in 1626, and the number and proportion of the enslaved there were the highest of the Northern colonies/states until 1827, when slavery ended in the state. By 1664, when the British seized the colony of New Amsterdam, the enslaved composed about 20 percent of its population, and about a fifth of the Blacks in the colony were free. These proportions are similar to those in the Chesapeake region at the time. On the eve of the American Revolution in 1771, McManus (2001 [1966]: 199) reports, there were almost 20,000 enslaved in the colony of New York, or 12 percent of the population. Greater numbers were concentrated in New York City and its surrounding counties, but

Table 1. Enslaved Population in the North in the Eighteenth Century

	1750			1770			1790		
	Number enslaved	Total population	Percentage enslaved	Number enslaved	Total population	Percentage enslaved	Number enslaved	Total population	Percentage enslaved
Connecticut	3,019	111,280	2.7%	6,462	183,881	3.5%	2,764	237,946	1.2%
Maine					31,257	0.0%	0	96,540	0.0%
Massachusetts	2,423	180,000	1.3%	5,249	235,308	2.2%	0	378,787	0.0%
New Hampshire	550	27,505	2.0%	674	62,396	1.1%	158	141,885	0.1%
New Jersey	4,606	71,393	6.5%	8,220	117,431	7.0%	11,423	184,139	6.2%
New York	13,548	76,696	17.7%	19,062	162,920	11.7%	21,324	340,120	6.3%
Pennsylvania	2,872	119,666	2.4%	5,561	240,057	2.3%	3,737	434,373	0.9%
Rhode Island	4,697	33,226	14.1%	4,697	58,196	8.1%	948	68,825	1.4%
Vermont					10,000	0.0%	16	85,539	0.0%

Sources: The numbers of enslaved in 1750 and 1770 come from McManus (1973: 199–214). However, he cautions readers to recognize that the censuses should be viewed as estimates; the dates presented are the closest population counts to the two dates. In addition, he notes that in some colonies the numbers are reported for "Negroes, blacks, and slaves," terms that were often used interchangeably at the time. As a result, some free Blacks are included and the number of enslaved is overestimated; at the same time, he points out that because the enslaved were taxed in most places, the numbers are probably low estimates as people sought to avoid taxation.

The numbers of enslaved for 1770 for Pennsylvania, New York, and New Jersey are from Nash and Soderlund (1991: 7), whose number of the enslaved includes the number of Blacks minus their estimate of those who were free at the time. The numbers for 1790 come from the U.S. Census.

The total population estimates come from three different websites that all offer the same numbers for each colony/state and are drawn from Historical Statistics of the United States: Colonial Times to 1970, issued by the Census Bureau, which cites as its main sources archival research and the statistical work of various scholars: "Estimated Population of American Colonies: 1610 to 1780"; https://web.viu.ca/davies/h320/population.colonies.htm Chuck Springston, "Population of the 13 Colonies 1610–1790," October 28, 2013; and http://thomaslegion.net/population_of_the_original_thirteen_colonies_free_slave_white_and_nonwhite.html. Other websites that provided similar numbers are no longer available. These sites do not completely agree with each other, but the differences are modest and are best attributed to estimates, since regular censuses were not conducted until 1790. The 1750 and 1760 numbers are often projected from the state or town censuses closest to that date.

there were higher percentages of enslaved people in Kings, Queens, and Suffolk counties and parts of the Hudson River Valley, all of which were farming regions at the time (White 1995).[2] These areas were also the slowest to free enslaved people even after gradual manumission began. In each, the proportion of slave owners who were Dutch throughout the period of enslavement was particularly high (White 1991: 18–21), and the Dutch slave owners in New York and New Jersey were among the last to free them (Hodges 1999: 164).

English colonists in New England (and their Native American allies) captured and enslaved Pequots during and after the Pequot war. Massachusetts captured Indian fighters in the 1630s and enslaved them, but this was unsuccessful because they would not work hard and often escaped, so Governor John Winthrop sent the captured Indians to the Caribbean to be sold. The ship returned with Africans, who became the first enslaved Blacks in the colony. New Jersey's enslaved population was concentrated in East Jersey, where planters from Barbados settled and built large plantations in the seventeenth century, and in this area of the state the proportion of enslaved people was similar to New York while Nash and Soderlund (1991: 7) place the enslaved population of the state at closer to 7 percent.

Pennsylvania's enslaved population in 1770 was smaller than either of the other mid-Atlantic colonies at 2.3 percent (Nash and Soderlund 1991: 7). The proportion in Philadelphia, the largest city in North America at the time, was higher, at 7.5 percent, with about 1,400 enslaved Blacks belonging to 590 slave owners (Nash 1988: 33). After this date, the enslaved population in Philadelphia began to decrease as the Quakers, who had debated resolutions on the question of slavery for some time, moved toward stronger opposition. They decided first in the 1750s that members of their meetings should not buy or sell slaves and then in the 1770s that one could not be a member of the Society of Friends and own slaves. Some who rejected this decision joined other religious communities. New Englanders owned fewer slaves than the other colonies, with the exception of Rhode Island, whose proportion was second in the North to New York until after the Revolutionary War.

The numerical high point of slavery in the North was in the third quarter of the eighteenth century. The numbers began to decline by the start of the Revolutionary period. Enslavement then dropped more quickly toward 1800. But the change was not uniform throughout the region. For example, in New York City the numbers of enslaved people actually rose between

1790 and 1800 (White 1995: 1–2), while in Philadelphia the pattern was the opposite. Philadelphia had just over one hundred free Blacks on the eve of the American Revolution, and by 1800 they numbered over 6,000, while the number of enslaved was less than half of what it was 25 years earlier (Nash and Soderlund 1991: 18). New Jersey was more similar to New York. It was the site of the largest number of battles in the Revolutionary War, but the enslaved population there did not decline at all until after 1800 (Gigantino 2015: 66–71).

Historians have proposed three major explanations to account for the shift in the last quarter of the eighteenth century. One is the Revolutionary War, which caused social disruption in regions where fighting took place or was threatened. Many enslaved people took advantage of this disruption to escape captivity and headed either to Canada or toward the sparsely populated western territories; others were granted freedom for serving in the Continental Army, sometimes as substitutes for their owners, or when they defected to the British who promised freedom to escaping slaves. While this might have been important in some areas of the North, White (1991: 54) argues that in New York, where the number of enslaved increased after the war, slavery's end is more usefully seen as resulting from the city's growth and early industrialization in the early nineteenth century.

An example is Titus (also known as Tye), who in 1775 fled from his Quaker owner in Monmouth County, New Jersey, after the owner refused to free him on his twenty-first birthday (Malcolm 2009: 51; Gigantino 2015: 43). He headed south—an unusual choice for a runaway. Only when he reached Virginia did Titus learn that Lord Dunmore, Virginia's Royal Governor, who was now in Norfolk, had promised freedom to any enslaved person who fled to the British. He joined the newly formed Ethiopian Regiment, composed of three hundred Black soldiers, most of whom had escaped in the Tidewater region. The early battles in which he participated were disasters, and the regiment lost at least half its men in battle, and then more to smallpox.

The survivors, including Tye, escaped Virginia and soon sailed north to join the British forces converging on New York. Titus and others were gathering on Staten Island. The survivors from the Ethiopian Regiment were merged into the new Black Brigade. Titus was among the better trained and more experienced in this group. He also found himself close to his former home in New Jersey, where he knew both the terrain and a number of the enslaved people. He soon became a leader of the new group. The first battle to chase Washington from Brooklyn was a rout for the British, in which Titus and the Black Brigade participated.

The next winter, Titus was sent to northern New Jersey, asked to form an independent unit of Blacks and runaway white indentured servants, and given the honorific title of "Colonel" (Malcolm 2009: 141). Their activities were coordinated with the Queen's Rangers, a guerrilla-style group in the British army. Titus and his men would often work with them and local Loyalists as they engaged in nighttime raids on Patriot farms and freed their slaves. Tye continued his raids in New Jersey and was promoted to Captain and then to Colonel and was "the most prominent of the former slaves fighting for the British" (Malcolm 2009: 170). The fighting and plundering became more and more vicious, and Tye was widely feared. In North Jersey, Patriots and Loyalists were attacking each other's homes and property regularly. Soon Tye was in the area of Shrewsbury, where his former owner still held enslaved people. He must have delighted at being able to attack the home and liberate the enslaved there. Tye stepped up daring raids and fought several pitched battles. By September 1779, his luck was running out. He and others attacked the home of Captain Josiah Huddy, who was home, and after successfully capturing him, their band was caught by a group of Patriots. Titus was wounded, developed lockjaw, and soon died at age twenty-six, having freed a number of men and women and inspired others. He died a free man and "as a soldier, with dignity" (Malcolm 2009: 180–81): "The attacks of Colonel Tye and the black guerrilla fighters . . . instilled genuine fear among white slaveholders throughout New Jersey and destabilized the racial order. They wondered that if Tye could be so destructive against his former owners, how their slaves would act if they gained freedom. . . . The fear of black revolt and the images of black violence against whites caused many to question if abolitionism, making steady progress in Pennsylvania and New England, was right for New Jersey" (Gigantino 2014: 52–53).

In mid-1775, George Washington began to recruit soldiers for what would become the Continental Army. That November, Lord Dunmore issued the declaration that promised freedom to any slave who left his American owner and joined the British forces. One consequence was the decision by several thousand Blacks to cast their lot with the British.[3] Some, but not all, of these people were taken to Canada either during or at the end of the war. Soon the Americans announced that Blacks could serve in the army; Americans felt they needed to make a similar offer to the enslaved who served, and most Northern states did so. At the time, there was also a sense among a good number of Northerners that slavery was on the wane and in response to the situation chose to free the people they owned. Some historians point to the advantage that owners would no longer be responsible for supporting their former slaves in old age, when they could no longer engage in productive work. However, without clearer evidence we can hardly say how important this motive was.

A second and more diffuse explanation for the drop in the enslaved population in the North after 1776 is that the colonists' revolutionary rhetoric ("all men are created equal") convinced some people in the region that slavery was wrong and inspired them to free some of the people they had enslaved. At the same time some religious groups such as the Quakers finally took a much stronger stand against slavery, which created an atmosphere where granting freedom seemed to a number of slave owners like the right, or at least the necessary, thing to do (Nash and Soderlund 1991). Obviously, since we have no public opinion data from this period, the claim that there was a significant shift in white beliefs in the North during this period rests on inferences from public debates, newspapers, and the actions of some of the new state governments.[4]

A third explanation for the rapid decrease in the North's enslaved population was the increasing opposition from non-slaveholding whites, who feared the enslaved threatened those working in cities and towns in the new industries in the region. In contrast to the South, the enslaved in the North worked in a wider range of jobs and acquired a greater range of skills, often leading white workers to see them as dangerous competition (Zilversmit 1967: Chapter 2, Berlin 1998, 2003).[5] Not only did white workers fear competition from enslaved Blacks, but Nash (1988) and others argue that even in the colonial period there was a strong preference for indentured white workers over enslaved Blacks—they were just not always available. Nash provides data from Pennsylvania, for example, showing that during the Seven Years' War, when the number of whites able to immigrate to the colonies significantly decreased, there was a parallel rise in the importation of enslaved Blacks. With the onset of the American Revolution, challenges to Northern slavery and calls for abolition increased. Northern abolition, however, was generally very gradual, and the rates at which it occurred varied widely across the states. In no way, however, were abolitionists in favor of equality.

For whatever combination of reasons, by the early nineteenth century, the majority of Blacks in the North were no longer enslaved. Nor did they have equal rights as citizens. Generally they were treated as outcasts living in segregated worlds, with limited job opportunities, and they were targets of severe discrimination.

As for the details of the daily lives, personal relationships, and the perceptions and thoughts of the enslaved in the North, we have very limited knowledge. Literacy rates among the early generations of the enslaved were miniscule, and we have little today in their own words. As a result, we are dependent on official record keeping and the diaries of whites, who were often the slave owners, for much of what we know.

Notable exceptions to this generalization include the poetry of Phillis Wheatley, who was the first published African American woman,[6] and the findings from Blakey's research on the remains of those disinterred at the African Burial Ground in New York (LaRoche and Blakey 1997; Blakey 1998, 2001).

Another exception is Venture Smith, an enslaved man who purchased his freedom and that of his family and dictated his life story, which was published in 1798. He wrote that he was born in Guinea in 1729 and brought to Rhode Island at age eight (Smith 1798).[7] "It is the only extant account by an African American that links West African memories to a life completed in the United States" (Stewart 2010: xiv). Smith's narrative is one of the few firsthand accounts of an enslaved person in the North. In it, Smith describes his early years in West Africa, his capture, the voyage first to Barbados and then New England, and his purchase by Robinson Mumford, the steward on the boat that transported him. He arrived in the colonies as a young boy in 1739. For the rest of his life he lived near the Long Island Sound in Rhode Island, Long Island, and southern Connecticut. Four different men owned Smith, and he describes some of the trials and tribulations of being enslaved. At the same time, his account shows the complexity of enslavement and the ways that, at times, he was able to maneuver the situation in his favor to improve his life, although at times he was treated harshly and beaten.

While Mumford still owned him, Smith and three other men stole a boat with the idea of escaping to Mississippi, but they got no farther than Long Island. Soon after, Mumford sold him to Thomas Stanton, Smith's second owner. Smith had married at twenty-five, and Stanton later bought his wife Meg and his child. A few years later, Smith had a huge conflict with Stanton during which Stanton's wife attacked Meg, and then Stanton attacked Smith with a large club a few days later. Smith went to the local Justice who told him to come back again if Stanton attacked him. On the way home, Stanton and his brother attacked Smith, who beat both of them but soon found himself in shackles and his legs locked. He was soon sold to a man whose goal was to sell him at a profit. With his perilous situation in flux, Smith was able to say that he wanted Colonel O. Smith as his owner. Colonel Smith soon agreed to let Venture purchase his freedom, which he eventually achieved at the age of thirty-six through selling produce from the land he had obtained and earning enough money to complete his purchase.

Venture Smith then moved to Long Island to work and earn money to purchase his two sons, then Meg, and, two years later, his daughter Hannah. He also occasionally bought a Black man to work for him, but most of them ran away. His son Solomon died of scurvy while on a voyage. When he was forty-four and had freed Meg, he sold all his property on Long Island and moved to East Haddam, Connecticut, where he was able to purchase a small plot of land that gradually grew to one hundred acres over the years.

He worked hard and his large and strong body was broken down as he dictated his story at age sixty-nine. Interestingly, he focused almost entirely on his work and the money he earned at various parts of his life, and we do not learn nearly as much about what he is feeling or his family relationships. Unlike most enslaved people from this period, the burying ground containing Venture and Meg's remains is known, and, with the permission of their descendants, archaeologists excavated their remains, which yielded only limited DNA information as to their origins (Strausbaugh et al. 2010).

Local census counts and estate and probate records are among the most specific official records that tell us the numbers of enslaved people and the places they lived and toiled. Black marriages were recorded in parts of the North as well, especially where marriage of the enslaved was encouraged as a way of promoting stability. There are also sales records and diaries of white slave owners that record their purchases, sales, and the hiring out of enslaved Blacks, a common practice in the North (Hodges 1999: 83). Court records, especially from New England, are especially rich. The region allowed enslaved people to bring lawsuits, and they seem to have done this quite often (Gerzina 2008; Adams and Pleck 2010; Hardesty 2016; O'Toole 2016). Freedom suits were one form, beginning in 1716. In Massachusetts, women filed fourteen (Adams and Pleck 2010: 127). Often, the enslaved were permitted to engage in independent economic activities such as selling produce from their own gardens and keeping whatever money they made or earning some money when their owners hired them out to others. Some rented themselves out as laborers and others participated in petty trade at town markets. Some enslaved people did paid work in their free time and, in this way, were able to purchase their own freedom. Once free, some managed to purchase freedom for their family members as well.

Shifting economic conditions meant that the enslaved often moved from rural areas to towns, sometimes between seasons, and were frequently sold. This unstable life prevented the establishment of communities (Berlin 1998: 57). Frequent sales and permanent threat of sales made family life very difficult to create or sustain. It was also hard for couples to live together, since often they would be owned by different people. A consequence was that the Black population in the region did not reproduce itself; only the continued importation of enslaved people kept it from shrinking during the colonial period. The isolation of many farms and the short growing seasons meant that both the owners and the enslaved performed many different tasks throughout the year.

For example, we know about Adam Jackson, an enslaved man who lived in or near New London, Connecticut, his entire life, through the diary of Joshua Hempstead Jr. a third-generation New Londoner and a skilled shipbuilder and carpenter until his wife died following childbirth, at which time he chose to farm and devote himself to his nine children. During Hempstead's life, New London grew into a small coastal port city of small famers, shipbuilders, traders—and the region of New England with the highest number of enslaved people. He kept his daily diary for forty-seven years, from which Allegra di Bonaventura (2013) learned a great deal about Adam, whom Joshua bought in 1727 and owned for thirty years before his death. The city records show that a short time later, Adam was a taxpayer and apparently a free man. The diary and countless other documents di Bonaventura used offer a rich and fascinating account of New London's early years. She points out that Joshua's diary "remains one of the great records of everyday life in slavery and renders Adam one of the best-documented enslaved men in America's English colonies" (di Bonaventura

2013: 288). It "allows a rare view into Adam's daily activities over more than three decades, a unique and sometimes unexpected portrayal of an early American bondsman that defies easy stereotypes" (291).

Both of Adam's parents—John, who arrived from Africa or the West Indies in 1686, and Joan—were free Blacks. Their former owners, John Rogers, the leader of a small religious community, and Samuel Fox, a Rogers follower, had freed them around 1700, at a time when there were very few free Blacks in New England. However, Adam, who was born before his mother was freed in 1702 or 1703, remained Fox's property until his death in 1727, when Joshua bought Adam from the estate. At the time, Joshua was getting older and fewer of his children were available to work his farm with him. Often he and Adam worked together, but Joshua was increasingly involved in his work as a selectman, lay lawyer, county surveyor, assessor of estates, and justice of the peace, who in effect served as the local magistrate.

He quickly learned to trust Adam, even when they were not working together, and he often sent him to one of his farms eight miles away, where Adam would work for two or more days at a time before returning. "As Adam became integrated into the work of the farm, even taking a primary role, Joshua would be able to devote more of his time to serving both his grown children and a growing community" (di Bonaventura 2013: 249). Adam was not socially isolated, and the diary describes work he did with at least eighty other people—many of them English—and makes it clear that he had authority, particularly over younger coworkers, including the white ones (291). Adam also worked with a range of people, including some who had come from Africa and others who were free Algonquin or Africans. At times, he worked unsupervised and to earn money for himself. Joshua quickly "displayed his trust in the young man's competence and character" (297), especially on his 200-acre Stonington farm, often running the operations and staying alone there for several days at a time.

John and Joan Jackson had a hard life that reveals the vulnerable position of Blacks in the North at the time. They could initiate lawsuits, which Rogers and his followers, including the Jacksons, did. Soon after John arrived in New London at about the age of eighteen in 1686, Rogers purchased him. Di Bonaventura reports that at this time most slave sales were between people who knew each other and often involved just one slave purchase at a time. John Jackson soon became John Rogers's servant and disciple. After being freed, Jackson continued to live at Mamacock, Rogers's homestead, working as his servant. This is not very surprising, as he did not possess special skills and he clearly got along with Rogers and his family. Soon he built a home on the grounds and stayed for many years. Jackson would soon marry Joan, who was enslaved to Fox, a neighbor, so they could not live together until the Foxes, who were followers of Rogers, freed her in 1702 or 1703.

John and Joan Jackson faced immense challenges that illustrate how precarious Black lives were in the colonial period even for free people. In di Bonaventura's account, the Jacksons' vulnerability jumps off the pages and I am confident that almost no other Blacks at the time in the same situation would have even tried to do what John Jackson successfully did to keep his family together. By 1710, John and Joan had four more children. Following the law, they were free, since the mother's legal status determined that of her child at birth. However, Samuel Beebe, Rogers's brother-in-law and a Rogers follower, had grudges against Rogers, claiming that his wife Elizabeth (Rogers's sister) got short shrift in the distributions from their father's will and demanded Joan in a court claim. Of course, if this was granted, it would also mean that Beebe would then own Joan's six children (di Bonaventura 2013: 148–49). Beebe won the suit in New London, probably because of Rogers's unpopularity there. He then took Joan and her young son Jack to his house on Plum Island near Orient Point on Long Island, where she soon gave birth to another child, Rachel.

Jackson and Rogers then hatched and carried out a plan to go to the island at night, seize the three, and returned home to New London. Joan was quickly hidden and Rogers and Jackson were arrested and convicted. Meanwhile, Rogers's son had obtained ownership of the three Jackson children living in Mamacock, probably to protect them in return for work. Beebe soon found Joan in Rhode Island, and he sold her and her children to John and Mary Livingston.[8] Unable to pay the fines he was assessed, John Jackson indentured himself to Livingston to be near his wife and in the hope that he could acquire land at the end of his indenture as payment for his work (di Bonaventura 2013: 161). Soon Rachel died (166), but in 1713 Joan delivered a healthy boy, Jeremiah (Jerry). By 1714, Livingston had embarked on another failed venture, and in desperate need for money he sold Joan and her young children and leased out his home.

John Jackson, however, did not give up and fought back. He recognized that his chances to gain any land at the end of his indenture were over, and he decided to become a peddler working the coast from New London to Boston. Perhaps, di Bonaventura says, Rogers helped him. Jackson decided to file suit in a Massachusetts court, claiming that Joan and the children were free and could not be sold. He won in the lower court, and even though Livingston appealed and tried to influence the judge, he was not successful. However, Jackson did not get Jerry back for another two years, when the Court threatened to arrest the man who had bought him if he did not turn Jerry over. Then Jackson filed another suit to try to get Jack, which failed. Rogers freed three of the four Jackson siblings. It was not clear why he didn't free Abner, who went on to be a highly skilled master artisan, working as a cooper. Perhaps he was too valuable to be freed. Di Bonaventura (2013: 280) reminds us to that "the Jacksons . . . were a family on the edges of the English mainstream. Perhaps only the patriarch, John, had experienced a sudden captivity in a different culture, but all the Jacksons nevertheless face the challenges of forced servitude, separation, and prejudice. . . . However, John Jackson had fought the enslavement of his family every step of the way and succeeded beyond all measure."

The Northern slave system was different in a number of ways from the system in the South, which was built around larger farms and plantations and the cultivation mainly of cash crops such as tobacco, cereals, and rice in the colonial period. In contrast, most Northern slaveholders owned a small number of people—most often one or two—who generally lived in the same house as their owners and their families. Even in the region with the largest plantations, eastern Rhode Island, the size of holdings was under two dozen (Fitts 1996, 1998).

One theme in some recent studies shows how enslaved people in the North often exercised agency despite the inequality between themselves and their owners.[9] Sometimes this was done through direct negotiations, as was the case with Venture Smith and some of his owners and Adam Jackson and Joshua Hempstead. There are many examples of Northern owners permitting the enslaved to find a new owner to whom they would be sold, to individuals negotiating how much of the money that they earned when they were rented out they could keep or to obtain permission to sell produce they raised in local markets and keep the money they earned doing so. Indirect exercise of agency is seen in a variety of ways: working more slowly, breaking tools, stealing food, taking longer to return when running an errand, and sometimes simply refusing to do something they were told to do.

Life for the enslaved in the North was more diverse than in the South. A good number of enslaved men in towns and cities were trained in crafts such as carpentry, metalwork, and various jobs associated with the shipping industry, such as sail makers, shipbuilders, and, in many cases, sailors (White 1991:11). In Pennsylvania and New Jersey, some worked in rural iron foundries and tanneries. During the colonial period, when Northern slavery was strongest, the economy was very small scale, which meant that slaveholders were often forced to either sell or rent out their slaves as their economic fortunes or the seasons changed. Growing seasons were much shorter, crops were more diversified than in the South, and generally owners and other members of their family worked alongside the enslaved in the fields, all doing the same tasks. Both enslaved men and women often developed a wide range of skills (Berlin 1998). Hardesty (2016) argues that the binary distinction between enslaved and free is not adequate to describe Black people in colonial Boston. He argues that the concept of "unfreedom" is a continuum to suggest a range of ways that "slaves learned to navigate and manipulate" their individual situations to their advantage at times. At the time, Boston was "a society in flux," its social order ambiguous, and "enslaved Bostonians took advantage of this ambiguity, . . . fighting to reshape the boundaries of their enslavement, seeking greater autonomy from the master class, and forcing their way into Euro-American society to demand a place within it" through individual and not collective action (Hardesty 2016: 3–7). Sweet (2003: 227–28) similarly makes a case that the end of slavery resulted from increasing autonomy and the actions of the enslaved themselves to take advantage of changing conditions that made ownership less advantageous.[10]

Despite these distinctive features of slavery in the North, some large-scale farms, often described as plantations, used enslaved labor. Located in eastern Rhode Island in the Narragansett region, eastern Connecticut, and the Hudson River Valley and eastern Long Island, the largest of these farms had more than twenty enslaved people. Griswold (2013) calls them "provisioning plantations" because, starting in the mid-seventeenth century, many of the crops they grew or the livestock they raised were for export to the Caribbean islands to feed the enslaved Blacks growing sugarcane on large plantations there. Newport, Rhode Island, was a crucial port for this commerce. Traders gathered foodstuffs from different places and shipped it to the Caribbean islands, where some of the traders and growers had relatives who owned sugar plantations.

The story of hardworking farmers on small New England farms eking out their existence is a central part of New England's own narrative of its early economic development. Less commonly heard is the crucial role that slave traders played in New England and New York in the growth of shipping, commerce, and nascent industries. Northerners owned the vast majority of ships from North America involved in the triangle trade between Africa, the Caribbean islands, and the colonies. In Africa, they purchased captives to be sold in either the Caribbean islands or the South. On the islands they purchased sugarcane and molasses used to manufacture rum in colonial factories, most of which were located in New England, and much of which was used, in turn, to purchase enslaved Africans. This trade was very lucrative and resulted in eighteenth-century capital accumulation among the Northern traders in Boston, New York, New London, and especially Rhode Island. In some cases, traders themselves or members of their family earned a high return off of plantations they owned on the islands, worked by enslaved people (Farrow, Lang, and Frank 2005; DeWolf 2008; Manegold 2010). Over several generations this produced some very rich people who formed a large part of the country's early economic and social elite, and whose families profited from this wealth over many generations.[11]

There was no stigma to being a slave trader, especially before the American Revolution. Many of the traders became political leaders and benefactors of the early colleges and universities in the region, such as Brown, Harvard, Princeton, and Yale (Wilder 2013). "The Puritans not only justified slavery, but gave it a triple sanction. Slavery was defended upon economic, spiritual and legal grounds" (Greene [1942] 1969: 60). By the time that U.S. slave trading legally ended in 1808, these wealthy men and their families were in a position to finance and run many of the early Northern textile mills and factories at the start of the country's industrial era. By the eve of the Civil War, when the country was producing 60 percent of the world's cotton, New England had 472 cotton mills, and large New York banks were crucial in financing the production of cotton and factories' finished goods, which illustrate the seamless links between Southern slavery and Northern industrial development (Berlin 1998; Farrow, Lang, and Frank 2005: 26; Baptist 2014).

Rarely did ships arriving in Northern ports with enslaved Africans have large numbers to be sold, as traders almost always went to the islands and/or Southern ports before returning home. Those who were enslaved in the North generally had been in the Caribbean, as Northerners preferred people who had been partially acculturated, able to speak at least some English, and less likely to be vulnerable to New World diseases, having survived the long and dangerous journey by boat from Africa and having lived in the Caribbean where they were "seasoned" for a few years (Berlin 1998: 47–50).

Yet one of the rarely repeated stories in early American economic history is slavery's indirect impact on the North. Folkloric accounts of hardy New England farming portrayed farmers (white ones, that is) clearing the boulders from their fields to build walls, plowing the soil, and working hard while planting and harvesting to scrape out a living. Surely such people existed, but there were also larger enterprises and some small farms, especially in southern New England, Pennsylvania, New York, and New Jersey, that relied on enslaved labor even when white landowners worked in the fields as well. And, more to the point, the shipbuilding and ancillary economies that relied on or were enmeshed in slavery were a huge part of the vaunted "maritime" New England tradition, and the investments and stockholding in the same enriched families intergenerationally. In understanding slavery, the deep symbiosis between regions and economies, even without direct slave ownership, is critical. Few Americans' hands are "clean" of the taint of a slave economy, in other words, whether they owned slaves directly or not.

After 1800, when Northern slavery was declining, cotton production in the South was quickly rising with the invention of the cotton gin and the establishment of plantations. Although the British were the largest market for Southern cotton, newer, small Northern textile mills needed the raw materials as well. Many of these early factories were built using the capital earned earlier in the slave trade, which officially ended in 1808. What this meant was that the North's early industrial economy accumulated the start-up capital, in effect, from the slave trade, and then used the money to obtain the crucial raw materials for production grown and shipped with slave labor (Bailey 1998)—producing a close relationship between "the lords of the lash" and "the lords of the loom." Another consequence is that "merchants and manufacturers with economic ties to the cotton and sugar plantations of the South and the Caribbean transformed higher education in the antebellum North" (Wilder 2013: 285). What is clear is that the growth of the Northern economy was fully implicated and dependent upon enslaved people and not built mainly on the backs of hardy yeoman farmers and their families.

Baptist (2014) summarizes the direct and indirect effects of Southern slavery and its significant impact on nineteenth-century Northern economic development.

> At every stage of the march from seed to mill to consumer, entrepreneurs of one kind or another sliced into tranches the margin of profit generated on the backs of enslaved African Americans, plated each slice, and distributed it to an actor in the world economy. . . .
>
> Next come the second-order effects that comprised the goods and services necessary to produce cotton. There was the purchase of slaves. . . . Then there was the purchase of land, the cost of credit for such purchases, the pork and corn bought at the river landings, the axes the slaves used to clear land and the cloth they wore, even the luxury goods and other spending by slaveholding families. . . .
>
> Third-order effects, the hardest to calculate, included the money spent by millworkers and Illinois hog farmers, the wages paid to steamboat workers, and the revenues yielded by investments made with the profits of merchants, manufacturers, and slave traders who derived some or all of their income either directly or indirectly from the southwestern [meaning Mississippi Delta] fields. (Baptist 2014: 321)

In general, even on the Narragansett plantations, the enslaved did not live in separate structures. In both the cities and rural areas they were likely to live in the same homes as their owners—often sleeping in attics, kitchens, back rooms, or small additions to a house. In many cases, they ate the same food and sometimes sat at the same table with their owners and their families. There is some disagreement among writers about whether this is an indicator of greater equality between owners and the enslaved in the North than in the South, where this practice was far less common. Greene ([1942] 1969) and others say that slavery in New England was more benevolent than its Southern counterpart. In contrast, Fitts (1996, 1998) emphasizes that Northern practices in Narragansett of different eating arrangements, segregated seating in churches, and separate burial grounds all clearly communicated important status differences, limited rights for the enslaved, and white desires to exercise control over them (also see Greene [1942] 1969: 284–85). While recognizing some differences between the lives of the enslaved in the North and South, White (1991: chap. 4) comes down firmly on the side that it was brutal in each but for different reasons, concluding that "the idea of a benevolent slave society was a chimera, a self-deceiving myth propagated by New Yorkers in a vain attempt to distinguish themselves from the evil that they perceived to exist in the South" (113).

An interesting practice in New England slavery was the annual "election" of "Negro Governors" that occurred throughout the region, "which was followed by an elaborate inauguration ceremony terminating in feasting and games" (Greene [1942] 1969: 249). Owners fitted out their slaves in the best cast-off finery, and slaves often rode to the events on their owner's horses or even in his carriage to reflect their enslaver's opulence (250). How much control these Governors had over their constituencies is unclear, since records show that the courts handled criminal cases against enslaved Blacks. However, Greene suggests that they probably handled more trivial disputes among Blacks and even petty cases brought by the slave owners (254). In addition, he perceptively suggests that while this practice suggests gradual cultural adoption, "it also shows the paternalistic aspect of New England slavery . . . [and] was a subtle form of slave control, for, by inducing the slaves to inform on and to punish their fellows, the threat to the masters' security was minimized. Psychologically it served as an outlet for the pent-up ambitions of the more aggressive Negroes and their fellows and thereby tended to make the Negro more complacent in his bondage" (255).

Writing about these same practices more than four decades later, Piersen (1988) emphasized that these rituals, probably dating from the early eighteenth century, were both an imitation of white people's elections and meant to honor African royalty or their descendants in their community. He stressed that these sometimes weeklong events were important as times when the enslaved were outside their owners' purview, but that whites permitted the events partly because they indirectly enforced social norms. For these events, whites were expected to provide fancy clothing, food, and drink, which reinforced their own status. Piersen concludes that the events were indeed hybrid in nature and were one of the many ways that African traditions were combined with white cultural practices in the lives of the enslaved (chaps. 10–11). As early as Dutch New Amsterdam, yearly celebrations combined African and European cultural expressions, and in places such as Philadelphia and other cities, some of these events mocked the hierarchical world in which the enslaved lived.[12]

Enslaved and free Blacks in the North were tightly controlled by slave codes that were passed in all the colonies starting in the late seventeenth century (Greene [1942] 1969: 128), although the codes were not the same in all places. What is especially important to remember is that even after abolition in Northern states, Blacks continued to have many restrictions on their movement and far fewer rights than whites, although both were nominally citizens. For example, Blacks generally were not able to vote or to serve in the military or on juries, and no laws protected free Blacks from job discrimination. Free Blacks in Massachusetts were required to work on roads a certain number of days each year at the discretion of local selectmen, and in Pennsylvania if fines could not be paid, some justices ordered free Blacks to be returned to servitude.[13]

In New England, an effort was often made to teach some of the enslaved how to read and write, as well as to convert them to Christianity and have them get married and baptize their children. While their attendance at church was often encouraged, the seating was almost always segregated, with Blacks only able to sit upstairs in a balcony or in the pews in the rear of the church.

Slave codes often limited the number of Blacks who could gather together in towns and cities and the hours when they could appear in public places and required the enslaved to have written permission from their owners to travel outside the area in which they lived and worked. Often, but not in New England, Blacks could not own property, testify in court, or learn to read and write. Many codes sanctioned owners to severely punish their enslaved people, and whenever there were any manifestations of protest, punishments were often severely increased. In addition, they specified much harsher punishments for Blacks than for whites committing the same crimes. Lepore (2005a: 57) points out, "New York's slave codes were almost entirely concerned with curtailing the ability of enslaved people to move at will, and to gather, for fear that they might decide, especially when drunk, that slavery was not to be borne and one way to end it would be to burn the city down." Often owners decided upon and administered what they considered the "proper punishment" for their own slaves (Lepore 2005a: 80–81). Any signs of protest, let alone violent resistance, increased white fears, which almost invariably led to the tightening of the restrictions on both enslaved and free Blacks.

Slave resistance was present and, in part, a response to the slave codes, daily humiliations, and other severe restrictions imposed on the enslaved. The existence of resistance makes it clear that not all Blacks were willing to continue to live as enslaved people even if the treatment in New England or elsewhere might have been relatively benevolent in comparison with the South or the Caribbean islands. As with enslaved people in the South, some enslaved in the North committed suicide rather than remain enslaved (Greene [1942] 1969: 256). Others chose to attempt to escape even though the punishment if they were caught was often severe, such as being whipped or sold to the islands to work on a sugar plantation. Escape attempts in the North were relatively common, and newspapers from the period had many advertisements offering rewards for runaways, but we have little idea about the success rate. Some reached Canada and found freedom. Others who succeeded cast their lot with Indian communities, often marrying and raising families in them.

Occasional slave rebellions and attacks on white farms and houses occurred from time to time in the North, the South, and in the Caribbean. "Plots to burn the metropolis flowed freely across the Atlantic and up and down the seaboard. When they were true they were terrifying. When they were delusions, they were droll" (Lepore 2005a: 56). Reports of these attacks frightened whites who feared Black crime and potential revolts. Their response was to tighten controls on the enslaved population. In 1712 in Manhattan, twenty-four enslaved Africans plotted a rebellion. They accumulated weapons and set fire to the outhouse of a white baker; when he and others arrived to put out the flames, they were ambushed, seven were killed, and nine others wounded. The response was a series of hurried trials in which twenty-one Blacks were convicted, eighteen of whom were executed (Hodges 1999: 65).[14] Soon afterward New York further tightened its slave code, restricting both free and enslaved Blacks. In 1741 in New York, purportedly of larger scale and seen by some as a class-based reaction to conditions in the city, a series of ten fires were set, the first of which almost entirely destroyed Fort George at the southern tip of Manhattan (Harris 2003: 43). Others followed shortly thereafter. More than two hundred enslaved Blacks and a few whites were suspected of participating in this conspiracy. Thirteen were convicted and burned at the stake; seventeen were hanged; one cut his own throat; eighty-four men were sold in the

Caribbean; two white men and two white women were hanged as the ring-leaders; and seven were banished from New York (Lepore 2005a: xii). Lepore, however, questions whether this was actually a rebellion or an effort on the part of some white political leaders to use the events for their own political gains.

Emancipation occurred gradually and peacefully in the North. Interestingly, it should be pointed out that ending the slave trade for the states in the region was much more quickly and easily achieved. During the Revolution, Vermont, which had broken off from New York, became the first state to outlaw slavery and included a ban in its 1777 constitution. There were only a handful of enslaved people in Vermont at the time. However, despite the constitutional ban, the 1790 census still showed sixteen enslaved people in Vermont.[15] Manumission societies formed in many states, often dominated by prominent white political and economic leaders. Sometimes, as in New York and New Jersey, a good number of their members were slave owners themselves and often not particularly effective. White (1991: 11) suggests that Blacks themselves played a far more significant role in pushing for their own freedom.

Massachusetts, which had been the first colony to legally recognize slavery, more ambiguously ended it. Many attribute its demise to a series of court decisions in the early 1780s that freed individuals but did not clearly rule that slavery must end throughout the state O'Brien (1960). The most famous one involved Quock (also spelled Quok at times) Walker, yet it was not published until many years later. However, Malcolm (2009: 227–28) argues:

> The [State's] Supreme Judicial Court ultimately determined that Quock was a slave but in the process of ruling on Walker's rights, the chief justice, William Cushing, found slavery inconsistent with article 1 of the state's new constitution, which declared: "All men are born free and equal." Cushing's pronouncement that slavery was inconsistent with the Massachusetts constitution caused confusion. The case turned on the narrower issue of whether an individual promised his freedom had been denied it. Moreover, the court opinion with Cushing's comments was not published for some years. But together with several other cases, the Walker case effectively ended slavery in Massachusetts.

New Hampshire, which earlier was part of Massachusetts, had a small enslaved population, mainly in and around Portsmouth, since at least 1645, when a Massachusetts slave trader brought several captives from Guinea to the small city and sold them (Sammons and Cunningham 2004: 16). The size of New Hampshire's enslaved population was never large. McManus (1973: 200) reports that it was 656 in 1775, less than 1 percent of the colony's population. It fell rapidly during the Revolution as a number of whites freed their slaves, who then served in the Continental Army, often in place of their owners or to help meet a town quota. Portsmouth had the state's largest enslaved and free Black populations but it was never more than 4 percent of the city (Sammons and Cunningham 2004: 4).

The New Hampshire's constitution declared "all men are born equal and independent," with natural rights, "among which are enjoying and defending life and liberty." This was very close to the language that some feel led, via the courts, to the end of slavery in Massachusetts. But there are no judicial records from New Hampshire to indicate that this was construed there as ending slavery. Many clearly felt it did, but whether for all slaves or only to children of slaves born after 1783 is not clear.

Slaves were removed from the rolls of taxable property in 1789, but the act appears to have been for taxing purposes only. The 1790 census counted 158 slaves; but in 1800, there were only eight. Portsmouth traders participated legally in the slave trade until 1807. No slaves were counted for the state in 1810 and 1820, but three are listed in 1830 and one in 1840.

A commonly accepted date for the official end of slavery in New Hampshire is 1857, when an act was passed stating that "no person, because of descent, should be disqualified from becoming a citizen of the state." The act is interpreted as prohibiting slavery. By a strict interpretation, however, slavery was outlawed only on December 6, 1865, when the Thirteenth Amendment went into effect (ratified by New Hampshire, July 1, 1865).[16]

An interesting follow-up to the story of New Hampshire's abolition is that in 1779, twenty Black Revolutionary soldiers from the state petitioned the New Hampshire legislature for an end to slavery there. The General Assembly did not act on the petition but pledged to consider it at a more convenient time. More than two hundred years later, it was discovered in the state archives. In 2013, the 150th anniversary of the Emancipation Proclamation, as a memorial for a recently uncovered burial ground for Blacks in Portsmouth was being planned (see Chapter 7), the legislature took up the bill and overwhelmingly approved it, which meant that the fourteen of the twenty who had originally submitted the petition but died as slaves were freed retroactively when Governor Maggie Hassan signed it (Irons 2013).

Pennsylvania passed a gradual abolition law in 1780 (amended in 1788) that established a pattern that Rhode Island, Connecticut, New York, and New Jersey all followed within the next twenty-four years. This law, like the ones adopted in the other states, showed that these legislatures continued to view the enslaved as property, recognizing the need to compensate owners for their loss. The act prohibited the future importation of enslaved people into the state and specified that a child born to an enslaved woman would be free but subject to indenture until age twenty-eight to reimburse their enslavers for raising them (McManus 1973: 161). What this meant in practice is that if a female born into slavery in 1779 gave birth to a child thirty-five or forty years later (e.g., 1818 or 1819), the child would not be free of indenture until 1845 or 1846. This illustrates how gradual the law was. The law, as amended in 1788, specified that people from other states could bring enslaved persons into Pennsylvania, but after six months the slaves could petition the state for their freedom.

In practice, the manumission of enslaved people in Pennsylvania that started in the early 1770s was relatively rapid, although there were still some enslaved in Pennsylvania as late as 1847. At the same time, legal freedom did not necessarily alter the lives for most former slaves in the state. Although they could own property, move more freely, and better protect their families, many did not have the resources, skills, or opportunities to take advantage of the change in legal status. Often, they became indentured servants under a long-term agreement and continued living with their former owners or with other whites who had purchased their indentures (Nash and Soderlund 1991: chap. 6; White 1991: 48–49). In addition, a good number of free Blacks found it necessary to bind out their children into indentures with white families, given their very limited economic opportunities (Nash 1988: 76). In 1790, half of the free Blacks in Philadelphia lived in white households; the proportion dropped to 39 percent in 1810 and 27 percent a decade later (Nash 1988: 161).[17] Family formation was difficult, and Blacks faced harassment from immigrant whites and were unable to work in many of the city's newly developing industries. Pennsylvania first allowed Blacks to vote upon being freed if they met the property qualifications, but it specified that Blacks could not vote when it adopted a new constitution in 1838.

In 1784 both Rhode Island and Connecticut passed gradual abolition bills that were similar to what Pennsylvania had passed four years earlier. In the mid-eighteenth century, Rhode Island had the highest proportion of enslaved people in New England with the heaviest concentration in the eastern part of the state in the Narragansett region. As in Pennsylvania, slavery did not end quickly in Rhode Island, and the 1840 census reported that there were still five enslaved Blacks living in the state.

The pattern in Connecticut was similar, where the earliest mentions of enslaved people were in 1639 in Hartford, but not many slaves were in the colony before 1700. Yet, by the eve of the Revolution, 25 percent of all property inventories included slaves. New London County, an industrial center that also contained large slave-worked farms, became the largest slaveholding section of New England with the highest number, but not the highest proportion, of enslaved people in the colonial period.[18] After three failed attempts in the 1770s, Connecticut finally passed a gradual abolition law in 1784. Its gradual manumission law, however, meant that there were still fifty-four enslaved people reported living in the state in 1840, the last year slaves were counted in their census. The legislature abolished slavery entirely in 1848.

In New England, as elsewhere, it should be noted that granting freedom was not the same thing as granting rights, and throughout the North the rights of free Blacks were severely restricted and were considerably less than those of whites (Melish 1998).

By 1771, the total number of enslaved Blacks in New York was just under twenty thousand, which was 12 percent of the population and down from the slightly more than 14 percent in the middle of the century (McManus 1973: 209–10). The proportion in the city was even higher— almost 18 percent in 1771 (Hodges 1999: 274–75). Despite the turmoil of the Revolution, the British occupation of the city for almost the entire war, and the many battles fought in the state during which a number of enslaved people escaped, the state's enslaved population increased. After a series of tumultuous debates in the New York, the legislature finally passed a gradual abolition bill in 1799 that specified that "the males became free at 28, the females at 25." Until then, "they would be the property of the mother's master. Slaves already in servitude before July 4, 1799, remained slaves for life, though they were reclassified as 'indentured servants.'"[19] Slavery in New York ended much more slowly in the hinterlands than in the city itself (White 1991: 50–53). Pressure to end slavery in the state continued to build, and, in 1817, the legislature voted to free all enslaved people in the state on July 4, 1827. Blacks in New York celebrated the day, July 4, privately to not antagonize whites, but on July 5 they "held a grand procession, an oration, and a public dinner" (Hodges 1999: 223).

McManus (2001: 175–76) argues that once it was clear that the state was heading toward the adoption of abolition, owners increasingly found ways to sell the enslaved to Southern states, where they could fetch a profit. As in the other states, once slavery ended in New York, the formerly enslaved living there were hardly citizens with full rights. For example, in 1828 in New York only 298 of 29,071 Blacks were eligible to vote (Hodges 1999: 191). "Slavery did not prevent Negroes from acquiring economic expertise; rather free society prevented them from using their skills and talents after emancipation" (McManus 2001: 195–96). The shifts in this period led to Black community creation through churches and the opening of a few segregated schools began. Some of this shift was tied to the reality that Blacks were no longer a source of skilled labor and were excluded from newly emerging factory jobs (White 1991: 54). At the same time, there was a rise in race-based violence including mob attacks against Blacks (Hodges 1999: chap. 8). During this period, the Black population increased but nowhere near as fast as that of whites did through immigration. As a result, employment opportunities decreased, and jobs Blacks once dominated, such as female domestics, were taken over by Irish immigrants (Hodges 1999: 243). A Committee of Vigilance formed to protect resident Blacks as well as help those escaping enslavement in the South avoid slave catchers (Hodges 1999: 245–48; Foner 2015).

Enslavement in New Jersey was harsh and especially slow to end. Abolitionists were weak in the state, especially in the east where slavery was most deeply entrenched. The debate over abolition in New Jersey emphasized that the enslaved were property and stressed the need to compensate slave owners for any loss of property if the enslaved were freed. When the state finally passed a gradual abolition law in 1804, the slave owners retained the right to sell their slaves to states where the practice was legal or into long-term indentures, provisions that were only ended in 1818. In 1830, of the 3,568 Northern Blacks who remained enslaved, more than two-thirds were in New Jersey. The 1804 law specified that children of slaves were required to serve their mother's owner until twenty-five if male and twenty-one if female. This shifted the financial burden of abolition away from the owners to the slaves for a term, making them repay the cost of freedom (Gigantino 2015: 97). The law also included an abandonment clause that required slave owners to care for a slave's children until they reached the age of one year, modeled after the one New York had adopted five years earlier (Hodges 1999: 170). After that they could be abandoned to the overseers of the poor, who would be paid $3 a month to maintain them—often then paid back to their owners for supporting the children. Opposition to this system grew as it quickly became so expensive that it consumed 30 percent of the states' budget (Hodges 1999: 171).[20] In 1806 it was abolished, but not for those children already abandoned. Abuse of the system caused its total termination in 1811 (Gigantino 2015: 106–7). In 1846, the state symbolically ended slavery but what it really did was reclassify all former slaves as "apprentices for life," which once again changed little in their lives (Gigantino 2015: 215). They were only free after the Civil War because of the Thirteenth Amendment, which New Jersey's legislature voted against.

When slavery in the North gradually ended in the decades following the Revolution, there was no effort to integrate the free Black population into the social and economic fabric of Northern society. On the contrary: most Northern whites, even if they thought that slavery was wrong, did not believe that free Blacks were capable of being full citizens. Within a short time of gaining their freedom, Blacks in the North found themselves treated as second-class persons in many ways. Free Blacks were subject to many legal restrictions quite similar to the Jim Crow laws adopted in Southern states after 1876. Discrimination in social, economic, and political areas was the rule. Called the Black Codes during slavery, these laws limited Blacks formally and informally by restricting their ability to participate in politics, sit on juries, marry whites, own property, and work in certain jobs.

Curfews in many towns and cities only applied to Blacks, and some municipalities refused to let Blacks live inside the town or city limits. In many areas Blacks were harassed and unable to work in jobs open to whites. In many places, Blacks could not vote even if they owned property; in others, where the right was first granted (although not used by many), it was withdrawn later.[21] New York, which granted free Blacks few rights was described in the 2005 New-York Historical Society exhibition as "inventing Jim Crow." By 1820 when white immigration was increasing, tension between Blacks and the newly arrived whites grew and produced regular race riots and attacks on Blacks and their neighborhoods in cities such as New York, Philadelphia, and Providence (DuBois [1899] 1967; Nash 1988; Sweet 2003: 351–97; Clark-Pujara 2016: 101–9).

Historians have pointed out that a number of Northern slaveholders were more than willing to free their slaves at this time because they realized it would mean that they would no longer be responsible for those too frail or too old to work any longer. In some states, such as New Jersey, slaveholders were compensated for their "loss of property" when their slaves were freed. More than a few slaveholders, realizing that manumission was near, sold their enslaved people to the South even when this was illegal. Federal laws starting in 1793 authorized efforts to capture fugitive slaves and return them to their owners, and more than a few unscrupulous operators seized free Blacks, claiming they were escaped slaves, to take them to the South where they were sold into slavery.[22] In sum, the lives of free Blacks in the post-Revolutionary period were hard and rarely were they able to achieve even a modest level of social or economic security.

Melish (1998: xiii) emphasizes that once most of the enslaved in New England were freed, there was a significant effort to erase the memory of slavery along with a strong hope that those Blacks living in the region would leave or somehow disappear: "I discovered that the narrative of New England slavery was not untold exactly, but it was a kind of private narrative, told in discrete, isolated places from which it had never emerged to disrupt the public narratives of a 'free, white New England.' In fact, a virtual amnesia about slavery in New England had a history almost as old as the history of local slavery itself." It was assumed that somehow the formerly enslaved would disappear—not that they would be integrated into society as citizens. Of course, this was not what free Blacks wanted (Melish 1998: 79–80). With emancipation, Melish argues, the white project became the removal of Blacks from the region. Attempts to do this included symbolic ones, such as portraying Blacks as dangerous strangers, emphasizing race as a Southern problem, characterizing New England slavery as mild and/or brief, removing Black corpses from burial grounds, conducting "roundups and 'warnings-out,'" rioting and vandalizing Black neighborhoods, and encouraging colonization (return to Africa) (Melish 1998: 2).[23]

The American Colonization Society was founded in 1816, and slave owners and former owners were among its sponsors, as were some abolitionists. At one point, it had 150 branches in the country. Tomek (2011) describes it as part of an effort to preserve white society, and many New

Englanders were especially enthusiastic about its proposals. The support can be explained simply: "The South . . . was afraid of them; the North did not want them" (Ottley and Weatherby 1967: 68–69). However, few free Blacks had any desire to move to Africa, having lived in the United States for several generations, and mounted a number of protests against the idea.

The fact that anti-Black sentiment was so strong and the fruits of emancipation were so meager in terms of improvement in people's lives is often not recognized if we fail to see enslavement as only part of the economic system in the country. McManus (1973: 188) points out that "emancipation freed Negroes from the control of individual masters but left them in bondage to white society," then adds:

> The gradual abolition of slavery in the North brought into sharper focus the economic determinants of the system. . . . The bitter paradox of emancipation in the North is that it excluded blacks from the economic opportunities needed to make a go of freedom. . . .
>
> The fact that Northern emancipation took the form of economic displacement made it easier for whites to accept the idea of legal freedom for Blacks. . . . Northern slaveowners lost nothing when their slaves became free, and the system of public compensation adopted by some states actually provided the masters with a windfall. (McManus 1973: 196–97)

Although few people link the North in memory to slavery, there is much that *might* have been remembered, and known, as even the preceding brief overview has revealed. Why, then, has this narrative been forgotten? Probably one reason is that Northern slavery ended slowly; it did not disappear at one moment in time and through a dramatic event or events. In fact, White argues that its end was often more rooted in individual actions, including negotiations between the enslaved and their owners, than in legislative action. Once it had become certain that slavery would eventually end, it must have seemed easier for many owners to secure several years of trouble-free service, or a cash payment from their slaves, rather than face the risk of losing both their slaves and any possible recompense when their increasingly restive human property decided to abscond (White 1991: 149).

Consider the three ways to facilitate memory recovery—narratives, ritual expressions and enactments, and visible public and commemorative landscapes. The absence of all three played a critical role in diminishing

awareness of the North's slave past and inhibiting the formation and preservation of collective memories of it. Not only were none of them common
as reminders of slavery's past in the North; in addition, most Blacks living
in the North today had ancestors who migrated from the South or did so
themselves, which also lessens their own direct connection to, and awareness of, the region's earlier history.

Rather, white Northerners starting in the first half of the nineteenth
century—either consciously or, often, but not always, unconsciously—
erased memories of slavery in the region (Minardi 2010, 2012). Its towns,
cities, and states produced little readily accessible evidence or narratives
about Northern slavery; there were no significant rituals or other cultural
expressions such as literature, theater, or artwork that recounted the experience of the Northern enslavement; and the symbolic landscape in the North
had few distinctively visible markers such as statues, memorials, restored
houses or other buildings, historical plaques, or other prominent signs that
slavery had been present in the region, or explanations of how and where
it was practiced and ended.[24]

Minardi argues that William Cooper Nell's book ([1855] 1968) documenting Blacks who had fought in the Revolution "disrupted the prevailing
narrative of a 'free' New England simply by putting enslaved and formerly
enslaved people onto the landscape of memory" (Minardi 2012: 96). However, "Yankee culture confined the memory of individual New Englanders
of color to other kinds of spaces, more private and less explosive than the
Revolutionary battlefield" (Minardi 2010: 96). The absence of accounts
from the perspective of the enslaved certainly contributed to the absence of
narratives and memories.[25]

The topic of Northern enslavement was rarely raised in public settings
in the North, so narratives about it were never disseminated. Occasionally,
local town histories would include some details of both enslaved and free
Blacks who lived in them (Sheldon 1893, Smith 1905, 1906). At the same
time, there was far too little use of local records that contained references
to, and information about, enslaved and free Blacks in the North. When
researchers more recently sought information on slavery in the North, they
were able to find quite a lot about its practice and magnitude (Greene
[1942] 1969; Litwack 1961; McManus 1973, 2001; Nash 1988; Berlin 1998;
Melish 1998; Sammons and Cunningham 2004; Berlin and Harris 2005b;
Gerzina 2008; Manegold 2010; di Bonaventura 2013; Hayes 2013; O'Toole
2016).

Melish (1998) argues that the narratives that emerged about Northern life, especially in New England, stressed the values of individual hard work, independence, and religious freedom, leaving little room for a more complex and complicated account that included slavery and the slave trade's role in the region's growth and development. This pattern of omission is quite widespread in the North. For example, among the many whites and Blacks with whom I have spoken in the course of my research, no one in Philadelphia where I live (other than historians) seems to be aware that William Penn and many other Quakers owned slaves in the colony starting in the 1680s, that Quakers were some of the colony's largest slave owners, that it was not until the eve of the American Revolution that they took a hard-line position in opposition to it (Nash 1988), or that some of the early fortunes in the state came from slave trading or plantations in Maryland and Delaware that provided the capital for early industrial growth (Seitz 2014). Only in recent years has this begun to change. An example of this pattern is Philadelphia's Chew family (see Chapter 6). Benjamin Chew, who served as Chief Justice of Pennsylvania during the colonial period, was at one point the largest slave owner in the state with multiple plantations in Maryland and Delaware. He never showed any interest in freeing any of them. Rather, he built the Cliveden mansion in Philadelphia's Germantown section, and his descendants later used his accumulated wealth to build large factories to acquire more riches (Nash and Soderlund 1991: 146–47; Seitz 2014).

Similarly, there is scant public memory about the region's early history of slave trading and the ways this produced many of the North's early civic and political leaders, including many founders and early leaders of prestigious universities before 1800 (Horton and Horton 1997: 5). "As their American identities evolved, merchant families became the sponsors and patrons of colonial colleges," Wilder (2013: 49) reports. Ties between Princeton and the South were particularly strong, and Southern planters frequently sent their sons there. When colleges were established in the South starting at the end of the eighteenth century, Princeton graduates often played a key role in them.

In the decades before the American Revolution merchants and planters became not just the benefactors of colonial society but its new masters. Slaveholders became college presidents. The wealth of

the traders determined the locations and decided the fates of colonial schools. Profits from the sale and purchase of human beings
paid for campuses and swelled college trusts. And the politics of the
campus conformed to the presence and demands of slaveholding
students as colleges aggressively cultivated a social environment
attractive to the sons of wealthy families. (Wilder 2013: 77)

There were a number of enslaved people in the cities and towns where
these schools were located, and many enslaved people built the school
buildings and performed the most labor-intensive jobs on the campus.
Many faculty members were slave owners as well. Princeton had nine presidents in seventy-five years, all of whom were slave owners (Wilder 2013:
chap. 4). In the nineteenth century, scholars at the leading colleges and
universities moved away from religious justifications for slavery and turned
to scientific racism.[26] When the American Colonization Society emerged
and advocated removal of Blacks to Africa, it had strong roots on college
campuses in the North (Wilder 2013: chap. 8).

Only in the first decade of the twenty-first century have the stories of
the link between slavery and many of the early founders of these prestigious
schools resurfaced. In 2003 Ruth J. Simmons, a descendant of former slaves
and the first African American President of Brown University, whose
founding family had earned a good deal of its wealth in the slave trade,
responded to some students' and graduates' discomfort about the university's historical amnesia concerning the slave trade. She appointed a Steering Committee on Slavery and Justice to investigate and issue a public
report on the university's historical relationship to slavery and the trans-
atlantic slave trade. The report, published three years later after extensive
research and community discussions, detailed ways many of Brown's
founders and early patrons, including members of John Carter Brown's
family, were involved in the slave trade. For example, "about thirty members of the Brown corporation owned or captained slave ships, and many
of them were involved in the slave trade during their years of service to the
University" (Simmons 2007: 59).

The report offered a number of specific proposals about how the uni-
versity could constructively address its history (Brown University Steering
Committee on Slavery and Justice 2006). In her 2007 lecture at Cambridge
University marking the bicentennial of the end of the British slave trade,

Simmons focused on the problem of the forgotten story of the slave trade in the North. Her lecture, "Hidden in Plain Sight: Slavery and Justice in Rhode Island," pointed out that it is still very hard for many white Americans to face this part of their past directly (Simmons 2007). Similarly, Melish (2009) describes the Rhode Island Historical Society's resistance to making the story of John Brown's involvement in the slave trade part of the society's tour of his mansion in Providence. This reaction is not uncommon throughout the North when the issue of slaveholding and trading on the part of ancestors surfaces many generations later. In short, the story of the links between the university's early years and slavery were not hidden; rather, no one wanted to see and acknowledge them. This pattern is hardly unique to Brown, however.

Yale's three hundredth anniversary celebration in 2001 included a tribute to its "long history of activism in the face of slavery," focusing on the abolitionist faculty members who befriended the enslaved Africans who had seized the ship *Amistad* that arrived in New London, Connecticut, in 1839. Yale also created the world's first center for the study of slavery located at the university (Zernike 2001). However, a research paper published by three Yale graduate students charged that the school had ignored its less honorable side. This included the use of money earned from slave trading for its first scholarships, endowed professorships, and library endowment. "It honored slave traders when choosing figures to chisel as 'Worthies' on the tower at the center of its campus" and chose the names of slave traders for eight of its twelve residential colleges (Zernike 2001).[27] In April 2016, Yale announced it would not change the name of Calhoun College, but would no longer use the term "master" to describe faculty members who head the residential colleges. Instead, the title would be changed to "head of college." A few months later, in July 2016, a worker in Calhoun College's dining hall used a broomstick to smash a stained-glass panel that pictured enslaved Blacks carrying bales of cotton that he considered degrading.[28] The following fall, Yale's Committee to Establish Principles on Renaming issued its report, and two months later Yale announced it would change the name of the building (Remnick 2017).

Yale was not the only distinguished institution in the North that benefited from slavery and the slave trade but soon forgot about it. So did Harvard Law School, endowed by money from the Royall family, which was earned in the slave trade and on Isaac Royall's large sugar plantation

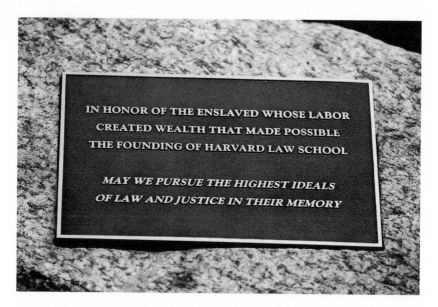

Figure 4. The plaque placed in front of Harvard Law School in September 2017 to recognize the enslaved people whose labor was crucial in the establishment of the school. Photograph by Jon Chase.

in Antigua. The Royall family shield became Harvard Law School's emblem (Manegold 2010; Zernike 2001). Starting in 2007, Sven Beckert and Katherine Stevens taught a seminar at Harvard, inspired by what Brown University had done, that investigated Harvard University's ties to slavery and culminated in an online report and website "Harvard and Slavery: Seeking a Forgotten History."[29] In 2016, following protests from students and faculty, Harvard decided to change the law school's shield (Annear 2016). In 2017, Harvard placed a plaque in front of its Law School acknowledging early dependence on the labor of enslaved people for its founding (Figure 4).

There were demonstrations and discussions at Princeton University in 2015 and 2016, around the issue of Woodrow Wilson's views on race and his very racist policies as President of the United States. The protests wanted the College to acknowledge his past more fully and change the name of the Woodrow Wilson School of Public and International Affairs. In April 2016. Princeton decided to retain the name but also appointed Martha Sandweiss, a professor of history there, to head a group to make a report on its past ties to slavery. Princeton, founded in 1746, issued a detailed report and posted a good deal of material on the web outlining its very long history of ties to slavery on November 17 (Schuessler 2017).[30] The report on the Princeton Slavery Project explained that the first nine Princeton presidents were slaveowners during their lives. It also pointed out that in 1766 the president, Samuel Finley, sold a good deal of his property including enslaved people on the front lawn of his campus house. Princeton had strong ties to the slaveholding South and between its founding and the outbreak of the Civil War, forty percent of the students came from that region. There was tension and sometimes fighting between the Southern white students and free Blacks in the town as well as tensions between Southern and Northern whites on the campus. In addition, in 2016, Rutgers and Columbia Universities also wrote reports on their ties to slavery, and a Rutgers University committee published a book on its connections (Fuentes and White 2016).

At other times, the topic of slavery was not ignored so much as refocused—on the North's moral superiority, its peaceful abolition of slavery, its opposition to slavery's western expansion, and its end to the practice nationally through the Civil War. These accounts did not include the more complex reality that there were pockets of abolition resistance among Northerners who continued to profit from the unpaid labor in the enslaved states south of Pennsylvania. Nor was there any clear recognition of white workers' strong fears that free Black labor threatened their own employment, and their refusal to work with free Blacks in almost all industrial jobs after abolition in the North. Similarly, the story of white discrimination and violence against Blacks in the North in the nineteenth century is rarely recounted.

Northern denial and avoidance of the topic of enslavement in the region were quite effective, particularly because there are so few distinctive reminders of slavery in the North's public or commemorative landscape. Northern slavery quickly became invisible, both physically and symbolically. This differs from the South, with its plantations, its broad range of historical sites, monuments and memorials, flags, heritage groups, and cultural expressions such as novels, films, and history books. In the few cases where the enslaved in the North resided in separate buildings, these were often made of poor materials that were not preserved, or they were later improved in such a way that any connection to their original inhabitants was forgotten:[31] "The role of slaves in the agricultural North was reflected in the dwellings in which their owners housed them. No lines of slave cabins surrounded the slaveowner's Great House as an architectural embodiment of the relationship between master and slave. Instead, like other rural workers, slave farmhands were reduced to *near invisibility* by being stuffed into garrets, back rooms, closets, and outbuildings" (Berlin 1998: 56; italics added). Furthermore, after 1800, the tremendous growth and development in the North led to many colonial era buildings and other structures once associated with enslavement being destroyed or built over. Even when the buildings remained relatively unchanged, little about them directly communicated their past association. House tours—such as those at the Brown and DeWolf mansions in Rhode Island or Cliveden in Philadelphia, where enslaved people lived and toiled—rarely mentioned the enslaved until quite recently.[32]

Perhaps the most enduring potential markers of the North's slave past might be the many, often small, cemeteries in which Blacks were buried because whites refused integration even after death. Berlin (1998: 62) argues that, "because white northerners excluded Black corpses from their burial grounds, the graveyard became the first truly African-American institution in the northern colonies, and perhaps in mainland North America." Most of these, however, were not visible on the landscape with the passage of time, and consequently both enslaved and free Blacks buried in them were rendered doubly invisible and forgotten.[33] Sometimes the sites were used for development, as in the case of the large African Burial Ground in Lower Manhattan or the many small Black burying grounds in the oldest parts of Philadelphia. Alternately, they were paved over for roads, as in Portsmouth, New Hampshire, or a playground in South Philadelphia, or left unattended and overrun for years as in the Hudson River Valley or New Jersey.

This same pattern occurred in many places in the North, both large and small. Burying grounds for Blacks and mulattoes, including potter's fields, were in many cases long forgotten and built over for housing or commercial buildings.[34] For example, Madison Square Park, Washington Square Park, the site of the Waldorf-Astoria Hotel, Bryant Park, and Zuccotti Park (the site of the 2011 Occupy Wall Street protests) were all once potter's fields in New York City.[35] So was Washington Square—once called Congo Square, one block from Independence Hall in Philadelphia. Some older burial sites have been overgrown, and there are now plans to clean them and restore the gravestones.[36] In many cases, it is no longer possible to know the names of those buried at these sites. However, archival records are often useful for discovering the locations where both free and enslaved Blacks were buried, and, in some cases such as Portsmouth, markers and memorials have been or are being built that inform the public about the earlier existence of enslaved Africans in these communities.

The stories of these sites reveal how much African American history in the North has been literally as well as figuratively buried and remains unknown to this day. When the physical markers of the past are no longer visible in a society's landscape, the narratives about the past begin to disappear, along with the memories of the people and events that made up a group's past. The lack of a Black presence from the visible public and commemorative landscape in the North takes many forms and goes far beyond just burial grounds.

Another notable feature of Northern towns and cities is the absence or scarcity of monuments, memorials, statues, or even historical markers acknowledging African Americans in visible public places, including parks or museums. Architectural historian Kirk Savage (1997: 3) was interested in "how the history of slavery and its violent end was told in public space—specifically in the sculptural monuments that increasingly came to dominate public space in nineteenth-century America." He found that although Blacks were about 20 percent of the U.S. population at the start of the nineteenth century—and a good deal higher in some states—they had almost no representation in the public landscape. He reports that there are no known images of Blacks, slave or free, in marble or bronze before 1860, although there was a project in South Carolina in the 1850s, never completed, to build a large sculpture of Black slaves working in the rice and cotton fields (Savage 1997: 16, 31).[37] If we look at paintings and other representations in museums from this period, we find a minimal, if any, Black presence, and when Blacks are present, it is more often than not in a subservient role.

Statues and public memorials are visible, and sometimes controversial, identity markers, but drawings and images in books, newspapers, magazines, and museums are even more common and can variously reflect and shape perceptions of minorities in society. Virtually all of these reinforced the rhetoric of inherent racial differences in abilities that existed from the days of first settlement in North America. By the nineteenth century these ideas about inherent inferiority were "refined" around an ideology of science "bolstered" by cranial measurements and crude evolutionary rhetoric that emphasized why Blacks' inferiority made their citizenship impossible (Gould 1981).

For many decades, this negative portrayal of enslaved Africans and Free Blacks was the dominant narrative about Blacks in popular culture. Even abolitionist imagery was often highly unflattering (Savage 1997: chap. 2). Melish (1998: chap. 5), for example, describes the common use of crude caricatures of Black people, speaking a strange dialect, in Northern broadsides published in the first half of the nineteenth century.[38] "The overall strategy of such broadsides was to ridicule the public activities of free people of color as imitation citizenship—ridiculous and pathetic efforts to assume the forms of civic participation and a public identity whose substance they were incapable of understanding" (Melish 1998: 177). Melish argues that this reinforced the idea of removal, distancing, and exclusion. Its consequences are seen most concretely in legal discrimination and widespread white support in the North for colonization for a significant period before the Civil War and severe discrimination and exclusion after it, during the Jim Crow era.[39]

For years, almost all of the public voices in the North, as in the South, were white. Africans and African Americans did speak out, but few whites had any interest in listening. In the nineteenth and early twentieth centuries there was a germinal Black press, and Black leaders throughout the North often addressed the issues of the day, but few whites paid any attention to what they wrote. David Walker's militant *Appeal to the Colored Citizens of the World*, published in 1829, was a significant repudiation of the American Colonization Society's paternalism, but it was only understood by a minority of whites (Davis 2006: 258). As is typical in majority-minority situations defined by great power differences, whites in the North continued what started in the early nineteenth century, forcing Blacks to live apart and wishing that they would leave. Even after the civil rights movement was in full swing, housing segregation and discrimination were typical throughout the North, and whites strongly opposed any change (Sugrue 2008; Coates 2014).

Even this short overview of what we know—and is available to be known—about Northern slavery obliges us to consider why this awareness is so recent and still so partial in terms of collective memories. On the other hand, amateur and professional historians have uncovered a good deal about Northern slavery over the years, and their research has slowly moved from the fringes of their discipline to a more prominent position in the last few decades (Berlin 2004). Public interest and awareness has increased greatly through television documentaries, museum exhibits such as the hugely successful "Slavery in New York" at the New-York Historical Society in 2005 and 2006, and increased newspaper and magazine attention to rediscovered sites such as the African Burial Ground in Lower Manhattan and the President's House/Slavery Memorial in Philadelphia. More historical markers and tours in the North now discuss the topic as well. African American interest in the past also has risen dramatically since the 1970s, with more exploration of family genealogy, history, and DNA testing.

Access to emotionally engaging narratives facilitates historical memory recovery—particularly narratives that emphasize the experiences of specific people, and visible sites associated with slavery in the North on which the narratives are recounted, with ritual events linked to them. The rediscovery of the African Burial Ground in New York and the public reaction to it offer a good example of how recovery of collective memories is possible and goes beyond the detailed, often admirable accounts historians have provided, even though in this case we do not know the names of any of the thousands of people buried there. Of course, personal stories of enslaved people that capture the public's imagination are not always easy to tell, although even a few facts about how particular people lived and worked when told well can go a long way to making a story powerful (e.g., Smith 1905, 1906).

Consider the public reactions to the character Kunta Kinte in Alex Haley's book *Roots* and its television adaptation or to Solomon Northup's story told in his book, later adapted as the Academy Award–winning film *Twelve Years a Slave*. In these two cases, the stories were compelling largely because they were told from the perspective of specific people with whom readers and viewers could easily identify and feel their emotions—the pain they suffered as enslaved people, their struggles to alter their situation that never ceased, and the joy they could still feel at times.[40] The historical record contains clues to where we may find the location, if not the richly detailed personal stories, of former slaves and their communities. A simple effective step might be for public historians to examine old maps and census records that will reveal where many enslaved people lived and worked and make them known as former sites of slavery. Much of this also is the work for archaeologists, historians, and museum professionals. They can offer the public opportunities to better understand the past in specific places and to integrate it more fully into what we pass on to succeeding generations.

Certainly, an attrition of collective memories occurs with the passage of time, but that is not the only reason why we have so few regarding enslavement in the North. To explore this question more completely, we need to examine what forgetting means on the collective level, and how it is similar to, and different from, individual forgetting.

Chapter 3

Slavery and Collective Forgetting

Indeed, historical narratives arise from the willingness or desire of communities to remember or forget.

—Katherine Howlett Hayes, *Slavery Before Race*

Collective forgetting about enslavement in the North meant that many Americans have little to no awareness that it was found in all parts of the region, that there were thousands of enslaved people, and that it lasted more than two centuries. Few realize that ending slavery in the North occurred slowly, that emancipated and freed Blacks in the North had far less than full rights, that the most important slave traders in the country were Northern ship owners and merchants from New England, and that among the slaveholders were a good number of Quakers and Puritans. In exploring the question of how and why events and people important at one point in time are later forgotten, it is useful to examine collective forgetting as a distinct process, with its own dynamics, rather than simply the opposite of collective remembering.

To do this, I begin with two central issues: first, I examine the distinction between the individual and social dynamics of storing and retrieving collective memories. Second, to move beyond the assertion that slavery in the North was forgotten, I consider specifically how and why this took place through a discussion of six theoretically plausible explanations for its occurrence. The source of this collective forgetting is rooted in the absence of the three critical components of collective memory—the disappearance of narratives about past events and people involved in them, the weakening and gradual disappearance of ritual expressions and enactments built around these events and people, and the loss or destruction of visible public, commemorative landscapes and objects that earlier marked the existence of Northern slavery. While the prominence of each of the three key components of collective memory often change, they are commonly viewed as "eternal" or unchanging when they are first created. In reality, however, popular understandings of their meaning and content often shift over time in ways that affect what is remembered about the past. Central to this argument is an appreciation that the past is not unchanging and an awareness that what is remembered and forgotten is determined in great part by contemporary needs and priorities.

Collective forgetting, like collective remembering, differs from what takes place for individuals because collective processes are not simply an aggregation of individual ones. They are not simply individual dynamics writ large. To understand the differences between collective and individual memory, it is useful to recognize that the emphasis in contemporary psychological approaches to memory are on how specific memories are stored in our brains. Of course, there are complicated questions about how the storage works: does it result from individual conscious decisions ("I have to remember to buy a nice bottle of wine for dinner tonight") or what dynamics make it so difficult, if not impossible, to erase a memory, as in the case of a traumatic experience or the death of a close friend.[1] The parallel to collective processes breaks down partly because society does not have storage mechanisms that are parallel to the individual brain. It preserves collective memories in other ways—through shared narratives, ritual expressions and enactments, visible public and commemorative landscapes, and objects such as monuments, memorials, and museums. As Mary Douglas (1986: 70) points out, "Public memory is the storage system for the social order. . . . Some patterns of public events get stored there, others get rejected." While these may be strengthened or weakened over time as are memories in our individual brains, these changes don't occur in the same way.

Forgetting for individuals is more complicated than a conscious act of removing something that had previously been stored in our brain. But how does this happen? Can we just decide to forget? Probably sometimes we can and do, but often we do not and cannot. In fact, we might hypothesize that the harder we try to forget something, the less likely it is to be forgotten. More important, it is naive to think about forgetting as primarily a conscious decision. Some forgetting isn't willed at all but occurs as our brains work less efficiently and cells die, or when time passes and more recent events assume a more prominent role in our memory. To the extent that memory depends on social and emotional cues and connections, memories of events and people lose their importance over time. Connerton (2009) suggests that the mobility of modern society and the physical changes in places that we once knew intimately, such as the neighborhoods in which we once lived, further exacerbate forgetting. Repression and suppression also have their own dynamics and are very different from a conscious decision to forget.

Collective memories across generations can be transmitted and found in the stories people hear and recount in a variety of ways. These include face-to-face conversations, media presentations, books, the rituals and ceremonies found in both small groups and large public events, and in the sacred places and objects that are reminders of people and events from the past. While each of these can be analogous to memories stored in the individual brain, access to them requires a further step: it involves people interpreting their content and meanings in ways that differ from how an individual processes his or her stored memories. These sources of collective memories are external to individuals, although their content can certainly be internalized when we remember the story about an event, our feelings about a ritual, or the visual and emotional sensations of visiting a historical site.

Perhaps one way to distinguish individual and collective memories is to suggest that individual memories result from direct experiences, and while these primary memories can be transmitted as second- or third-order memories to others, their content, affect, and intensity will rarely be the same. As a result, successive generations almost invariably understand the narratives, rituals, and public sites that mark the past differently than those who directly experienced the events or people portrayed in them, since how memory storage works is different in each.

The meanings of collective memories and the emotions they evoke invariably change over time. Sometimes, as fewer and fewer people pay attention to them, the memories lose their emotional valence. In this way, we can see a parallel between individual and collective forgetting. One example with which I have become familiar in the recent years is the ongoing salience and visibility of the American Civil War in some parts of the United States, and the lack of the same in others. Sites such as Civil War battlefields in Virginia or at Gettysburg draw thousands and even millions of visitors each year, and reenactors regularly stage battles fought a century and a half ago (Horwitz 1999). In contrast, Philadelphia's Civil War Museum, which housed thousands of artifacts, closed in 2008 because of the building's poor condition, lack of funds, and lack of public interest.[2] The large monuments in the city that mark the sacrifice of Pennsylvanians in the war are almost totally unrecognized by local residents and visitors as Civil War memorials.

The changes to (or loss of) a monument's meaning and significance are particularly interesting, in great part because the people who commissioned it intended it to be "set in stone" (or metal) for time immemorial, to teach "timeless lessons" to future generations. Yet this is often not the result, as succeeding generations are likely to fight about the significance of a monument. They might ignore, alter, or even remove monuments once they no longer feel significant or when they express anachronistic sentiments (Levinson 1998). Is this collective forgetting, or collective redefinition of the meaning of the past, or both?

As we examine the content of collective memories a crucial feature is inclusion and exclusion from the narratives, rituals, and public sites in a community. Carefully looking at these will show that those included are rarely the only ones involved in the events that are marked. For example, despite the fact that slavery was the central cause of the American Civil War and more than 200,000 African Americans—many of whom were formerly enslaved—served in the Union armies, the postwar reconciliation between North and South and Civil War commemoration almost exclusively involved white Americans. It ignored the experiences of Blacks, the war's consequences on their lives, and the postwar segregation and discrimination in the South and North that went virtually unaddressed for almost another hundred years (Linenthal 1993; Blight 2001).[3]

Not all collective forgetting occurs for the same reasons or in the same ways. Connerton, who has written about collective remembering and forgetting (1989, 2009), identifies seven forms of forgetting, each of which involves different agents and dynamics (2008).[4] In his analysis, he notes that the same events can produce both memories and forgetting. He argues that following World War I, there was "an orgy of monumentalization; memorials to commemorate the fallen all over Europe" (Connerton 2008: 69), while at the same time more than ten million mutilated survivors were ignored, as "the sight of them was discomforting, even shameful. They were like ghosts haunting the conscience of Europe. The living did not want to remember them; they wanted to forget them" (Connerton 2008: 60).[5] Young (1993: 5) makes the same point: "In effect, the initial impulse to memorialize events like the Holocaust may actually spring from an opposite and equal desire to forget them."

In *How Modernity Forgets*, Connerton (2009) discusses how collective life facilitates forgetting in modern society. He considers denial and ignorance, but his emphasis is on modern social practices that produce changes in physical sites that promote forgetting. He argues that place-rooted connections among people in modern society are significantly weaker than in earlier forms of social organization. Place memory is especially important for Connerton, and he emphasizes that memory "depends essentially upon a stable system of places . . . [and] remembering relates implicitly to the human body and that acts of memory are envisaged as taking place on a human scale" (2009: 5). This is useful, although perhaps too categorical or absolute, for there are other ways that memories can operate. These include memories created through mass media experience involving events thousands of miles away (Dayan and Katz 1992). Production in modern society likewise stimulates a loss of memory with its impersonal methods and short product cycles; as a result, Connerton argues, the loss of memory triggers new institutions and practices, such as computer storage devices and government archives, to preserve memories that we no longer easily store in our daily lives.

In some situations, the presence of groups of people or their stories of past events are never discussed or publicly recognized, but it is inaccurate to say that they are forgotten, since communities continue to have an awareness of their existence. One example is families or friendship groups where no one talks about the person who is an alcoholic, even though everyone recognizes his or her addiction. Another is seen in communities where minorities are clearly treated differently than others but no one speaks about it. In these situations, dominant social groups often naturalize their privileged status rather than posing questions about minorities who are treated as invisible in a variety of ways. In these situations, it is not quite that the minority group or individual members of it are "forgotten" as such; rather it is more that they are variously ignored and their needs, views, and presence are simply not considered important. If we search public documents and the landscapes of such communities in the past, we would find scant evidence of minorities in them, as if they did not exist or were forgotten. Yet they did exist and are not so much forgotten as ignored—which amounts to almost the same thing.

Narratives frame who matters within a community, who should matter, and who can be ignored. This last dynamic is very relevant to thinking about how the memories of Northern slavery did not survive, since whites had little incentive to maintain the memory of this past. This forgetting was not accidental but intentional. Many Blacks, as well, did not dwell on this unhappy period. One result was a tacit collusion between whites and Blacks that led to an absence of collective narratives, shared rituals, and recognizable landscapes associated with enslavement. Absent these cues, and with incentives to forget about the past, it is not surprising that Northern slavery quickly receded from the region's collective memory.

How does collective forgetting occur? To distinguish between memories that persist and those that do not we need to recognize that on both the individual and collective levels, mostly unconscious decisions are continually made that selectively retain or forget memories of certain events, people, and their associated emotions. The remainder of this chapter considers six theoretically plausible explanations for collective forgetting in the case of slavery in the North.[6]

Over the years when I have described this project to people, a common reaction has been that the almost complete forgetting about enslavement in the North is due to white racism. I want to spend some time contemplating this frequent response. While the existence of white racism is consistent with what took place, it is more useful as a "context condition" than something that should be understood as a plausible explanation for the dynamics of collective forgetting and recovery memories of slavery in the North. I see white racism as a very general concept that fails to identify precisely how and why forgetting took place. In addition, it sheds little light on why and how this forgetting took place for a large number of African Americans in addition to whites.

More important is the implication that forgetting about enslavement is the only possible consequence of white racist beliefs. But if this is the case, does that mean that white racism did not exist in the South, which not only did not forget its slave past, but, following the Civil War, reinstitutionalized it in Jim Crow laws as well as less formalized systematic discrimination that persists today? If this is so, it means that white racism accounts for both Northern forgetting and Southern Jim Crow, which is hardly satisfactory. As a result, white racism offers too general an answer to the question of forgetting about Northern slavery. Thus, without denying white racism's existence or importance, I have sought more proximate and precise explanations for what took place. In addition, invoking white racism too easily suggests that white beliefs are more homogeneous than they actually are and implicitly suggests that the behaviors to be understood arise from a few beliefs or a single coherent set of beliefs (see, e.g., Feagin 2013).

Finally, the concept of white racism as a central factor in both the forgetting and then the recovery of memory of Northern slavery seems to me to focus only on the role of whites in the process, while leaving little room for the actions and beliefs of African Americans. It would almost be saying, or at least strongly implying, that only whites were responsible for the loss of the collective memories of Northern enslavement and that the recovery of the memories is also only attributable to changes in white attitudes. Black action and agency are certainly present in this process.

What follows is a review of ways that social forgetting might occur, with greater specificity than the general allegation of white racism. The evidence from stories of slavery in the North for the six kinds of forgetting discussed here is indirect in most cases, to be sure, and these modes of forgetting would not apply equally to all contexts. But these phenomena, I contend, help us to understand the forgetting and, later, the remembering of slavery in the North.

First, we do not often acknowledge that present needs and problems determine what from the past is most useful for individuals and groups to remember. Crucial here is the ability to make cognitive and emotional connections between the present and past. When this linkage is successful, the past provides both negative and positive "lessons" relevant to the present. When this not possible, the salience of past events fades more quickly. Slavery is an interesting case in point, as there are many African Americans who see a direct connection between it and current patterns of discrimination and deprivation in the Black community, while a vast majority of whites see no linkage between the two. People who believe there is such a connection and that it is tied to the existence of white privilege are far more likely to support reparations to Blacks than those who see no relationship between the two (Coates 2014).

Forgetting often results from the decline and eventual lack of relevance of past events for the present, so that memories of them fade and eventually slowly disappear. When communities fail to recount stories about past events or people, when they are not marked or celebrated, and when there are few if any sites dedicated to recounting the collective memories of them—because the communities do not see a link between the memories and the present—the past recedes.[7] When immediate witnesses who experienced events themselves are no longer accessible due to either emigration or death, the memories are likely to fade unless people in a community make an effort to maintain them. Of course this is not automatic, and memories persist over generations and in some cases grow stronger, rather than weaker, even when personal direct linkage to the past weakens.

It is *not* the proximity of past events, as the slavery case shows, that matters as much as their perceived relevance to present circumstances and challenges. After all, many groups make claims based on long ago events, such as the Serbs whose claims to Kosovo are based on a 1389 battle they lost, Northern Irish Protestants who draw lessons from battles fought in the late sixteenth century, and Jews who justify the state of Israel on the basis of the Roman destruction of ancient Israel and its Second Temple in A.D. 70. For these groups it is not *when* these events took place, but the "eternal lesson" they represent that makes them relevant in the present.

Sometimes there is a deliberate effort to draw a hard boundary between the past and present as a way of delegitimizing claims that the past provides a relevant model for the present. An example is arguments over discrimination and the need for affirmative action. Some support the 2013 U.S. Supreme Court decision that invalidates sections of the Voting Rights Act because they believe the conditions that originally justified the act are no longer present. In contrast, the court's minority argued that significant discrimination still exists against minorities in some parts of the country and the protections of the act need to remain in place.

Second, forgetting often occurs with the destruction or significant modification of sites associated with memory. There are many ways that specific places become associated with strong memories. Sometimes they grow from intense personal experiences; others arise from the emotional experiences of others—past and present—while some are rooted in the regularly repeated narratives and rituals associated with a site that heightens its emotional significance, either for just a few people or a large community. However, retaining place memories is far from automatic, and Connerton (2009) argues that in modern societies place memories are quite precarious. Changes to once-familiar sites promote forgetting.

Connerton's analysis distinguishes between memories of memorial sites and mundane places. Memorial places are highly evocative of events because of what occurred on them. However, I would add that there are some memorial sites far from the location of the original events. An obvious example is the Vietnam Veterans Memorial in Washington, thousands of miles away from the site of the war. The power to name a memorial site is the power to define, as well as to redefine, what memories are important and how a commemorative landscape is maintained, altered, or remembered. Ironically, Connerton notes, memorials are inspired by a fear or threat of cultural amnesia. Yet "the relationship between memorials and forgetting is reciprocal: the threat of forgetting begets memorials and the construction of the memorials begets forgetting" (Connerton 2009: 29), meaning that once the memorials are built, people often feel less need to take individual responsibility for the preservation of the memories associated with them.

Ordinary place memory (what Connerton calls locus memory) involves the many mundane daily locations and activities associated with individual and small group lives. Obvious examples include the homes we grow up and live in and the streets and neighborhoods where we live, work, and play. The memories of such places are highly personal, and the connectedness produces what he calls "encoding of a sedimented tradition" (Connerton 2009: 31). While we easily develop such memories, Connerton argues that the combination of high physical mobility in modern life as well as continual changes in the built environment leads to destruction and reconstruction of buildings, neighborhoods, and road networks. These alterations in the environment promote higher levels of forgetting (Connerton 2009: chap. 4).

While the memories associated with a landscape and objects on it can fade and eventually disappear, in some cases the sites and some objects or parts of them can be "rediscovered" and the forgotten stories recovered, as has taken place with former battlefields and burying grounds. For many centuries, European rulers searched for evidence of each nation's historical past through archaeology. The matter is complicated, however, as sites or objects recovered do not come with complete explanations of what they are and mean. They require interpretation, and their meanings at the time the sites are "rediscovered" are often not the same as when they were first created. The story of the African Burial Ground in Lower Manhattan presented in the introduction illustrates this point. Its "rediscovery" in the late twentieth century produced narratives and rituals emphasizing enslavement and suffering that are surely different from what would have been said about them in the eighteenth century. The National Park Service Visitor Center displays objects used to control the enslaved Africans, such as shackles, chains, and whips. By making these objects visible and putting them in a context where people could learn the story of what slavery looked like in early New York, the memories of the practice are, at least partially, recovered. Similarly, the ceremonies, rituals, and memorials around the disinterment and reinterment of the remains of those exhumed at the site provided a powerful emotional connection for African Americans in New York.

Third, incentives for forgetting or remembering, whether provided by the larger society or one's primary group inner psyche, can be positive or negative. Some memories produce a good deal of pain and discomfort that individuals and groups seek to avoid. Traumatic events obviously fall into this category. For example, people involved in serious auto accidents often afterward have no memory whatsoever of what happened. In other situations, people and groups need to work hard to forget (or we could say suppress) painful memories. One individual strategy is simply not to talk about events such as war experiences or other things the individual wants to forget. There is at least anecdotal evidence that this is exactly what a high percentage of returning war veterans do, whether they personally had traumatic experiences in war or not. So do most rape victims. Similarly, many victims of traumas such as a physical assault or internment during the Holocaust are often very reluctant or unwilling to discuss them, even with family members and especially their own children, many years later.[8]

This same strategy is used on the collective level, when events are simply not spoken about or publicly remembered. Examples include the French defeat in Algeria (although this has changed somewhat in recent years) and the Dutch amnesia about their acts of violent repression in Indonesia in the late 1940s. Forgetting can be one reaction to a devastating defeat, but interestingly it is not the only possible reaction to loss. In some cases, losses are remembered more vividly than victories. Sports fans often dwell on tough defeats in contests they expected their team to win more than those games in which they prevailed. For large groups, losses such as the battle of Kosovo for Serbs in 1389 and the U.S. Civil War for Confederates also fit this pattern, in which the loser's memories are far more enduring than the winner's.[9]

O'Toole (2016:273–77) ends her analysis of enslavement in Little Compton, Rhode Island, by echoing Melish (1998) when she identifies the town's efforts to forget about its past history: "Once slavery ended in Little Compton, the community tried to forget it. For much of the nineteenth and early-twentieth centuries Little Compton joined with hundreds of other New England communities in efforts to minimize the history of slavery and forced indenture in the region. If mentioned at all, northern slavery was described as a gentler, somehow better institution than the practice in the South. Little Compton even congratulated itself because its slavery was better than South County [Narragansett]" (O'Toole 2016: 274).

She notes that, "despite half a century of important academic efforts, the existence of slavery, and more specifically the widespread nature of slavery in New England, remains a surprise to even well-educated members of the public" (O'Toole 2016: 273). O'Toole bases this on evidence from visitors to Little Compton in recent years, and it is consistent with what I have seen in Philadelphia, New York, and elsewhere. She points out that Little Compton's early historians did not deny slavery's existence, "but they wrote about it in a way that made every master seem kind and every enslaved person loyal." In the twentieth century a few stories, including those of the Richmond family of Little Compton, dominated anecdotes that were repeated, and "describe warm, respectful relationships between the successful Richmonds and their responsible, loyal, talented slaves." These stories were truthful in some ways, but many details were at odds with the historical record, creating "an inaccurate, overly positive, public perception of slavery in Little Compton" (O'Toole 2016: 275). Consequently, slavery was portrayed "as a small-scale, short-lived benign curiosity rather than a harsh significant economic and social institution that endured for 150 years and impacted hundreds of people, enslaved and free" (276).

In a more obvious example of memory erasure, authoritarian regimes punish individuals or groups who publicly try to keep certain memories alive through published materials, ceremonies, or public discussions. Examples abound and range from cases in which past events are simply ignored to those in which supporters of past regimes who actively work for the public preservation of memories about them are severely punished. The objects of memory suppression can be wide ranging and include minority languages, historical events, past heroes, and more. At the same time, regimes—and their supporters—emphasize their own accounts of the past, with their own events, heroes, and ritual events.

Hegemonic narratives developed following events such as a war are very clear incentives for rethinking the past and its meanings. An often cited example of this in the United States is the "Lost Cause" narrative in the South in the decades following the Civil War, which argued that the war was about constitutional principles and ways of life, not slavery, which Jefferson Davis described as simply "an incident" (Blight 2001). This narrative was quickly adopted and virtually unopposed in the South, while whites in the North soon repeated many of its key parts, and this shared narrative became an important basis for the postwar reconciliation between the regions (Blight 2001; Linenthal 1993). Slaves, in this account, were well treated and content with their position. Slave owners were kind and provided economic security, health care, Christianity, and civilization, for which the enslaved were grateful. "No argument in the Lost Cause formula became more an article of faith than the disclaimer against slavery as the cause of the war. In reunion speeches, committee reports, and memories, it is remarkable to note the energy Southerners spent denying slavery's centrality to the war" (Blight 2001: 282). The narrative emphasized that the war was lost because of superior Northern numbers and resources—not for lack of Southern commitment or bravery.

The Lost Cause argument that slavery was an "incident" but not a cause of the Civil War is at odds with the dominant view of historians over the past half century (McPherson 1988, 1997; Dew 2001). This elaborate and, to some, compelling account of the Civil War in the years after the war is a particularly good example of how a narrative coalesced around a few beliefs and did more than just reflect them. It also shaped beliefs and behaviors over decades and limited the possibilities for effective Black-white dialogue in the North and South, once the Lost Cause narrative achieved hegemonic status among whites in both regions by the turn of the twentieth century. Its core assumptions about Black inferiority gained wide acceptance, appearing in political rhetoric, popular literature, and war memories. All of this continued to meet the contemporary needs of some whites more than a century after the war ended.

Whites did not search widely to understand the African American perspectives that were sharply at odds with the romantic vision of Southern antebellum life, best captured in *Gone with the Wind*. These perspectives received little attention from whites until the civil rights era. For more than one hundred years after the war, most whites had little or no knowledge of what African Americans felt, not because their views were unavailable, but because Blacks were considered uninformed and/or ignorant and were treated as socially invisible. When the National Association for the Advancement of Colored People (NAACP) began to actively campaign for a national law against lynching during and after World War I, most whites and elected public officials did not support it (Francis 2014). For the most part, whites readily accepted the views of the few Blacks who said what they wanted to hear and systematically ignored dissonant views that challenged their own strongly defended positions. Often the few whites who resisted the dominant position in both the South and the North were socially ostracized and even harassed for articulating their views.

There was also little to no attention in these accounts to slave resistance, to the work conditions on many plantations, to the open rebellions, including those in New York in the eighteenth century, to white fear and violence that fueled attempts to control the enslaved, and to the large number of enslaved people who risked their lives to escape to Indian territories, a free state in the North, or Canada. On many plantations, not just those in the South, there were also countless acts of sabotage both large and small, informal organization among the enslaved to slow down work to make it more manageable, and theft from stocks of food and other goods to improve their living conditions. None of this is consistent with the "happy and grateful slave" narrative, which is central to the Lost Cause narrative that slavery was not a central cause of the war.

A "forgotten" event in Colorado in 1864 toward the end of the Civil War is instructive here. The territorial Governor John Evans sent Colonel John Chivington's Colorado volunteers to Sand Creek, where they massacred Southern Cheyenne and Arapaho, under the pretext that the Indians were organizing a rebellion and were somehow allied with the Confederate army (Kelman 2013). Of the hundreds killed in the raid, about two-thirds were women and children. Some of Chivington's officers opposed the attack and refused to participate in it on the grounds that it was not needed and that the reasons given to justify it were spurious. The events set off decades of violence between whites in the region who wanted Indian land and the tribes in the area who tried (and eventually failed) to fend them off.

Whites celebrated the battle as a site of victory, and it was later listed on the Civil War memorial in Denver, along with other battles in which soldiers from the state fought. Most whites in the region saw Chivington as a hero in the years after the raid. While there were three hearings—one held by the army and two in Congress—at which Chivington's account of the battle was challenged, his emerged as the dominant narrative. Very gradually the true story of the events came out in recent decades, and, as Kelman (2013) explains in great detail, what actually took place became clearer to most, but not all, people.[10] Sand Creek was declared a National Park Service site and named the Sand Creek Massacre National Historic Site in 1997. In December 2014, 150 years after the massacre, Colorado Governor John Hickenlooper became the first leader of the state to apologize for the shameful event.

Fourth, fear of painful memories promotes forgetting. People who experience a severe trauma directly or indirectly often fear its possible repetition and take action to prevent it. Not only are people in this situation unlikely to speak freely about what happened to themselves, but also they will do little or nothing to offer a narrative, engage in ritual actions, or develop memorials, monuments, or museums where the events they experienced are publicly marked. They fear that publicly recounting their trauma might lead to its future recurrence. This can produce not only self-silencing but also efforts to silence others, and over time it can lead to (collective) forgetting.[11]

We have seen this in the case of Holocaust survivors, Japanese Americans who were removed from their homes and interned in camps during World War II, and victims of sexual violence. Takezawa (1995) writes that when the children of the Japanese Americans who had been interned during the war began to demand reparations in the 1970s, many in the older generation were furious with them because they were fearful that political agitation and reparation demands would result in new punishment and repression, rather than in the formal apology and reparations they eventually received. Fear powerfully silences deep concerns between, and sometimes within, communities. As a result of fears and vulnerabilities, people avoid issues that everyone knows about but is unable to broach in public and sometimes even in private settings. It is the "elephant in the room" (Zerubavel 2006). Blacks and whites have a very hard time engaging with each other in conversations about reparations for the centuries of exploitation their ancestors experienced.[12]

Another example is seen in the story of the June 1921 race riot in Tulsa, Oklahoma, which virtually wiped out the entire prosperous Black neighborhood of Greenwood, sometimes referred to as the "Negro (and later Black)

Wall Street." It resulted in as many as 300 Black (and some white) deaths, the destruction of more than 1,200 homes and businesses and twenty-three churches, and ten thousand people were left homeless (Ellsworth 1982; Staples 1999; Madigan 2001). Only a few years earlier, Blacks had called Oklahoma "the promised land" and had migrated to the territory (after 1907, the state) in large numbers. It had several dozen all-Black towns. At the time, Tulsa, the fast-growing oil-boom city, was strictly segregated under Oklahoma law, and Blacks could not shop in the downtown white stores. One result is that Blacks in Greenwood built successful businesses, and there were a number of professionals in the community. Even though Blacks were unable to work in the oil fields or local industries at the time, there were more jobs for them in and around the fast-growing city than in many other parts of the country. But this did not mean Black life was easy, and by 1921 the revived Ku Klux Klan received wide support from whites, including the owner and editor of the local afternoon newspaper, the *Tulsa Tribune.*

The spark that led to the riot was a fast-spreading story that a young Black male, Dick Rowland, who shined shoes in a downtown office building, made a sexual advance toward a white female elevator operator in the building. When the *Tribune* published a story the next afternoon with the headline "To Lynch Negro Tonight," an angry white mob bent on inflicting its notion of justice on the perpetrator and on Blacks in Tulsa more generally soon gathered outside the jail where Rowland was being held.[13] Clearly, lynching and similar acts of intimidation of Blacks in the country at the time fed the mob's anger. Talk of violence that had been building over time stoked the flames of racial animosity in the city.

The sheriff was determined to prevent a lynching, which he did. However, as an armed white mob grew in size, firebrands demanding swift "justice" stoked the crowd. When word of the gathering mob reached Greenwood, a group of armed Black World War I veterans drove to the courthouse, offering to protect Rowland, and only left when the sheriff assured them that he was determined not to let the mob seize the prisoner. Later in the evening, they returned and, when whites challenged them, shots were fired. Once again, the Black vets returned to Greenwood, while the white mob continued to grow and reached about two thousand people. Rumors of armed Blacks moving throughout the city increased white fears. Groups of armed whites advanced toward Greenwood. There were exchanges of gunfire throughout the night, and by morning the whites gathered at the edge of the neighborhood and increased their shooting. World War I–era planes flew over the area and various reports said they dropped bombs and incendiary devices and fired guns from the air. Blacks returned the gunfire in an effort to defend the neighborhood but were outnumbered and soon began to withdraw toward the north of the city. Whites began entering Greenwood, first looting homes and then torching them, destroying shops and churches and shooting often unarmed residents. The governor sent in the National Guard, which restored order mainly by rounding up Blacks.

More than six thousand Blacks who could not flee were herded into the city's Convention Hall and its minor-league baseball park, which served as detention centers. The dead were often piled in the streets, and many were buried in unmarked graves soon afterward. "Tulsa's African-American district had been turned into a scorched waste land of vacant lots, crumbling store fronts, burned churches, and blackened, leafless trees" (Franklin and Ellsworth 2001: 24). The city first promised to help rebuild Greenwood, but it never did. Rather, in an effort by whites to gain control over the area, Tulsa passed ordinances demanding impossible building standards that Blacks could not meet. Only attorney B. C. Franklin's successful court suit, filed to challenge the regulations, halted their implementation.[14] The African Americans who remained in the city were left to their own devices to rebuild their homes and businesses and re-create their community over the next few years, which they did. Insurance companies refused to pay any of the almost two hundred damage claims that Blacks filed with them, citing a riot-exclusion clause in the policies, although white claims were often paid (Weller and Grossman 1999; Staples 1999).

The story of the 1921 riot and destruction received a great deal of national coverage in its immediate aftermath, but it was soon widely forgotten, "and once the riot slipped from the headlines, its public memory also began to fade" (Franklin and Ellsworth 2001: 25). The 2001 report of the Oklahoma Commission to Study the Tulsa Riot pointed out that "for many years the Tulsa race riot practically disappeared from view. For decades afterwards, Oklahoma newspapers rarely mentioned the riot, the state's historical establishment essentially ignored it, and entire generations of Oklahoma school children were taught little or nothing about what had happened" (Franklin and Ellsworth 2001: 24).

The city's leaders had little incentive to remember the events of 1921. As the 2001 state report noted:

As the years passed and, particularly after World War II, as more and more families moved to Oklahoma from out-of-state, more and more of the state's citizens had simply never heard of the riot. Indeed, the riot was discussed so little, and for so long, even in Tulsa, that in 1996, Tulsa County District Attorney Bill LaFortune could tell a reporter, "I was born and raised here, and I had never heard of the riot." . . . For some, and particularly for Tulsa's white business and political leaders, the riot soon became something best to be forgotten, something to be swept well beneath history's carpet. . . . Nowhere was this historical amnesia more startling than in Tulsa itself, especially in the city's white neighborhoods. (Franklin and Ellsworth 2001: 25–26)

For African Americans in Greenwood the events were sometimes discussed in private but not publicly, and an ongoing sense of vulnerability hung over the community: "Fearful that speaking evil would summon it to life, most Black Tulsans banned the riot from conversation and no longer spoke of it to young people and newcomers . . . [as] 'Black folks lived with the fear that the whites who had come once might come again'" (Staples 1999).

There were occasional publications about the riot, but none was widely read. By the 1950s its occurrence, let alone details about what happened, was hardly known even in Tulsa, except by the people who had lived through it. Then in the 1950s W. D. Williams, a history teacher at Greenwood's Booker T. Washington High School, told students working on the school yearbook that when he was a junior in the school in 1921, there was no prom that year because the whites in Tulsa had destroyed the community. A young student, Don Ross, challenged Williams, saying that he had grown up in Greenwood and none of his older relatives had ever said anything about the riot. How was that possible? Williams's response was to show him an album he kept with photos of the destruction, the corpses piled on trucks, and the homes on fire. He told him about his father's effort to defend the community and the family's loss of its home and business. Over the following days Williams took Ross to meet and talk with other survivors who told of their own experiences. It changed Ross's life. He had always been interested in history and went on to edit a magazine, *Oklahoma Impact*, which published white ex-veteran and freelance writer Ed Wheeler's account of the riot in 1971 after the Tulsa Chamber of Commerce magazine, which had originally commissioned the story, decided not to print it on the grounds that it was "too inflammatory" (Staples 1999; Madigan 2001). Ross went on to represent Greenwood in the state legislature and was central in getting the events publicized and the appointment of a state commission to investigate the riot in 1996.

Breaking what has been called the "conspiracy of silence" (or what I have been calling a form of collective forgetting) in Tulsa was not easy. Writer Ed Wheeler was threatened repeatedly by whites angry because he was investigating the riot. By this time, however, there was support in the Black community from many people who felt strongly that the story needed to be told.

Few felt this as strongly as those who had survived the tragedy itself, and on the evening of June 1, 1971, dozens of African American riot survivors gathered at Mount Zion Baptist Church for a program commemorating its fiftieth anniversary of the riot. Led by W. D. Williams, a longtime Booker T. Washington High School history teacher, whose family had suffered immense property loss during the violence, the other speakers that evening included other fellow riot survivors. (Franklin and Ellsworth 2001: 29) Gradually there were more investigations of the events of 1921 (see, e.g., Ellsworth 1982), and the survivors in Greenwood increasingly spoke about it publicly. They organized to build a cultural center in 1989 that told the story of the riot. Seven years later they built the Black Wall Street Memorial, a plain black granite wall inscribed with the names of the people who had suffered and died in the violence. The History Channel made a film about the riot and *60 Minutes* and PBS broadcast several stories about it. The Oklahoma Commission's work was widely covered in the press around the country.[15]

While fear of publicly discussing what happened in 1921 in Tulsa gradually faded, it took three quarters of a century for the story to be told and for the Oklahoma government to acknowledge it. The Oklahoma Commission (2001) recommended reparations, in the form of:

1. Direct payment of reparations to survivors of the Tulsa Race Riot.
2. Direct payment of reparations to descendants of the survivors of the Tulsa Race Riot.

3. A scholarship fund available to students affected by the Tulsa Race Riot.
4. Establishment of an economic development enterprise zone in the historic area of the Greenwood District.
5. A memorial for the reburial of any human remains found in the search for unmarked graves of riot victims.

The state legislature did not accept the commission's recommendations. When the legislature failed to pass reparations and the courts refused to order them paid, Johnson (2012) argued that both the city and the state supported a series of nonmonetary reparations and did not admit any culpability for the riot-related offenses.

Fear cast a long shadow over the Tulsa race riot and was a prime motivator for silencing any public recognition and discussion of the events of 1921. Those whites who actually participated in the looting and killing, as well as their descendants, harbored fears of an arrest and trial. For many whites in Tulsa, especially those who had nothing to do with the riot, but who did have some knowledge of what transpired over the two days in 1921, fear was probably not as important as feelings of shame and/or guilt, which often motivate collective forgetting and silencing. It seems plausible that, among members of the city's white elite, these sentiments played a role in their unwillingness to acknowledge or discuss the events of 1921.

An easy parallel suggests itself between the trauma of the Tulsa riot and enslavement in the North or South. In each case, there was little incentive for the victims and their descendants to publicly mark the events, for fear that doing so would only invite more repression and silence. This is understandable, when people without power or voice need to be careful about the risks they are willing to take. Of course, a few people wrote articles and even books about their experience as enslaved people both before and after the Civil War, and several thousand formerly enslaved people were interviewed in the 1930s by the WPA project. But they were only a small proportion of those willing to do this publicly.

Fifth, shame and guilt cause pain for individuals and groups and incentivize forgetting. Psychologists carefully distinguish between the two, arguing that guilt arises from realization that someone's actions may have injured another, whereas shame is a feeling that develops from the sense that something dishonorable or improper was done by oneself or one's group. At the same time, it is understood that the two emotions are often interrelated and that distinguishing between them in specific situations is often difficult. In addition, laymen frequently use the two interchangeably and understand that many actions can set off both emotions. This is particularly the case if we assess collective, and not just individual, actions, which is why I consider the two together here.

One widely used strategy to attempt to avoid feeling either shame or guilt is forgetting, which operates both individually and collectively. When people experience shame or guilt, they often work hard to repress the source of these feelings and are reluctant to share them with others. When groups experience them, one result is a lack of public attention to their source. For example, people or events that produce shame or guilt are rarely discussed prominently in the media, are not written about in school texts, and are not visible in museums, memorials, monuments, or public celebrations. As a result, there is little to no social support and few institutions promote memories about the events that caused the shame or guilt in a community; people or groups who do feel ashamed are obliged to deal with these feelings on their own.

Shame and guilt linked to repression result in topics that are taboo—publicly ignored and often punished if they are raised in public or even in some private settings. In extreme cases, they can involve punishments such as social ostracism or even physical attacks and expulsion from a community. While there is no doubt that shame and guilt can induce people to silence others, self-repression is the most common response in both individuals and groups to avoid thinking about painful topics. Incentives to forget are largely internal. Groups or individuals are careful to avoid topics that are emotionally painful to themselves.

Anger is another emotion closely related to shame or guilt. Faden encountered these reactions as the executive director of the Mark Twain Boyhood Home and Museum in Hannibal, Missouri, when she made its presentation less nostalgic and included the previously ignored enslaved boy Jim and a discussion of slavery. The museum lost its largest donor after these changes (Faden 2012: 252–55).

Slavery often produces feelings of shame and guilt for both whites and Blacks in the United States, although not for the same reasons or in the same ways. "Freedpeople and their descendants could be ambivalent about remembering slavery—albeit with very different motivations from white New Englanders. . . . For many people, memories of individual heroes better served the political priorities of the mid-nineteenth century, when Black leaders were seeking to assert themselves as capable citizens, than did narratives stressing victimization and the 'dark past' of slavery" (Minardi 2012: 96). Hurmence's (1984) short edited book based on slave interviews in the Library of Congress includes Sarah Debro, who said, "My folks don't want me to talk about slavery, they's shame niggers ever was slaves" (61).

Given the changing social and political norms over time, today a good percentage of whites are uneasy and ashamed that their ancestors owned other human beings. Because this practice is now seen as so completely wrong, it is easy for those living today to feel not only a sense of shame or guilt on behalf of their ancestors but also acceptance of the judgments that people who were slave owners were "bad or evil people," although when the topic is raised they may rejoin, "well it was a different time."

A number of people have described New Englanders' reaction to the region's slave past as one of denial. As Harper (2003) notes: "Early nineteenth-century New Englanders had real motives for forgetting their slave history, or, if they recalled it at all, for characterizing it as a brief period of mild servitude. This was partly a Puritan effort to absolve New England's ancestors of their guilt. The cleansing of history had a racist motive as well, denying Blacks—slave or free—a legitimate place in New England history. But most importantly, the deliberate creation of a 'mythology of a free New England' was a crucial event in the history of sectional conflict in America."[16]

Beginning in 2012, Harvard Professor Henry Louis Gates, Jr. produced and hosted *Finding Your Roots,* a program on PBS in which he interviewed famous Americans from a variety of fields and explored their recent and not-so-recent backgrounds. The research in some cases turned up information that poignantly illustrates the argument made here about shame and guilt as a motive for forgetting about the past history of enslavement in many white families.

In interviews with actors Kyra Sedgwick and Kevin Bacon, husband and wife, Gates revealed to each that they had ancestors in the North who were slaveholders in the eighteenth century—something that had disappeared from their families' memories at some point.[17] Sedgwick's great-great-great-great-grandfather Theodore Sedgwick was both a slaveholder and a leading voice for independence in Massachusetts as one of the authors of the 1773 Sheffield Resolves, which reads like an early version of the Declaration of Independence. He later served as a delegate to the Continental Congress.

In the 1770s, records show that he owned at least two enslaved people. However, in 1781, he was one of the two lawyers who brought the *Brom and Bett v. Ashley* "freedom suit" to court, and he was also a lawyer in the Quock Walker case, the decision that helped to end slavery in Massachusetts. He also litigated the western Massachusetts case that freed Bett who took the name of Elizabeth Freeman. Subsequently, she was hired by the Sedgwick family as a domestic servant and is buried in the family cemetery on their property. Gates told Kyra Sedgwick that he was flabbergasted to learn that Theodore Sedgwick was an enslaver, since none of the stories he had encountered in his research ever mentioned that fact. Her response on hearing it was, "Oh, that's so sad."

Bacon too learned that he had a slaveholding ancestor—his great-great-great-great-great-great-grandfather Samuel Atkinson. Chris Densmore, the curator at the Swarthmore College Friends Historical Library, found Atkinson's will from 1775, revealing the story. Densmore also pointed out to Gates that even though most people are not aware that Quakers were often enslavers, as late as 1775 about 10 percent of them were still slaveholders.

> *Gates.* Did you ever think that your ancestors owned slaves?
>
> *Bacon.* Being from the North, no, but when we were getting ready to do this [program], it did cross my mind. I'd like to think it didn't happen.
>
> *Gates.* Are you surprised?
>
> *Bacon.* I'm kind of surprised on the Quaker side because I didn't ever really think of the Quakers as slave owners, especially since they were a persecuted people. . . . Such a disconnect there. The idea that you come to a place to practice religious freedom at the same time you think it's OK to own a human being.

In his interview with CNN's Anderson Cooper, Gates informed him that the 1850 Census reported that his ancestor Burwell Boykin, an Alabama farmer whose land was worth $6,000 at the time, also owned twelve slaves.[18]

> *Cooper.* Oh my God. That's incredible.
>
> *Gates.* Did you know about that?
>
> *Cooper.* I never heard anything about that. Having family from the Deep South I'm not surprised that there's some—you know—at least one slaveholder. But I always thought that

because my relatives were so poor that they wouldn't have had slaves. It's really depressing, especially when you see the ages and the fact that there are no names [on the page in the census book]. I just find it so disturbing.

Gates then shows him a page from the 1860 Census showing how Boykin died.

Cooper. Holy crap. . . . Killed by a Negro.

Gates. Boykin was murdered by a rebellious slave . . . beaten to death with a farm hoe.

Cooper. Oh my God—that's amazing. This is incredible. I'm blown away.

Gates. Think he deserved it?

Cooper. Yeah, I have no doubt.

Gates. It's a horrible way to die, Anderson.

Cooper. He had twelve slaves. I don't feel bad for him. Honestly, part of me thinks that's awesome . . . I feel bad for the man who killed him and I feel bad for the eleven other unnamed people who—God only knows what happened to them. . . . I wish I knew more, I wish I knew the name of the slave. When you think about how many people's names history never remembers and people whose stories are never told. It's shameful and I feel such a sense of shame over it. At the same time, it's the history of this country.

These three interviews all reveal that in none of the families was the story of their ancestors being slaveholders transmitted to the present generations. Is this because earlier descendants of the slaveholders felt guilt or shame about what their ancestors had done? Not necessarily, but watching the interviews it is clear that Sedgwick and Bacon were taken aback and expressed regret when they learned the news. It is not hard to read guilt or shame into their reactions. In Cooper's case, his explicit reaction contained shame, anger, and deep sadness.

WikiLeaks revealed in 2015 that actor Ben Affleck requested that Gates remove a part of his interview, in which Gates reported that Affleck's relatives on his mother's side had once been slaveholders. Gates agreed to do this, and in the process violated PBS's editorial standards. In a Facebook post about the deletion, Affleck wrote, " 'I didn't want any television show about my family to include a guy who owned slaves. . . . I was embarrassed. The very thought left a bad taste in my mouth.' In hindsight, he added, 'I regret my initial thoughts that the issue of slavery not be included in the story. We deserve neither credit nor blame for our ancestors and the degree of interest in this story suggests that we are, as a nation, still grappling with the terrible legacy of slavery' " (Collins 2015).

Affleck's mother and other family members in recent years had been active and vocal supporters of civil rights laws, so why did he ask for the deletion? Most likely owing to the great shame that he seemed to feel over this revelation about his ancestors. We all have things about our past, or that of our ancestors, that we prefer to not acknowledge, and in this country slavery is probably high up on the list.

A Southern historian once suggested to me that one reason it is so hard for many Southerners to accept the idea that slavery, rather than differences in the interpretation of the Constitution, was the primary cause of the Civil War is that it would mean that many would then view their ancestors as "bad people" and their actions as shameful. For whites in the North, the dynamic is different. A common Northern response is to simply focus on slavery as "a Southern problem," ignoring any of the evidence of its widespread existence in the North. Even when they admit that there was Northern slavery, some people elaborate that it was more benevolent and far more limited than in the South, or they emphasize that many Northerners opposed it at the Constitutional Convention. They construe the opposition as moral, not political, and even more often simply say that Northerners ended slavery in the Civil War. For others whose ancestors immigrated to the United States well after the Civil War, a common response is that their ancestors had nothing to do with it. They never acknowledge that many of the privileges their families enjoyed resulted from the many ways that whites have been, and still are, favored in terms of opportunities in American society, such as access to government-backed mortgages starting in the 1930s or high-quality schools for their children (Coates 2014).

For African Americans, a different dynamic likely results in discomfort thinking and talking about slavery. For one thing, given the almost universal history of earlier enslavement, it is agonizing to think of one's ancestors having been subject to the indignities and suffering of being enslaved. I have been told by a number of African Americans now living in the North whose grandparents or great-grandparents had heard stories about life during slavery from their own enslaved ancestors that the topic was often so painful that the older family members would say little or nothing about it to them, even when asked directly. This effectively communicated that slavery was not a topic they wanted to talk about with their own children or grandchildren. How was this done? Probably in the same way that Germans who were adults during the Nazi era were not at all willing to talk about it with the younger generations during the postwar period. One consequence of such silence is that younger generations quickly internalized the shame or even the guilt of their ancestors having been enslaved, and as a result they worked hard to avoid talking and reflecting about it themselves.

A sixth and final way that forgetting occurs is through reframing—although reframing can also promote recovery of collective memories at other times. "Reframing" does not necessarily entail total forgetting but recasts a memory away from the shame- or guilt-inducing aspects that often promote repression. One example that fits here is the focus by Germans in the immediate post–World War II period on their own suffering in the final years of the war, with little or no attention to German aggression and the millions who died in the Holocaust—issues that only received extensive public attention inside Germany decades later (Lind 2008).[19] Another is found in the Lost Cause narrative in the American South, described earlier, which emphasized the cruelty of the Northern armies, the benevolence of the Southern slave system, the irrelevance of slavery as cause of the war, and the South's legitimate, denied right of secession to make the claim that the South was simply smaller and outmanned but its cause more just (Blight 2001). Reframing events and people can also be useful in recovering forgotten and repressed collective memories, such as Northern slavery.

An interesting reframing example is O'Brien's (2010) account of the way that New Englanders told what happened to the region's original inhabitants, the Indians. She explains how they placed the Indians in a premodern category and constructed

> an origin myth that assigns primacy to non-Indians who "settled" the region in a benign process involving righteous relations with Indians and just property transactions that led to an inevitable and (usually, drawing on the Romanticism that conditioned nineteenth-century sensibilities) lamentable Indian extinction. Thus the "first" New Englanders are made to disappear, sometimes through precise

declarations that the "last" of them has passed, and the colonial regime is constructed as the "first" to bring "civilization" and authentic history to the region. Non-Indians stake a claim to being native—indigenous—through this process. (O'Brien 2010: xv)

The English settlers replaced the local culture with their own and marked the landscape with monuments, historical commemorations, place-names, and ownership, which is particularly evident at Plymouth, Massachusetts, and its rock, which symbolizes their mythic spot of origin. History begins with the advent of Europeans, and Indians "made no history" (O'Brien 2010: 20), while "local narrators engaged in a subtle process of seizing indigeneity in New England as their birthright" (51).

Reframing is sometimes called "rewriting history," but it does not have to mean changing the facts so much as using different language and casting past actions in a different light. In what he calls "the age of euphemism," Wilder (2013) discusses how in the nineteenth century Northern elites reframed the region's, and often their own families', history in new ways:

The northern elite was cleansing the stain of human slavery from the story of its prosperity. Some of the best-educated people in the nation were revising history to romanticize and sanitize their relationship to bondage. They erased their pasts as masters or reimagined their slaves as a lower order of adopted family—trusted, faithful, and beloved servants whom they had treated with dignity and human sympathy. They recast their enslavement of Africans into a tale of decorative servitude. . . . The great families distanced themselves rhetorically from the planters of the West Indies and the South—despite numerous shared surnames—by claiming histories as merchants, investors, and insurers, and then elevating underwriting, finance, and trade to high arts. Slave traders became Atlantic merchants, and the biggest firms received the greatest praise. It was an age of euphemism, populated with fragile lies, half-truths, and deflections. (280–81)

Minardi (2010) provides an interesting example of narrative creation that might be best viewed as framing rather than reframing, but is nonetheless illustrative. She reports that in 1795 Judge St. George Tucker, a professor of law at the College of William and Mary in Virginia, wrote to Jeremy

Belknap, the head of the Massachusetts Historical Society, a series of questions about slavery and emancipation in the state. After asking a number of his peers, Belknap responded, "Slavery hath been abolished here by *publick opinion*" (Minardi 2010: 13). Minardi writes, "In his response Belknap reinforced this connection between historical transformation and historical narration by intimating that Bay Staters had abolished slavery because it did not suit the narrative they were creating for themselves as forgers of freedom" (13). Belknap emphasized a widespread, popular response to the practice, rather than pointing to the state's 1780 constitution that included the words "all men are born free and equal," or the 1783 court decision that cited those words to judge slavery inconsistent with the constitution. Belknap's interpretation was widely accepted, and for decades "various historians (some with a nod to Belknap) claimed that slavery had been fundamentally at odds with the will of the people of Massachusetts during the Revolution. Over time, Belknap's 'publick opinion' argument mutated from a complex causal explanation of emancipation into an expression of a mythic identity for Massachusetts" (Minardi 2010: 14).

Making Massachusetts's opposition to slavery central to its Revolutionary heritage was indeed politically powerful in nineteenth-century debates about slavery and citizenship. However, as Minardi points out, the argument that public opinion was the key to freeing the state's slaves had divergent implications:

> On one hand, the claim the Bay Staters had already accepted emancipation absolved them from charges of complicity with the slaveholding South. On the other, civil rights activists could point to the Revolutionary forefathers' apparent consensus around emancipation in order to argue that succeeding generations should uphold the antislavery legacy. Whether used to justify complacency or inspire action, the argument that public opinion in Massachusetts firmly opposed slavery became, in the increasingly regionalized political discourse of the antebellum decades, a mark of the state's distinctive place in the history of American slavery and freedom. (Minardi 2010: 14)

Lawsuits from enslaved people demanding their freedom in the state increased during the Revolutionary period, before the Quock Walker case, and Belknap saw these as a sign of changing public opinion. "By vesting opposition to chattel slavery in the zeitgeist of Revolutionary Massachusetts, this historical explanation [Belknap's] gave weight to the idea that antislavery sentiment was integral to the patriot cause," Minardi (2010: 20) argues. At the same time, she points out that states' rights arguments and the still-strong ties between the mercantile economy of New England and the South and the Atlantic slave trade made it difficult to mount support in the region for abolition in the country (21).

For Northerners, placing themselves morally above the South required the disappearance of their history of enslavement from the region's collective memory, strong assertions of their own moral superiority, and a reframing and sanitizing the region's history and that of their ancestors. Bailey (1998: 6) offers an excellent example of this, citing Lillian Brandt's 1899 article on the Massachusetts slave trade: "The favorite theme for students of Massachusetts' relationship to slavery has been the growth of the sentiment against slaveholding and the early abolition of it within the state. When her connection to the slave trade has been considered, the tendency is to limit the inquiry to the number of Negroes brought into Massachusetts and the successive efforts to prohibit their importation. This is only a small part of the subject; the Negroes imported into the colony by no means measure the part played in the trade of Massachusetts citizens, capital and shipping" (Bailey 2006:6).

O'Toole (2016) offers good examples of reframing of slavery in her book on Little Compton, Rhode Island, drawing from the town's archives used in her careful research. In these examples, O'Toole provides several cases where people recording the town's history in the decades after slavery ended were, in fact, rewriting it in a direction that either ignores slavery, plays it down, or sanitizes it. She tells us that sometime in the 1840s, Little Compton's town clerk Otis Wilbour undertook the very large task of transcribing all of Little Compton's early vital records from their various books and ancient handwritings into a single, well-organized volume in his highly legible script. Otis Wilbour decided to edit one enslaved couple's marriage record, as follows:

> *Cesar Church and Sarah Peabodie both of Little Compton intend Marriage September 11 1731, married October 7, 1731 by Richard Billings.*
>   Otis eliminated Cesar and Sarah's race, status as servants, and master's names from the official record. He also gave the couple last names that, according to the earlier record, they did not really use.

In the 1840s, hundreds of Little Compton residents could still personally remember the presence of slaves in Little Compton, and a formerly enslaved man, Primus Collins, lived in town until 1858, but Otis did what he thought was proper at the time and rewrote Cesar and Sarah's record as though they were white and free. Because Otis edited a number of records for enslaved people of color in a similar way, his actions helped hide Little Compton's history of slavery from future generations. A similar obscuring of the history of slavery was happening all throughout New England in an effort to portray New England as a historically free, white society that stood in stark contrast to the slave-holding South. Otis' transcription muddied Sarah and Cesar's story. If Cesar had a more English-sounding name, we may never have looked deeper into the old record books to discover the truth about their race and their enslavement. Little Compton's original records remain our best hope for a more accurate understanding of the local history of slavery. (O'Toole 2016: 131)

A second example O'Toole (2016: 153) offers comes from a family memoir and genealogy:

When Joshua Richmond wrote about his ancestor Silvester Richmond in a massive family genealogy in 1889 he recorded that Silvester's will stated "To Nat and Kate their freedom." That was all; a very edited version of the truth, though, he did print Cate's runaway notice. In his later local history David Patten used Joshua's book as a source and simply reprinted "To Nat and Kate their freedom." For well over one hundred years readers of these histories were impressed with Silvester's decency for freeing his slaves. The story changes, along with our impressions, only when we returned to its unedited version in the primary source, Silvester's last will and testament.

Silvester didn't really free Natt and Cate. He freed them if they could raise their own freedom bond. Slave owners were required to post a substantial bond (between 50 and 100£) with the town when they freed a slave as a sort of insurance. If the freed person ever became "chargeable" to the town through disability, age or even idleness or drunkenness, the town would use the bond to provide for the person, saving tax payers the expense. Silvester did not want his heirs to shoulder the cost of Natt's and Cate's freedom bonds so he laid that expense on the two enslaved people as a condition for their freedom. Cate could not do it. For two more years, she worked as a slave in the Perez (Silvester's son) household. Finally, she could take it no longer, and in her old age, ran away. (O'Toole 2016: 152–53)

Whites in neither the South nor the North wanted to think much about how Blacks were doing after the Civil War and Reconstruction. Northerners told themselves that they had done the right thing in ending slavery, and Southerners, while explaining their defeat in terms of the Lost Cause narrative, did their best to reestablish the antebellum racial order through Jim Crow, sharecropping, prisons, and violence that recreated "slavery by another name" (Blackmon 2009). In the North, a more informal system that we should perhaps think of as "Jim Crow North" was characterized by segregation, inferior public services such as education, and job and pay discrimination. When Blacks and whites protested against these in the North during the civil rights period, white resistance was often high and sometimes violent (Sugrue 2008). In short, to the extent that Northern whites thought about race issues, including enslavement, they focused on the South and not what had happened, or was happening, in their own cities and towns. Blacks and their plight were simply ignored, even during the New Deal and Fair Deal years, when whites had little awareness that the major social legislation—particularly Social Security and the GI Bill—really was what Katznelson (2005) calls "white affirmative action" because their implementation was left to the states and localities as the price of Southern support and most excluded, or greatly limited, any benefits to Blacks.[20] While the implementation was far more exclusionary in the South than in the North across the board, where loans and mortgages were concerned, for example, the practices of Northern banks looked a lot like Southern ones (Coates 2014).

Reframing involves redefining contexts and concerns in ways that lead to a shift in meanings and memories. Behind this reframing is the common displacement of older events and narratives with new ones that have a higher salience or contextual relevance. Barry Schwartz's studies of how the American collective memories of George Washington and Abraham Lincoln evolved over time in response to changing contemporary needs illustrate this process particularly well. Schwartz emphasized ways that present needs are crucial in shaping the past because they define the central concerns that shape interpretations. Interestingly, Schwartz made it clear that the new interpretations of each former president were based not on new information about them but on the changing needs of the times (Schwartz 1991).

He analyzed Washington biographies over time and found a distinct shift from how he is portrayed before the Civil War when biographers saw Washington as a distant, gentle, and flawless figure, with little emphasis on his popularity. Washington's image as a gentleman soldier and a man of character is central to this early image (Schwartz 1991: 224), but it shifts in biographies after 1865, when he is much more likely to be portrayed as an imperfect man but one with whom people could identify personally. In the post–Civil War period, interest in Washington decreased and interest in Lincoln rose. As a result, after 1865, a more human and democratic Washington emerged in biographies, consistent with the more realist postwar paradigm that emphasized egalitarian values and human qualities, and more of a common man than in the past in ways that were more consistent with contemporary values (Schwartz 1991, 1997). Lincoln portrayals in the twentieth century moved from emphasizing that he had preserved the Union to his being the president who freed the slaves because of the changing needs of the times, not because of new historical information. When significant civil rights actions took place at the Lincoln Memorial or were tied to him through such acts as Lyndon Johnson's signing the 1965 Voting Rights Act in the same room and on the same desk that Lincoln had used to sign the Emancipation Proclamation, the shift was reinforced.

Both Northern whites and Blacks often had strong reasons not to develop powerful public narratives, ritual events, or visible public sites and objects around slavery's past. Whites wanted the story of their own past actions to be forgotten and many hoped that Blacks would somehow disappear from the region once slavery ended. Few Northern whites had any desire to treat the recently freed enslaved or their descendants as equal citizens, and free Blacks were generally barred from many jobs, had limited access to education, and suffered from discrimination in almost all domains of life. At the same time, they feared slave catchers might capture and send them South. The challenges of survival in daily life were more than enough of a trial, and in this context, dwelling on the evils of enslavement that they or their ancestors had experienced was not a high priority.

Given the many decades of little, if any, attention to Northern slavery, an obvious question is what changed in the past two to three decades that led to the partial recovery of the collective narratives that had all but disappeared. The next four chapters address this question directly through an examination of a wide range of former sites of slavery in the North and the rediscovery of what took place on and near them. They describe the process of recovering a past that was literally buried, with particular attention to three intense public controversies in Philadelphia. The first involves memorialization following the rediscovery that George Washington kept nine enslaved Africans a block from Independence Hall in a house that served as his home and office in the city while he was president from 1790 to 1797 and Philadelphia was the country's capital. The next two involve paved-over burial grounds in the city, which had been used as early as the 1750s and contain the remains of thousands of free and enslaved Blacks. They were forgotten until community groups demanded that the sites be protected and recognized as historically sacred places. In all three cases, the stories of the early generations of Blacks in the city generally are better understood in part because researchers have also learned something about specific people whose stories can be told.

Chapter 4

Enslaved Africans in the President's House

> *Public memory is the storage system for social order. . . . Some patterns of public events get stored there and others get rejected.*
>
> —Mary Douglas, *How Institutions Think*

As president, George Washington brought nine enslaved people to Philadelphia to live and work in his house between 1790 and 1797, when Philadelphia was the nation's capital. Once this was rediscovered in the early twenty-first century, many Philadelphians struggled for a decade over how to recount the past presence of slaves at a historical site that for six decades prior had focused exclusively on the country's story of freedom and liberty. In the process, Washington's reputation was somewhat sullied, and many people in the region learned more about slavery in the North than they ever knew before. The enslaved people came from Virginia, and all but one returned there after Washington's time in Philadelphia, but learning about their presence in the nation's capital nevertheless brought attention to the forgotten story of slavery in the city and in the North more generally.

This chapter is about an intense but never violent conflict that occurred just a few miles from where I live. It first interested me because the conflict resembled ones around the world that I had written about in *Cultural Contestation in Ethnic Conflict* (Ross 2007). That book focused on identity conflicts that were managed to varying degrees of success, and in which cultural issues played a central role.[1] Racially rooted conflicts in the United States, of course, have produced both kinds of outcomes over the years. Conflicts over inclusion and exclusion from sacred sites—both religious and nonreligious—can be particularly intense, as was the one described here about how to memorialize enslaved people at Philadelphia's Independence National Historical Park.

Independence National Historical Park (INHP) is a National Park Service site, located downtown, where it is said that extraordinary people did extraordinary things from 1776 to 1800. Visitors to the site, much of which has been restored to evoke colonial Philadelphia, are told about these events. Until recently, however, tour guides and the literature available to visitors at this National Park Service (NPS) site made little, if any, mention of the contradictory, discordant aspects of a history that literally juxtaposed freedom and slavery at this very place, in the country's Constitution, and in the lives of many of the founding fathers.

The President's House, torn down in 1832, was located just one block from Independence Hall, where the national narrative of freedom and liberty is celebrated. Only some facts are known about the house, and for many years very few people even had a sense of where the house had been. In the 1990s, the National Park Service introduced large-scale renovation plans for the block just north of Independence Hall. They did not plan to take any special note of the former house. Starting in 2002, after the actual site of the house was clearly identified, the probable plan of the building was published, the interior design as well as the residents of the house identified, an intense conflict arose over what the site should look like and how it should be interpreted on the INHP's mall. At the core of the disagreements were how to combine the paradoxical juxtaposition of slavery and liberty made visible in the blatant contrast between the treatment of anyone who was not considered white and the words of the founding documents—especially at a site that has incompatible commemorative and historical goals.

Independence Hall and the Liberty Bell have been sacred to Americans for a long time, although the hall and the specific places in and around it where the bell has been housed have changed a number of times since the 1770s (Nash 2010). The country's founders met at Independence Hall to write and adopt both the Declaration of Independence in 1776 and the Constitution in 1787. The bell was rung following the Declaration's first public reading on July 8, 1776.[2] This linked the two in the country's narrative, more than fifty years before the Liberty Bell was so named by abolitionists (Mires 2002; Nash 2010: 16–17).

Interestingly, despite the explicit association between the Liberty Bell and opposition to slavery, Nash (2010) describes how the Liberty Bell became a critical symbol of national unity and reconciliation following the Civil War. The Liberty Bell took seven "road trips" around the country between 1885 and 1915. Traveling by train, it was enthusiastically greeted in town after town along the way (Mires 2002). Three of these trips were to the former Confederacy, where large crowds gathered to greet it and celebrate the South's role in the American Revolution. Even Jefferson Davis, the former Confederate president, spoke in Biloxi, Mississippi, "on behalf of the Bell's power to help bind the nation's wounds" (Nash 2010: 80). It was featured at world's fairs in New Orleans, Chicago, and San Francisco and was the highlight of the celebrations in each city. Unlike the American flag, which was still a divisive symbol, the Liberty Bell was welcomed everywhere. The reason for this is not completely obvious but probably had to do with the flag's association with Northern armies in the Civil War, while the Bell was tied to the country's founding and was less symbolically connected to more recent, divisive politics.[3] In the twentieth century the Liberty Bell was an important symbol for Americans during both world wars.

During the Cold War, the Liberty Bell was a widely used symbol of freedom and democracy. Certainly, this was a significant factor in the Congressional decision to authorize the creation of Independence National Historical Park. The park was opened in 1956 and now encompasses fifty-five acres in the oldest part of Philadelphia. Before the park was created, the surrounding area contained a hodgepodge of stores and homes—many of which were in poor condition. As part of the propaganda war against Soviet Communism, the area around Independence Hall was eventually transformed into an impressive historical district that featured a large mall in the three blocks to the north, all of which now celebrate the story of the founding of the United States and its democratic history. The emphasis at INHP was on the eighteenth-century "miracle in Philadelphia."

The Liberty Bell is the most popular tourist site in the park, although many visitors take a tour of Independence Hall as well.[4] The National Park Service at INHP, as in many of its sites, is continually challenged to decide what narratives to present to visitors to balance the dual needs of history and commemoration as they shift over time.[5]

Up until the twenty-first century, enslavement was virtually absent from the park's displays and narratives. The President's House, which also served as the U.S. executive mansion, was where Washington signed the Fugitive Slave Act in 1793. Ogline (2004: 50) explains:

Over the years, a variety of interpretive programs had explored the early history of the executive branch of the federal government. But no one spoke of the slaves—not out of any deliberate conspiracy of silence, but because Washington's labor arrangements lay outside the park's field of vision. Founded to tell the stories of the Continental Congress and the Constitutional Convention, the park reflected the priorities and outlook of the larger society. . . . The history of slavery on Independence Mall has not so much been suppressed as considered irrelevant to the park's primary narratives: the political history of the late eighteenth century and the institutional history of Independence Square.[6]

That invisibility changed in early 2002 after independent historian Edward Lawler published his detailed research on the architectural details of the house (Lawler 2002b).[7] In early March historian Gary Nash, who had published articles and books on the colonial and Revolutionary periods and slavery in the city, appeared on a local public radio program. He discussed the significance of Lawler's findings and sparked intense interest in them. Among other things, Lawler's work explains in part why the house itself and its enslaved people were forgotten for so long. As early as the 1850s there was great confusion about the size, exterior appearance, and even the precise location of the house (Lawler 2002b: 6). Soon after John Adams left the house in 1800, it became a hotel, and after a short while it became a white elephant, as the block was transformed into an important commercial location, filled with storefronts. In response, the building's owner installed stores on the first story and boardinghouse rooms on the upper ones. In 1832, the building was gutted and only the exterior walls and foundations remained (Lawler 2002b: 52–59). Over the years there was a great deal of speculation about the house's design and location, and in the 1930s a WPA project built an inaccurate model of its design. Finally, in 1951, when the entire square block was cleared to make way for the mall on the newly established Independence National Historical Park, the exterior walls and foundation that had never been destroyed were taken down, since they were believed to have been built after 1832 (Lawler 2002b: 70–78).

There is no record of any attention to the enslaved Africans who had lived in the house from the time it was built until President Washington left, although this information was available to be known for decades: the Washington papers and correspondence that Lawler and others have used to learn about the enslaved people were at Mount Vernon and other archives. The National Park Service had known since 1970 that Washington had brought enslaved Africans to the city but did not think it was especially important. This is fully consistent with the narrative that says the lives of Black people didn't matter in U.S. history, and even if Blacks had known about the site's slave past, they were relatively powerless to change this narrative.

Soon after the public radio program aired, the *Philadelphia Inquirer* ran a front-page story (Salisbury and Saffron 2002) about Lawler's revelation that Washington had brought eight (later corrected to nine) enslaved Africans from his Mount Vernon plantation to live and work in the house during his presidency.[8] The rear of the house, where some of the enslaved worked and slept, sat on Independence Mall next to what would soon become the entrance to the Liberty Bell Center, then under construction (Mires 2009).

Up to this point, most people living in the city had never thought about slavery in Philadelphia and had simply assumed that Pennsylvania was always a free state, given its significant Quaker heritage. However, this was not the case. In fact, William Penn, the founder of the colony in 1682, owned at least twelve slaves in his lifetime (Nash and Soderlund 1991:12), and for ninety years or so many other Quakers were slave owners as well. In fact, Penn purchased 150 Africans within two years of his arrival, as he felt that the colony needed more workers. As a group, to recall, the Quakers only disavowed the practice on the eve of the American Revolution.[9] Pennsylvania's 1780 Gradual Abolition law, mentioned in Chapter 2, specified that persons born to an enslaved woman would not actually be freed for more than twenty years as a way to reimburse the owner for the cost of raising them from birth. In practice, this meant that people were enslaved in the state until the mid-1840s. A 1788 amendment to the law allowed residents of other states to bring their enslaved persons into Pennsylvania for a period of up to six months, after which the enslaved persons could petition for their freedom. When Philadelphia was the nation's capital, the Pennsylvania legislature considered a bill to exempt federal employees who were residents of other states from the law's manumission provisions, but it failed to pass. It was widely known that Washington was a slaveholder in Virginia,[10] but few people connected the dots that he and other founders of the country would have brought enslaved people with them on travels to Philadelphia in 1776 and 1787, and when Philadelphia was the country's capital.

When stories about Lawler's work appeared, many in the city asked why it had been "buried" for so long, since the NPS had known about the enslaved Africans for decades. This topic was uncomfortable and disturbing to many people. As I followed the story and sought to make sense of it, I was especially interested in the emotionally intense debates about what should be said and done concerning Washington and the enslaved Africans at INHP, and in the question of why there had been so little awareness, let alone knowledge, about Northern slavery and its role in the region's social and economic development.

A range of people including quickly formed Black citizen's groups, local historians, the press, and many citizens soon demanded that something be done to integrate the story of the enslaved Africans into the park's narratives, including those of the not-yet-opened Liberty Bell Center. The fact that the National Park Service apparently decided that this story was not sufficiently significant to make it available to the public only strengthened widespread anger, skepticism, and distrust.[11] Even with this initial attention, the NPS was very slow to recognize the political and emotional significance of the "rediscovery." The NPS proposed only the most modest symbolic gesture: a plaque on the site that acknowledged that Washington and Adams had lived in the house, that it once was on the corner of Sixth and Market Streets, and that Washington had kept enslaved Africans there while he was president. Although the NPS had access to Lawler's research a year before it was published, its position was simply that the plans for revising the mall were too far advanced to change, and that presenting the story of slavery in a block of the park that was to tell the story of freedom and liberty would be too confusing to visitors. Rather, Martha Aikens, the Park Service head at IHNP, herself an African American, suggested that people could learn more about Washington and slavery at the Deshler-Morris house, another NPS site, in Germantown, ten miles away, where Washington had lived for several months during a yellow fever outbreak in 1794.[12]

Three citizens' groups quickly formed to challenge the NPS decision: Avenging the Ancestors Coalition (ATAC), led by attorney and activist Michael Coard; Generations Unlimited; and the Ad Hoc Historians group, composed of local historians, all of whom were especially interested in pushing the NPS to tell the more complex, braided history of slavery and liberty in and around the new Liberty Bell Center.

The local media were filled with stories about Washington's enslaved Africans, and national papers soon picked up the story. Editorials and columnists overwhelmingly supported the idea that the NPS needed to do far more than put a historical marker on Market Street in front of where the house once stood. By early summer, the NPS transferred Superintendent Aikens to a different position in Washington and appointed Dennis Reidenbach as the new head of INHP. Reidenbach was more willing to reevaluate the plans to mark the President's House site and tell the story of enslavement in it.

On July 3, 2002—three months after the story first broke—ATAC and Generations Unlimited organized a demonstration that drew at least five hundred protesters in front of the future home of the Liberty Bell.[13] They called the adjacent site of the President's House "a crime scene" and bounded it with yellow police tape. Speakers evoked graphic images of slavery and called for the construction of a slavery memorial on the site of the house that abutted what was to be the new entrance to the Liberty Bell Center (Achrati 2002). A week later, the House Appropriations Committee in Washington adopted an amendment to the Interior Department's budget bill that called upon the NPS to appropriately commemorate the slaves who toiled in Washington's household while he lived in the city (Salisbury 2002a).

It would take eight and a half more years before the design and construction for the President's House/Slavery Memorial was completed. Soon a controversy erupted over the interpretive panels inside the Liberty Bell Center, which was to open the next year, in 2003. The initial panels barely mentioned slavery. The Ad Hoc Historians as well as local citizens and elected leaders in Philadelphia insisted that it was crucial to integrate the story of slavery into the center's exhibits and demanded that they commemorate the house itself and the enslaved Africans who toiled and lived there (Nash 2004; Lawler n.d.). They widely criticized the original text panels for the Liberty Bell Center as simplistic and incomplete and inconsistent with the NPS's policy of inclusion, adopted in the 1990s. NPS chief historian Dwight Pitacithley realized the interpretive and narrative possibilities, and in a communication to then Superintendent Aikens argued: "The potential for interpreting Washington's residence and slavery on the site . . . presents the National Park Service with several exciting opportunities [including] . . . the juxtaposition of slave quarters (George Washington's slave quarter's, no less) and the Liberty Bell [provided] some stirring interpretive possibilities. . . . This juxtaposition is an interpretive gift that can make the Liberty Bell 'experience' much more meaningful to the visiting public. We will have missed a real educational opportunity if we do not act on this possibility" (Nash 2004: 46).Pitacithley succeeded in involving the Ad Hoc Historians in the process of reviewing and rewriting the panels for the Liberty Bell Center, and in a short time a new set was prepared in which slavery was more prominent than in the original Cold War–style ones. Even so, groups remained uncertain and distrustful about the NPS's intentions and especially where it stood on the matter of creating an appropriate memorial for the President's House and a marker of some kind on the part of the house closest to the Liberty Bell Center entrance, which was being widely referred to as the "Slave Quarters," although it was not the only part of the house where enslaved Africans slept.

A great part of the confusion arose because the NPS continued to waver, saying it was not certain about where the enslaved Africans slept, and insisting that until it had definitive proof, it could not use the term "Slave Quarters." In addition, despite the fact that many have moved on from using the term "slaves" to "the enslaved" to reflect the active role of the "enslavers," the NPS often called them "servants." This was common in the eighteenth century and continued at NPS sites around the country in the twentieth century, although it failed to distinguish between white indentured servants and enslaved Blacks. The NPS continued to refer to the area as the "servants' hall," since some of the people who slept there might not have been enslaved. Only in 2004 did the Park Service begin to describe the area as "slave quarters" (Mires 2009: 231).

Finally, there was still the unresolved commemoration question, since the NPS had agreed to tell the story of slavery but not necessarily to include a memorial (Salisbury 2002b, 2002c). Following a meeting in October 2002 with NPS officials, Michael Coard said, "The officials are now saying the right thing, but I won't believe them until they begin to act on their word" (Moore 2002a). It is fair to say that the historians involved generally agreed with Coard and the community groups. They also recognized that pressure from elected officials and the meetings with the NPS pointed toward the likelihood of NPS change (Lawler 2002a).

After a series of small group meetings and discussions involving the NPS, community groups, city officials, and the Ad Hoc Historians, the Park Service commissioned a preliminary design for the President's House/Slavery Memorial site from the Olin Partnership of Philadelphia and Vincent Ciulla Design of Brooklyn, which had previously worked on the Liberty Bell

Center. They announced that there would be a public meeting at the nearby African American Museum in early 2003 to discuss the proposal. The packed meeting was raucous and passionate. Clearly, many people were upset and very distrustful of the NPS, thinking that the design was a fait accompli and angry that there had been no chance for significant public input. There was general booing from the audience when a distinguished African American historian characterized Washington as a relatively benign owner (Mires 2009: 227).

While slavery was certainly a central element of the proposal for the site, there was great skepticism about some parts of it. Some people were concerned that the Park Service still had no plan to fund future construction. Others were angry that there was insufficient African American participation in the design and in the plans for the future construction, and still others complained about the specific language proposed to describe both the enslaved and the enslavers. The Park Service's "clumsy attempts to control the tenor of the debate were met with direct, even loud, personal abuse. In heated language, people assailed the process by which the draft design had come into being" (Holt 2003).

In contrast, Coard emphasized that there was reason to celebrate the decision to install a memorial on the site. "Keep your eyes on the prize," he said (Salisbury 2003b), stressing the NPS's change of position. "To go from completely denying to designing is a monumental prize for us. We got them to make a 180-degree turnaround. Can you imagine a community group forcing the federal government to listen to our concerns and to begin implementing our input? Now I think we will be on our way" (Wilson 2003). For a time, discussion and puzzling about funding possibilities increased as a new head of the park service at INHP, Mary Bomar, took over. She had very successfully headed the NPS in Oklahoma City at the memorial site of the 1996 bombing and was seen as an ideal person to deal with the controversy over the President's House site.

Bomar said she liked working with people and would involve all relevant parties in any decisions. Her earliest success was working with the city to reopen Chestnut Street in front of Independence Hall, which had been closed following 9/11, to the dismay of many local residents and merchants. It was soon clear that she understood the need for a more complete presentation of the role of race in early American history in the park, along with the inclusion of the Black experience in the city from its earliest days. This meant explicit recognition and discussion of slavery as well as the free Black community in Philadelphia, which was the largest in the country in the 1790s, most of whom lived in and around what is now INHP.

Bomar, like other NPS employees, was cautious in what she was willing to commit the NPS to doing, although both the activists such as Coard and the historians found her open and thoughtful. For example, she, like others, was uneasy about calling the area in the back of the house, often referred to as the "smokehouse," as the Slave Quarters, as Lawler and the Independence Hall Association (IHA) had done on their comprehensive website (USHistory.org), which covered the controversy based on Washington's correspondence with his Secretary Tobias Lear (Lawler 2002b). Bomar said that while Washington had first wished to change the smokehouse to the Slave Quarters, there was no definitive evidence that the area was transformed before he moved to the city. She added, "Our research and analysis show that Washington quartered his slaves and servants by function, that is, some slept in the main house, some in the servants' hall next to the kitchen and some near the stable. Since Washington mixed free and enslaved people in all of these lodging arrangements, we see no valid argument for designating a particular area as 'slave quarters.'"[14] No one involved directly disputed these points but for a variety of reasons, there was great appeal in designating a particular area as "the slave quarters."[15] Lawler responded to Bomar, expressing displeasure and charging that "erasing the smokehouse and its addition from the footprint of the house— seemingly, to avoid having to deal with the issue of the 'slave quarters'—is deceptive and intellectually dishonest, will not make the controversy go away, and is an open invitation for new and accelerating charges of duplicity by INHP."[16] Hardly a meeting of the minds.

In early July 2003, ATAC again marked its "Black Independence Day" event at the house's site as they had the year before and issued a position paper including the demand for "a culturally dignified, historically complete, physically dramatic and timely installed and/or timely presented *commemorative project* as well as other permanent memorializing acknowledgments—with substantive and ongoing input from the African American community—to *honor* primarily *the* eight *Africans* who were brutally *enslaved by President George Washington at America's first 'White House,'* which was located *in Philadelphia* near the current Sixth and Market Streets site of the new Liberty Bell pavilion."[17] That same day the *Christian Science Monitor* ran a long story about the conflict, focusing on the role of slavery in the development of the American economy. The authors quoted Harvard economic historian Sven Beckert's statement that "the center of our economy was cotton," from which both the North and South profited. "The old history separated 'American capitalism' and 'democracy' from 'slavery.' In the 'new history,' the three are organically connected" (Teicher and Robinson 2003).[18] It also pointed out the crucial role that debates about slavery played at the Constitutional Convention, at which twenty-five of the fifty-five (46 percent) delegates were slaveholders. Others were previous slave owners. Benjamin Franklin was on such attendee. He once owned slaves before he became an abolitionist very late in life, a conversion that Waldstreicher (2004: 235–39) sees as politically expedient rather than a deeply held belief.

Meanwhile, funding was still not identified for the project, and people became impatient with what they perceived to be NPS foot-dragging. The Ad Hoc Historians issued a press packet with their views on the controversy. Demonstrations were planned for October 9, 2003, the day when the Liberty Bell would be moved to its new home. Coard denounced "the omission of a marking for the slave quarters" as a fundamental flaw in the NPS design to date. "It's five feet from the entrance of the Liberty Bell Center. How can you not address it?" (Salisbury 2003c).

The bell's move came off smoothly, and during the dedication ceremony Philadelphia's Mayor John Street announced that the city would contribute $1.5 million toward commemorating the enslaved Africans who lived and worked in the President's House next door. Rep Joe Hoeffel announced that he and other local members of Congress were working to complete the funding for the project (Salisbury 2003a).

The next month, the NPS hosted a roundtable of fourteen experts to seek a consensus about the interpretation of the historical evidence. Lawler, one of the members of the group, submitted a minority report that included corrections, additions, and some disagreements with the consensus document. Once again, there was considerable focus on the issue of the smokehouse and "Slave Quarters" and the absence of the term in the Olin/ Ciulla plan. Historian Charles Blockson objected to calling the enslaved people African Americans for the simple reason that they did not have any of the rights of Americans at that time.

In July 2004, the news broke that Lawler's most recent research revealed that Washington had brought to Philadelphia a ninth enslaved African named Joe who worked as a postilion—a footman for the president's coach—and a groom in his stables. The news became the centerpiece of what had become ATAC's yearly July 3 event. Coard emphasized the lack of progress toward the promised memorial: "It's taken so long to acknowledge these enslaved Africans because of the embarrassment that America feels about slavery. But we have three demands for the Independence National Historical Park. We want a physical manifestation, perhaps something like a waterfall; a verbal manifestation, like an explanation from the park ranger when giving tours and a footprint marking. We want people who visit this site to know they're crossing over hallowed ground—from the hell of slavery to the heaven of liberty" (Bolling 2004; Salisbury 2004b).

That fall, the NPS held a Civic Engagement Forum that featured a panel from the stakeholder groups and interested members of the public. It was organized around the five themes identified in the Olin/ Ciulla concept plan for the site: (1) The house and the people who lived and toiled there; (2) the Executive Branch of the U.S. government; (3) the system and methods of slavery; (4) African American Philadelphia; and (5) the move to freedom. All the topics but the second one elicited comments. John Adams, who lived in the house for almost four years after Washington, was never mentioned. Doris Fanelli, the IHNP historian, identified an additional theme of "History Lost and Found," which would emphasize how knowledge about the site changed over time and slavery was long lost from popular memory.

At the session, the issue of the "Slave Quarters" produced a good deal of interest. A number of people disputed the NPS position that no specific location of the house could be identified. Earlier in the day, Lawler and NPS archaeologist Jed Levin had marked the physical location of the buildings closest to the Liberty Bell Center entrance that they had been referring to as the "slave quarters." Two days later Lawler provided a tour of the area for Bomar and other NPS personnel after which Lawler and Bomar "agreed to place a sign on the brick pier at the site of the smoke house" with the wording "Smoke House/Washington designated that his stable workers, some of whom were enslaved Africans, be housed here." There were two subsequent meetings of the forum's planners and within a few weeks there was agreement from Bomar and the participants "to give the location the label 'Slave Quarters' [note the absence of the limiting article] indicating that it was one site, but not the only site on the property where enslaved Africans were housed" (Salisbury 2004a; Fanelli 2004).

The speakers and audience offered a number of comments that Fanelli identified as cultural values important to the themes: identity, memory and sense of influence of the past on the present, agency, dignity, and truth. Blockson emphasized the importance of interpreting the experience of all enslaved people on the site—not just those who had lived and worked there. Other comments emphasized the site's symbolic importance and the events there "as a representation of the conditions of slavery that the attenders' ancestors had suffered." One participant said "people are calling out to us from that site." The agency theme emphasized the triumph of individuals over their conditions and shifted the focus from master to slave (Fanelli 2004).

Those attending expressed strong feelings that the contractors and architects for the project should be African American and that the main focus needed to be on the enslaved residents of the house. Blockson said at one point, "I don't give a damn about the President's House. We wouldn't be here today if it weren't for the African American community" (Salisbury 2004a). On other occasions, I have heard some say that people can learn about Washington in hundreds of places in the United States, so this site should focus on slavery in general and his enslaved Africans who lived here, which so few people know anything about.

In September 2005, Congressman Chaka Fattah announced a federal grant of $3.6 million that was intended to complete the necessary funding for the project (Slobodzian 2005). The same day five of the Ad Hoc Historians and five INHP staffers met to clarify what they agreed and disagreed about. In their memo, the group identified sixteen points of agreement and only one disagreement—the level of architectural details within the perimeter walls of the agreed-to floor plan to make the visitor experience "real."[19] Stakeholders who had not attended the meeting were invited to offer comments to the document that was circulated. Coard sent one that reiterated his and ATAC's view:

Whether the commemoration is a statue, a series of statues, a waterfall, an eternal flame, a sculpture, a wall, a whispering corridor, or something else, it must be culturally-dignified, historically-complete, prominently-conspicuous, and physically-dramatic. In addition, it must be designed and constructed with the substantive (if not primary) input and participation of the descendants of Africans in America.

Furthermore, it must be appropriately-located, which means, e.g., at or near the 55 × 35-foot outline of the kitchen ell/servants' hall. Moreover, it must include slave quarters footprint markings at the entrance to the LBC [Liberty Bell Center].[20]

All was far from decided, however, as there were tough design and interpretive issues, as well as an archaeological excavation of the site ahead. More than five years passed before these were completed and this addition to the mall was ready to be open to the public in December 2010.

"The President's House: Freedom and Slavery in Making a New Nation" was now funded. The city and the NPS agreed on the membership of an Oversight Committee composed of a group of historians, civic leaders, NPS officials, and chaired by the Mayor's Chief of Staff, Joyce Wilkerson. It would make decisions concerning the design and construction, all of which would also require agreement from the Park Service, which would actually manage the site once it opened. City funds would be used for the design phase and the city would manage the construction (Salisbury 2005).

The questions of what would actually be built and what would be presented on the site now moved to the forefront. These two questions— especially the second one—were highly contentious, and it took several years and a lot of discussion and debate to decide. Even when the decisions were finally reached, some were angry that their important concerns were ignored. A recurring third issue concerned who would do the actual work and the extent to which African American contractors would be involved.

The first step was issuing a Request for Qualifications, to which twenty-one architectural teams representing more than one hundred firms and individuals responded. Almost exactly six months later, in March 2006, Mayor Street and the new INHP Superintendent Dennis Reidenbach[21] agreed on the six semifinalists after reviewing comments from the Oversight Committee, the city's Capital Program Office, and the Chief of INHP's Division of Cultural Resources Management. Mayor Street and Superintendent Reidenbach also authorized a research "dig" on approximately 45 percent of the previously unexcavated yard areas on the President's House site—those areas most likely to yield positive results, meaning artifacts directly associated with the enslaved people who had lived and worked in the house. The odds of a significant discovery were not high, but the Mayor felt strongly that the dig should occur, on the off chance that there were objects associated with Washington's household underground. As Superintendent Reidenbach explained, "Given a core theme of this project—to disclose fully the history of this site and to tell its forgotten truth—we have a responsibility to resolve any lingering questions people may have."[22]

Despite the widespread belief among archaeologists that a dig would not provide much information about the house or its inhabitants during the last decade of the eighteenth century, the city's Oversight Committee decided to proceed with it. After all, several people argued, a recent dig two blocks to the north prior to construction of a bus depot to be used for National Constitution Center visitors in 2003 had unexpectedly produced many interesting artifacts in and around the former home of James Oronoko Dexter, a once enslaved and later free Black man who lived there in the 1790s. Dexter was a founder of St. Thomas's African Episcopal Church, the first Black church in the city in 1792, and a founding member of the Free African Society in 1787 with the more well-known Richard Allen and Absalom Jones (Yamin 2008: 88–93).

In June the Oversight Committee hosted a public forum to consider plans for the President's House/Slavery Memorial and invited Howard Dodson, head of the Schomburg Center for Research in Black Culture at the New York Public Library, and Fath Davis Ruffins, curator of African American history and culture at the Smithsonian's National Museum of American History, to speak about "opportunities for teachable moments" at commemorative sites and to suggest implications for the President's House site design. Dodson, who had been involved in the planning and design for the African Burial Grounds in New York for the past fifteen years, spoke about the struggles to develop the site. He emphasized the resistance from government and white citizens. He spoke about the struggle for recognition and acknowledgment of New York's slave history and their eventual success.

Ruffins emphasized the ways that slavery and freedom have been intertwined in American history and the prevailing silence about slavery until recently. She noted that when the Smithsonian's National Museum of American History opened in 1964, slavery was left out—on the belief that it was a Southern problem, not a national one. However, today, she said, "that silence has begun to end" and "new narratives of the American past, which can acknowledge both freedom and slavery and their relationship to each other," are appearing. In fact, she pointed out that this was occurring internationally as well and talked about how West and Central Africa are now more clearly aware of their roles in the slave trade. She ended with a consideration of different kinds of sites that speak to the past and suggested that the President's House/Slavery Memorial site would not be a monumental site, but rather a commemorative, memorial one, more like the Vietnam Veterans Memorial in Washington.[23]

During the question and answer session, there was little interest in what the two speakers had discussed. Instead, there were a series of angry comments from the audience, demanding that African Americans be hired to work on the project, with a limited role for whites and the city's predominately white unions. The same theme dominated the July 2006 ATAC Black Independence Day celebration, which also stressed the progress made toward construction of the memorial and demanded that "today's free Blacks be selected to play a leading role in designing and constructing that monument. Now that we got the federal government to finally agree to this commemoration, now we go to the second issue" (Waters 2006).

Five proposed designs for the site were put on public view for comments at the Constitution Center from August 16 to September 19, 2006, and at the African American Museum from September 20 to October 1.[24] Visitors were asked to submit comments on them. *Philadelphia Inquirer* architecture critic Inga Saffron (2006b) found two of them successful at balancing the two different themes of the birth of American democracy and the stain of slavery, but none was really good enough, in her view. Two weeks later Saffron (2006a) suggested there were good ideas across the five that, if merged, would make for a superior design. Reactions to the designs revealed clearly the tension between focusing on the story of Washington and Adams and the establishment of the Executive Branch of the U.S. government versus the heretofore untold story of enslavement throughout the early United States. The site's small footprint and the absence of physical artifacts further limited the options to resolve this tension between the goals of history and commemoration.

Ongoing tensions between ATAC and Blockson's Generations Unlimited group again surfaced and demonstrated the strong emotions that the story of enslavement on the site evoked within the African American community. Blockson called for a public community meeting between them to "iron out" their differences. He added that displaying the designs at the Constitution Center before the African American Museum was a slap in the face to African Americans. He reiterated his view that the President's House as a tourist site was overshadowing the story of slavery and added,

"We should honor the enslaved Africans and not the house itself" (Hoffler 2006).

With great fanfare, the Mayor and the NPS Superintendent announced the winning design team in late February 2007. Kelly/Maiello, a local African American firm, won the national competition, and the Mayor declared, "I am sure there will be meaningful and substantial minority participation throughout this project—both when the words are written and the bricks are laid" (Salisbury 2007a). Richard Rabinowitz, with his American History Workshop team, was selected as the lead interpretive planner. They had developed the widely acclaimed "Slavery in New York" exhibit at the New-York Historical Society, as well as the creative work for the Birmingham Civil Rights Institute and the National Underground Railroad Freedom Center in Cincinnati. Well-known historians James Oliver Horton and Gary Nash would also serve on the team (Salisbury 2007a). The plan was to start construction as soon as possible and open the site in 2008.

This proved to be overly optimistic, for the archaeological dig produced some surprising findings that led to revisions in the site's design.

When the decision was made to conduct an archaeological excavation at Sixth and Market, there was no great expectation that it would yield abundant information about the original house itself, mainly because the location was built and rebuilt a number of times after the house was torn down in 1832, and any foundations and artifacts were thought to have disappeared long ago. After all, archaeological work in the area just to the south, which now houses the Liberty Bell Center, had produced thousands of objects of interest but no building foundations. However, that dig had unearthed one very interesting structure, in a section of the area closest to the Sixth and Market site. Archaeologists had discovered a large underground ice house that the wealthy Robert Morris, who owned the house at the time, had built after consulting about the design with his friend George Washington (Flam 2001).[25]

The excavation of the President's House site began in late March 2007 and was expected to last three to six weeks (Figure 5). Instead, it lasted four months. Several thousand artifacts were found, but none of them could be connected definitively to Washington, his family, or the enslaved Africans who had toiled and lived there. Contrary to expectations, however, the lower part of the house's foundations had not been totally destroyed. The dig exposed a lower level kitchen, once located in a small structure behind

Figure 5. Entrance to the archaeological excavation at the President's House/Slavery Memorial site, 2007. Visitors to the platform were able to watch archaeologists discuss the work they were doing and its significance with the public.

the house. It is likely that some of the enslaved Africans, including Hercules, Washington's chef, worked in this kitchen. The dig also excavated an underground passageway between the kitchen and the main house, through which enslaved people carried food to Washington's dining room upstairs. In addition, and unexpectedly, the excavation revealed the curved foundation fragments of the bow window that Washington had added to the State Dining Room to expand a ceremonial space where the public could meet the President as part of the house's enlargement after he moved to Philadelphia. A number of people have suggested that this was the model for the bow window in the White House in Washington, D.C.

The excavation was important in two additional ways. It generated an enormous interest in the house and its history in the city. The Park Service

Figure 6. President's House/Slavery Memorial Site, 2007 archaeological excavation. The dig uncovered the base of the walls of the house's foundation. On the far left side, the passageway goes from the lower kitchen at the back of the house to a stairway leading to the Washingtons' dining room. Immediately behind the President's House is the entrance to the Liberty Bell Center where visitors can view the bell. The windows of Independence Hall can be seen in the background.

constructed a platform from which people could look down into the pit (Figure 6) and talk with one of the archaeologists on the site about the house, its history, and the people who lived and worked there.[26] About 300,000 people visited the platform—some repeatedly—in its few months of operation, and their questions and comments clearly illustrate their engagement with the site's history. Because they were able to talk to the archaeologists about their findings, people developed a human connection to the site and its history. They learned details about the neighborhood in the 1790s, the house and its residents, including the names and brief profiles of the nine enslaved Africans Washington brought with him from

Virginia, and the different kinds of work each one performed. People were able to construct poignant stories for themselves about life in the house and the relationship among the twenty-five or so people who lived in it during Washington's time. The fragments of the building's foundations linked people emotionally across time.[27] One topic that came up again and again, especially for African American women, was speculation concerning Washington's sexual access to the younger enslaved women in the house and the assumption that he, like many slaveholders, regularly exploited the enslaved women for his own pleasure.

While there is not a great deal known about seven of the nine enslaved people, it is striking how even knowing their names, ages, and the kind of work each did promoted personal connections and affinities for visitors to the site. The most complete stories were about Ona Judge[28] and Hercules, the cook in the house, known for his fine meals. (See pages 146–152 below for the full list of enslaved Africans in the President's House.) "The excavation . . . ignited imaginations and intense conversations as more than 300,000 visitors watched archaeologists expose the symbolic foundations of Black slavery and governing white power in the literal foundations of the first U.S. executive mansion" (Salisbury 2008c). People not only wanted to know what had happened there long ago but also wanted to talk to each other about its relevance for the present. There were many reports of whites and Blacks talking together meaningfully about race in ways that are still relatively rare in the city. Many people forged personal connections with the past. Cheryl LaRoche (2007b), one of the archaeologists who worked on the dig and had previously worked on the African Burial Ground site in New York, wrote movingly about her experience saying, "My work on this site has been personally gratifying and life transforming. I had been thinking about and researching Ona Judge for at least two years before I began to work here. To walk the ground where she may have stood is for me a blessing of the rarest kind."

The ATAC's annual demonstration on July 3, 2007, included a funeral for the nine who had been enslaved in the house. Nine schoolchildren read eulogies and then simultaneously lifted the tops of nine cardboard caskets on the green grass, and black helium-filled balloons rose into the blue sky as the crowd chanted, "The nine are free, and so are we." One attendee was Peggy Hartzell, a descendant of one of Washington's brothers. She laid a red flower on each of the coffins. "I think it's a really good thing they've uncovered the slave quarters," she said, "and I don't think they should cover it up quickly. What you have to do is deal with it" (Salisbury 2007b).

The deep emotions the dig stimulated were especially clear to me after talking to John Dowell, a distinguished African American photographer in his seventies. Joyce Wilkerson, the Chief of Staff for Mayor Street, met with Dowell when the dig began, and asked him to take pictures of the excavation. When he got to the site he became irritated about what he was asked to do, angrily announcing that he took pictures of architecturally significant and historically important buildings, and *not* holes in the ground. Wilkerson begged him to take the pictures and Dowell relented, coming back a number of times. One day, he told me, he was down in the hole and he began sobbing uncontrollably, as he imagined that it was one of his ancestors who had been enslaved in the house, walking back and forth in the passageway carrying food from the kitchen to Washington's dining room. More than a few people noted that the very close physical proximity of the kitchen and passageway where the enslaved worked and the discovery of the bow window made the intertwined story of liberty and slavery all the more powerful.

Dowell's reaction reminds me of the emotions expressed at the Vietnam Veterans Memorial on the Washington Mall. The very ambiguity of these sites invites visitors to project their own connections to the story and elicits deep emotions.

When the archaeological excavation was completed, the Park Service held a ceremony on July 31, before returning the dirt to protect the foundations from the elements. A plaque with the names of each of the nine enslaved was placed within the walls of the kitchen, and there was an African libation ceremony that included pouring water from the Nile River and sand from Egypt to honor the enslaved who had lived and worked at the house. Archaeologists involved in the project, Michael Coard from ATAC, members of the city's Oversight Committee, and representatives of key elected officials gave short speeches. It was clear that the uncovering of the foundations of the house provided an important emotional connection for many people. "What the archaeologists found was a discovery that linked the present directly to the past. The foundation gave a visual aid to the story of not only the nation's first President, but of the slaves who were forced to labor there as well" (Hightower 2007). The passion of the conversations on the viewing platform and around the site was palpable as Cheryl LaRoche (2007a: 1), one of the archaeologists, pointed out: "archaeologists and other interpreters spent the summer engaged with a stream of impassioned, inquiring visitors gripped by the historical and moral significance of what emerged from the ground. Pointing out the foundations that survive and telling the story of what they represent has meant telling long-buried truth about the presidency, slavery, and the formation of the nation." Reflecting on her experience on this dig and the earlier one at the African Burial Ground in New York, LaRoche (2007a: 1–2) wrote: "Important African-American historical and archaeological sites frequently emerge only after lengthy public protest. . . . Sites born in protest create unique working conditions for public history professionals. In both cities, the public grappled passionately with the deeper meaning of freedom and personal liberty in the face of slavery. In Philadelphia, months of public discussion and media attention deepened understandings of slavery. Many people realized for the first time that slavery had existed in the North, and in cities, not just on southern plantations."

The archaeological excavation resulted in a broad consensus that the site design be modified to incorporate the archaeological findings, rather than simply reburying them when the dig was completed. The Oversight Committee, the Ad Hoc Historians, the public, and the press all endorsed this idea, so the next question was how best to accomplish the goal. Strikingly, the discovered fragments—and they were not much more than fragments—could excite people and provide a meaningful emotional connection to events and people from over two hundred years ago.[29] The strong emotions that the open dig elicited convinced planners that making part of the building's remains visible would help visitors better feel the power of the site. This meant further delay, but there was little opposition to the plan.

By December 2007, Kelly/Maiello devised four possible ways that the archaeology could be incorporated into the site—all of which would, of course, raise the cost of the project. In the end, the plan selected incorporated a large vitrine to allow visitors to look down and see parts of the building's foundations—including part of the kitchen, the underground passage from it to the front of the house, and the outline of the bow window. Some of the other designs included a stairway that would have taken visitors closer to the remains of the foundations, but these would have entailed more significant cost increases. With the adoption of the new design, a staircase heading to what was the location of Washington's second floor private office was scrapped. It was originally included to indicate that

Washington worked in the house, but also because it afforded great proximity to and a very clear view of Independence Hall.

The new design necessitated additional fund-raising and final decisions concerning the interpretive materials that would tell the story of the house. This story was to be presented through images, text panels, videos that would be shown on five wall monitors, and a memorial close to the Liberty Bell Center's entrance and symbolically located over the space where some of the enslaved had slept. The arrival of a new African American mayor, Michael Nutter, in early 2008 further delayed the project, as the new administration needed to first fully understand where the project stood, and what it needed to do and how to do it.

Nutter issued an official city tribute in honor of the 160th anniversary of Ona Judge's death. ATAC members and others gathered to mark the day at the site of the President's House, outside the entrance to the Liberty Bell (Salisbury 2008a). By April, design work on the site resumed in earnest, but largely behind the scenes. The public learned little about the new work, other than that it would now cost an additional $3 million, which would require both additional fund-raising and further schedule delays (Phillips 2008). Late in the spring John Dowell's stunning photos of the excavation went on display at the INHP Visitor Center, including some nighttime pictures of the open site at one end and the Liberty Bell on the other.

Stephan Salisbury, the *Philadelphia Inquirer* reporter who covered the story from the outset, reflected in a series of four articles on the role of archaeology in changing perceptions of the INHP's history and extending it far beyond the story of the founding fathers and their achievements. He argued that the digs during the construction of the National Constitution Center earlier in the decade, which had revealed artifacts associated with free Blacks living in the area, had contributed to this change, as well as the digs at the President's House/Slavery Memorial site the previous summer. "Archaeology has triggered the greatest change and precipitated the greatest renewed interest in America's civic origin," Salisbury (2008c) wrote, and enlarged our understanding of early free Blacks in the city. Salisbury noticed that some park rangers and guides on walking and storytelling tours were linking the story of the enslaved at the house to the Underground Railroad. They included the story in those of other historical African American figures and for visitors to African American sites in and around the park (Salisbury 2008b).

At ATAC's 2008 annual July 3 gathering at the site, reenactors played the part of those enslaved in the house, and the group celebrated its achievements to date. Coard told those assembled, "For Black folks, this is our Statue of Liberty; for Black folks, this is our Mount Rushmore. You can bet your ancestors are sitting here ecstatic about the work we've done" (Farrell 2008).

In the fall, the Mayor announced the city's formal decision to proceed with the project and raise funds to pay the additional cost. By the end of the year, construction preparations were under way, but with no sign that the additional funds were yet available. However, in January 2009 Governor Ed Rendell revealed a plan that recommended a $3.5 million grant from the Delaware River Port Authority (DRPA), which he headed.[30] This was approved a few weeks later, despite some objections from both the American Automobile Association and an editorial in the *Philadelphia Inquirer* on January 23, 2009, which asserted that DRPA funds should only be used for transportation needs.

As the actual construction got closer, the minority hiring issue heated up. In early May 2009, the city announced an information meeting for construction opportunities. Potential contractors angrily asserted that they were shut out of the bidding process, and many wondered why the general contractor for the project was white. In a city where the exclusion of minorities from lucrative construction jobs had been a contentious issue for decades, the tension was palpable. Some argued that only Black firms should be hired. "Just like you don't have Jews building Muslim mosques or you don't have Muslims building Jewish synagogues," one man argued, "we're not going to have white folks come in here and build monuments to the holocaust of enslavement for our people" (Hightower 2009). At one point, D. J. Keating, the general contractor whom Kelly/Maiello—the African American architectural firm—had hired, stood up and said he had no problem asking the city to release his firm from the contract. He and his associates then left the auditorium. After the meeting, however, Kelly/Maiello announced that they had no intention of releasing Keating from the project (Shipman 2009).

In late August, as construction plans were developed, the city announced that two-thirds of the subcontracts for construction would go to businesses owned by minorities and women (Salisbury 2009d). Coard said this was a good beginning for city construction projects, but that similar levels of minorities needed to be hired on other city projects. Sacaree Rhodes, an activist member of Generations Unlimited, said she would continue to battle for higher African American participation on this and other projects.

The "rediscovery" of the story of enslaved Africans living and toiling at the President's House in Philadelphia in the 1790s, which the National Park Service initially tried to ignore, generated a tremendous amount of interest and contestation over how to tell their story and how to memorialize them at Independence National Historical Park. Both African American groups, such as ATAC, and the Ad Hoc Historians saw this as an opportunity to provide a more inclusive account of the early United States that included the role of slavery and enslaved people in its growth and development. But differences and distrust among the parties over what exactly should be done quickly became emotionally intense and partially racialized. High distrust and suspicion emerged right from the start and the parties that had an interest or stake in the outcome rapidly expanded, making it increasingly difficult to manage constructively.

The intense controversy received widespread coverage in the media, and consequently both Blacks and whites in the city probably learned more about Northern slavery from it than they had ever known before. Those following the developments were surprised to learn that Philadelphia and other cities in the North had had significant enslaved populations, and many were angry that these stories had been hidden for so long—not just by the National Park Service but in schools and other historical sites in the region. More than one person I spoke to at the time asked, "Why didn't I ever hear about this in school or somewhere else?" As a result, a small physical space on one of the two most sacred sites in the country would have to address these large and emotionally charged issues in ways that would speak to a wide range of annual visitors. Could this be done well on a modest budget, and, if so, what would that require? The next chapter suggests a complicated answer to this question, in part, because the last two years of the project were as contentious as any and brought to a head the tensions over the narrative to be told on the site and its physical manifestations.

Explaining how and why "forgetting" slavery's past on this site is not simple, but several of the reasons easily grow out of the ideas offered in the previous chapter. A start is that attrition took place with the passage of time, meaning that direct connections to the events require written or oral narratives. Yes, there were records such as the Washington papers at Mount Vernon and some in Philadelphia, but people would have needed a reason to examine them to learn about what occurred—and apparently no one did this—and to have made them public. Second, sites of slavery such as this house were almost never marked in the North. In fact, very few people were even aware of where the President's House was located before Lawler undertook his research. Third, during the Cold War, the NPS (and the country) especially wanted a simple uplifting story about its country's founding and the first President during the Cold War period so that, so they made no effort to tell about slavery there. What they said and illustrated in INHP was not false so much as very incomplete. Enslaved Blacks were never considered to be central to the park's narratives, as Melish (1998) suggests they were also excluded in New England after manumission of former slaves there. Those who wanted the narrative rewritten to tell a more complete story were angry when they learned what happened, while those who wanted the site to focus more narrowly on the country's founding years as it had done since the park's founding, unable to accept the need for such a sudden shift, felt betrayed in hearing what was said publicly about the shameful behaviors and beliefs of the country's early years.

∽ *The Nine Enslaved Africans in the President's House*

Of the nine enslaved people who lived and worked at the President's House in Philadelphia in the 1790s, the most complete stories we have are those of Ona Judge, the young woman who was Martha Washington's seamstress and personal servant, and Hercules, the cook.[31] Both of them escaped from Washington's bondage.

ONA JUDGE

Ona's surname, Judge, was that of Andrew Judge, a white man who was her father and an indentured man in Virginia (Figure 7). George Washington had bought his indenture, and he became part of Mount Vernon's workforce. By the 1780s Andrew Judge had left Mount Vernon. At age ten, Ona began to work for Martha Washington in the big house and soon became an excellent seamstress as was her mother (Dunbar 2017: 9–13).

When the Washingtons moved to Philadelphia, then the nation's capital, they took Ona Judge and eight other enslaved people with them. Judge escaped when she left the house in Philadelphia one night in May 1796, after learning that Martha planned to make her a wedding present for her granddaughter

Figure 7. Ona Judge and the words she spoke—"I am free now"—when she reached New Hampshire after fleeing from Philadelphia in 1796.

Eliza, a "woman with a stormy reputation" (Dunbar 2017: 96), who could make life precarious for her. It would mean also that she would no longer be living at Mount Vernon with her friends and family after Washington's term was finished. With the help of free Blacks in the city, she took a boat to New Hampshire where she would live until her death in 1848 at the age of seventy-five. Soon after her escape, Washington posted ads for her capture and, after learning of her whereabouts, sent people in New Hampshire to try to bring her back to Virginia. They were unsuccessful. Less than a year after she had escaped, the president asked his Secretary of the Treasury Thomas Wolcott to help. Wolcott then sought out Joseph Whipple, whom Washington had named customs agent for Portsmouth. He tried to convince her to return to the Washingtons, and she finally agreed to meet him at the docks when he could arrange her departure. He notified her of the appointed day and time, but Ona had no intention to return and failed to show up (Dunbar 2017: 139–148). In early 1797 Judge married Jack Staines, a seaman, in nearby Greenland, New Hampshire. In 1799, Washington sent his nephew Burwell Bassett to New Hampshire to try to get Ona back to Mount Vernon. At the time, Staines was away at sea. Burwell arrived at her house where she was alone with her one-year-old daughter, Eliza. He tried to persuade her to leave, but Ona refused to agree to return to the Washingtons, telling him, "I am free and I choose to remain so" (Dunbar 2017: 166). She then fled to a small nearby town where friends protected her, and Burwell returned to Virginia empty-handed. Later that year, Washington died at Mount Vernon.

Ona and Jack had three children, but he disappeared after 1803, probably dying at sea. Ona and the children lived with another family in Greenland.

Life was hard, as the women struggled to support their children. Ona outlived her son and two daughters and worked hard to survive. She became literate and turned to religion for support. When she was interviewed in 1845 by an abolitionist newspaper, the *Granite Freeman*, she told them she had no regrets. "I am free, and I have, I trust, been made a child of God by the means" (Adams 1845; Dunbar 2017: 187).

When people watching the archaeological dig learned that Judge often slept near the Washingtons' bedroom so that she could tend to their younger grandchildren at night if they needed something, many asked about whether she was there to be available to Washington for sex. Clearly the possibility of rape and forced sexual relations between slave owners and young enslaved women was highly charged and made many people who visited the site, especially African American women, furious.

HERCULES

Hercules served as Washington's cook at Mount Vernon beginning in 1786. His wife was a dower slave called Lame Alice, a seamstress, and they had three children, Richmond (born 1776), Evey (born 1782), and Delia (born 1785). Alice died in 1787. Washington brought Hercules to Philadelphia in November 1790. Richmond came along as a kitchen worker. When he came to Philadelphia, the Washingtons granted Hercules some special privileges, such as permission to earn money selling "slops" from the kitchen. In addition, he was able to move around the city streets easily in his role as a skilled chef. Hercules developed a reputation as a bit of a dandy in Philadelphia, since he bought fine clothes with the money he earned. He knew the city well, went out of the house often, and enjoyed being seen around and about town. It was thought for a long time that he had escaped from the President's House in the city. However, in February 2010, *Inquirer* food critic Craig LaBan published a two-part article presenting recently found historical evidence at Mount Vernon that Hercules escaped during Washington's presidency but had not run away from Philadelphia as had previously been believed. Rather, he actually ran away from Mount Vernon on February 22, 1797, Washington's sixty-fifth birthday. Researchers now believe that Washington had sent him back to Virginia several months earlier where he was working as a menial laborer, and that he ran away while Washington was celebrating his birthday in Philadelphia (LaBan 2010a, 2010b). Little is known about his life afterward, although there were a few never confirmed sightings of him in New York in the early 1800s. He is the only one of the nine whose image we know, as he appears in several paintings including one by Gilbert Stuart in the Museo Thyssen-Bornemisza in Madrid (Figure 8). Less than a month after the escape, Louis-Philippe (later king of France) visited Mount Vernon. His manservant spoke with Hercules' daughter and "ventured that the little girl must be deeply upset that she would never see her father again; she answered, 'Oh! Sir, I am very glad, because he is free now' " (Lawler 2005b: 394).

Figure 8. Gilbert Stuart probably asked George Washington for permission to paint a portrait of his renowned cook, Hercules, on one of the several occasions the artist painted the president's portrait. Museo Thyssen-Bornemisza, Madrid.

MOLL

Moll, a dower slave, was a nanny for Martha Custis's two surviving children. She was about nineteen when she was brought to Mount Vernon following the January 1759 wedding of Martha Custis and George Washington, and so was born around 1739. She probably nursed Mrs. Washington's daughter, Patsy, until the sickly girl's death at age seventeen in 1773. There is no record of her having had a husband or children of her own. Moll has been described as the First Lady's personal maid in the New York and Philadelphia households, but she probably was primarily the nanny to her two youngest grandchildren. When she arrived at the President's House in 1790, it is likely that she slept in one of the divided rooms over the kitchen with either eleven-year-old Nelly or nine-year-old G. W. Parke Custis. The Washingtons do not seem to have worried that she would take advantage of the Gradual Abolition Act to obtain her freedom, and at least once she seems to have stayed in Pennsylvania beyond the six-month deadline. Moll was the only one of the initial eight enslaved Africans to work in the President's House for the whole six and a quarter years that Washington lived in Philadelphia and then return to Mount Vernon at the end of Washington's presidency. Tobias Lear's famous account of Washington's final hours records her standing at the door of his bedroom as he died on December 14, 1799. After Martha Washington's death in 1802, Moll would have become part of the household of one of the Custis grandchildren; it is not known which one.

Austin, a dower slave, was the son of Betty, a seamstress, who brought him as a baby when she came to Mount Vernon following the January 1759 wedding of Martha Custis and George Washington. The identity of his father is not known, but Austin was of mixed racial heritage. Beginning in the mid-1770s, he worked as a waiter in the mansion at Mount Vernon, and he appears also to have worked as a postilion, or footman for the carriage. During the Revolutionary War, Austin probably was one of the young men who accompanied Martha Washington on visits to her husband in the field. Austin was the half-brother of Ona Judge. His wife was another dower, now thought to have been a seamstress named Charlotte. Austin's position in the presidential household is unclear. First-person accounts of state dinners describe all the waiters as white, but it is possible that he served the family meals. Some of the purchases for him in the household account books seem related to the house and others to the stables, which may indicate that he performed a dual role at the President's House. Austin and Lewis List, a white servant, accompanied Washington and his secretary on a return trip from Mount Vernon in late October 1793, but Philadelphia was in the midst of a yellow fever epidemic so their destination became Germantown, Pennsylvania, ten miles northwest of IHNP. Initially, he and List may have been the entire staff of the Deshler-Morris House, which served as the executive mansion for two and a half weeks until the crisis was over. The following summer, the Washingtons vacationed at the Germantown house, and their staff likely included Austin, Moll, Hercules, and Ona Judge. The Washingtons trusted Austin to make long rides on his own, including trips from Philadelphia to Mount Vernon. He died on December 20, 1794, during one of these solo trips, after a fall from his horse near Harford, Maryland. He was survived by a widow and five children: two sons, Billy (born ca. 1782), Timothy (born 1785), and three daughters, Elvey, Jenny, and Eliza (probably born between 1786 and 1795). After Martha Washington's death in 1802, Austin's children seem to have been inherited by G. W. Parke Custis and probably were moved to Arlington House (now in Arlington National Cemetery).

Richmond was the son of Hercules and Lame Alice. He was born in 1776 and had two younger sisters, Evey and Delia. Because their mother was a dower slave, they also were dowers. Richmond was eleven when his mother died in 1787. Three years later his father asked Washington's permission to bring him to the President's House. Washington reluctantly agreed, and Richmond worked as a scullion in the kitchen for the first year in Philadelphia. Among his duties would have been sweeping the chimneys. He probably slept with his father and Christopher Sheels in a room on the fourth floor of the main house. Washington returned him to Mount Vernon in October 1791, and

Richmond probably worked there in the mansion kitchen. Richmond was caught stealing money at Mount Vernon in November 1796. Washington assumed that the theft was part of a planned escape attempt, possibly of the father and son together. Hercules did escape to freedom several months later, but alone. Washington demoted Richmond to a field laborer, and he was unmarried and working at River Farm in 1799. His fate and that of his sisters after Martha Washington's death in 1802 is not known.

GILES

Giles, a dower slave, worked as a postilion, or footman for the carriage, at Mount Vernon and sometimes as a driver. He appears to have been about the same age as Austin, a teenager in 1774, which would have meant he was born in the late 1750s. During the Revolutionary War, Giles probably was the young man who accompanied Martha Washington on her visit to the encampment at Valley Forge from January to June 1778. There is no record of his having had a wife or children. Giles accompanied Washington to Philadelphia in May 1787 for the Constitutional Convention, as did the general's body servant, Will Lee. The two Black men would have stayed with Washington in Robert Morris's house on Market Street, which three years later became the President's House. They returned to Mount Vernon in September. Giles was brought to New York in April 1789 to work in the stables of the presidential residence, and he probably accompanied Washington on his northern tour in October and November. A year later he was brought to Philadelphia and would have lived in the quarters adjoining the stables of the President's House. Giles drove the baggage wagon for Washington's southern tour in March through June 1791. Early in the tour he was somehow injured so severely that he was no longer able to ride a horse and was left behind at Mount Vernon when Washington returned to Philadelphia. Giles is not listed in the 1799 Mount Vernon slave census, which likely indicates that he had died.

PARIS

Paris, one of Washington's slaves, worked as a stable hand at Mount Vernon. He was younger than Austin and Giles, a teenager in April 1789, when he was brought to New York to work in the stables of the presidential residence. Paris came to Philadelphia in November 1790 and would have lived in the quarters adjoining the stables of the President's House. In March 1791 Paris accompanied Washington on his southern tour, but his misbehavior on the trip angered the president. As punishment, Washington left him behind at Mount Vernon and returned to Philadelphia without him. There was a good deal of sickness at Mount Vernon in the autumn of 1794. In late September or October, Washington's estate manager wrote him that Paris had died.

CHRISTOPHER SHEELS

Christopher Sheels, a dower slave born in about 1775, was the nephew of Will, also known as Billy Lee, who had been Washington's body servant throughout the Revolutionary War. In the postwar years, Will was injured in two serious falls and became incapacitated. Christopher assisted his uncle in attending to the president in New York in 1789, and when the capital moved to Philadelphia the following year, Will was retired to Mount Vernon and Christopher became the president's sole attendant. The teenager probably lived on the fourth floor of the main house in a room with Hercules and Richmond. The length of Christopher's stay in Philadelphia may have been as little as a year—he was back at Mount Vernon in January 1792. Christopher seems to have been one of the few Mount Vernon slaves who could read and write. He may have been taught by Will, who reportedly was an evangelical Christian. Christopher was close in age to George Washington Motier Lafayette, the teenaged son of the Marquis de Lafayette who lived with the Washingtons for more than a year in Philadelphia and Virginia beginning in April 1796. The two seem to have become friendly. Soon after the president's retirement, Christopher was bitten by a dog that was feared rabid and was sent to Lebanon, Pennsylvania, for treatment. He and young Lafayette traveled together for part of the journey. Several weeks later, Washington wrote the Frenchman of Christopher's recovery. In September 1799, Christopher requested Washington's permission to marry an enslaved African from another plantation, one who also seems to have been able to read and write. A few days later Washington intercepted a note sent between them outlining an escape plan and foiled it. Three months later Christopher attended to Washington on his deathbed. After Martha Washington's death in 1802, Christopher would have been inherited by one of the Custis grandchildren. Nothing is known of his subsequent whereabouts.

JOE

Washington mentioned "Postilion Joe" in a letter written October 19, 1795, toward the end of an eight-day journey from Mount Vernon to the capital. We can infer that Joe arrived in Philadelphia the following day with the rest of the traveling party. A postilion was a footman for the presidential coach, and Joe would have worked in the stables of the President's House and probably been housed in the quarters between the kitchen and the stables. It is not known how long Joe was in Philadelphia. He may have stayed until March 1797, the end of Washington's presidency. There is no documentation for Joe's exact age. As a dower, his absence from the Custis estate inventory likely means he was born after January 1759. Similarly, his inclusion as an adult in the 1786 Mount Vernon slave census implies that he was then over age fourteen. His wife, Sall, a seamstress, was born around 1769; Joe may have been about the same age. At the time he came to Philadelphia, they had three sons: Henry, age seven; Elijah, age three; and Dennis, age one. Sall and the children were owned by Washington and received their freedom following his death by the provisions of his will. They took the surname Richardson. Joe would have been one of the 153 dowers inherited by Martha Washington's grandchildren—it is not known which—following her death in 1802. Although he remained enslaved, Joe and Sall Richardson managed to stay together and had at least seven children, all of whom were free. Two of their sons were working at Mount Vernon in 1835.

Chapter 5

Memorializing the Enslaved
on Independence Mall

> *But where are the monuments, the memorials, and the museums on federal*
> *property that acknowledge the all-consuming horror of and the courageous*
> *resistance to and the long-overdue abolition of slavery? They are nowhere—at*
> *least not until now, right here.*
>
> —Michael Coard, ATAC, speaking at the inauguration
> of the President's House/Slavery Memorial,
> Philadelphia, December 15, 2010

One might think that once the design for the President's House/Slavery Memorial project had been selected and the money raised, the completion of the site would be quick and easy. Not exactly. The minority hiring issue persisted and continually resurfaced in a variety of settings, especially public ones. Equally visible were two other controversies—one over the physical design of the site and the second, even more contentious, over the content of its interpretive text panels, images, and videos. Each controversy had its own personality and dynamic, although they both elicited passionate reactions. Commemorative landscapes are often emotionally powerful, generically, so great attention gets paid both to their designs and to the stories told.[1] It is unsurprising, then, that a historical and memorial site in Independence National Historical Park entitled "Freedom and Slavery in Making a New Nation" would provoke intense controversy over design and narrative content as the project moved into its final phase.

The crux of the design controversy came down to differences in what people expected the site to be. While there was never any serious consideration of "rebuilding" the house that stood on the site in the 1790s—in part because the NPS is not authorized to undertake such a project and in part because the costs would be far too high—a significant debate raged over the importance of fidelity to the architectural layout of the original house. Some were outraged with what they felt were deviations from the actual "footprint" of the eighteenth-century house. Similarly, would interpretive materials emphasize the founding of the Executive Branch or focus on a twenty-first-century commemoration that recognized that the house of the country's first president and the executive office building were stained by the history of enslavement? How could the interpretive panels tell a compelling story that would not only commemorate the events at the site of Sixth and Market Street in the 1790s but also speak to a part of the country's past that was figuratively, and often literally, buried, as had been this building's foundations? How could any single proposal produce universal acceptance, when slavery is both historically monumental and, especially in the North, occluded from view?

In July and August 2009, a few members of the Ad Hoc Historians and the Independence Hall Association (IHA),[2] most likely at the urging of Ed Lawler, raised a series of complaints about the proposed physical design just as construction was finally about to begin. They objected that the layout of the proposed house site and some of the interior locations were not completely true to the building's original eighteenth-century footprint and felt that its value as a site of history would be compromised if this was not corrected. In contrast, most of the people I interviewed for this research, including a number of historians, believed that the deviations from the building's original footprint were relatively trivial and in no way detracted from the project's symbolic significance. Many people felt that the physical layout was secondary to the site's value as a memorial, and the concern unimportant. One way to think about this is whether the site's success would depend on its fidelity to the physical design of the house in which Washington and the enslaved lived or on how well it recounted the lives of the people who lived and worked in the house and the events that transpired there.

The three main objections to the proposed design were the size and shape of the bow window, the location of the Market Street façade, and the location of the Slave Quarters at the rear of the site.[3] Basically Lawler and the IHA complained that the dimensions of the proposed commemorative site deviated in some places from the actual dimensions of the house as shown in historical records and/or as gleaned from the 2007 archaeological dig. They objected that while the Oversight Committee was charged with assisting and advising on the project, the detailed plans were not distributed to them, so the IHA had to get a copy from the contractors. In particular, they objected that the architects had cut two feet from the front of the house; that the bow window was curved rather than octagonal, and almost four feet larger than the one in the design; and that the design moved the location of the Slave quarters away from the entrance to the Liberty Bell Center, which cut 3.5 feet off the kitchen ell. They asked for a meeting in the hopes that the design would be changed "in keeping with historical accuracy prior to groundbreaking." They requested peer review of the interpretive plan, including videos by historians, prior to finalizing and fabricating the interpretive panels (Salisbury 2009b).

The intensity of their anger is apparent in the published communications with the Park Service, in which they charged that the NPS had decided "not to abide by the documentary and archaeological evidence"[4] that they had delineated in their memo. They issued a statement expressing their great anger, and we might even say disgust, with the Park Service's approval of Kelly/Maiello's revised design, as seen in the following comments:[5]

It seems to be the whole lesson of the dig was the power of juxtaposition in a physical sense. Once we mess with that tangible reality, then we've sacrificed much more than accuracy, we've sacrificed the authentic, as far as we can discern it.

Wow—moving the slave quarters and making up a "fake" site more conveniently situated seems absolutely the wrong approach to me.

My fury stems from the screaming hypocrisy of the Park Service in this latest of its incarnations. . . . The Americans with Disabilities Act trumps verifiable history, and so do INHP budgetary priorities, widening the sidewalk a convenient foot and a half, complications of constructing the semi-circular exterior, and avoiding a traffic jam at the front door.

This is ground sacred to American history and now, as . . . pointed out, sanctified to African-Americans and to many more of us who have attended ceremonies of such sanctification there. This is ground where we've got to get it right, because we've gotten it wrong for four centuries. I can't tell you how offended I am at the cavalier indifference with which the architects and the Park Service worked. The arguments of convenience and cost that have been advanced, and that seem to have prevailed, would be fine for other projects. The adjustments, cut corners, fiddling with dimensions a bit here and a bit there, and switching of this for that are the things that happen routinely in the design of buildings. I resent that THIS building has been treated so routinely.

Sharon Ann Holt, one of the Ad Hoc Historians, wrote a separate angry e-mail to Cynthia MacLeod, the INHP superintendent, the next day, defending Lawler's complaints:

To state categorically that abstraction must prevail in these matters is just vile; the betrayal of trust and promises of collaboration is the purest of cynical self-serving power plays. . . . The real loser here will again be the city of Philadelphia, whose efforts to generate momentum around heritage are consistently undermined by INHP's inability to be a consistent, reliable, open, and effective part-ner. I had hoped that, under your leadership, INHP would cease to be Philadelphia's cultural black hole, where good ideas go to die. Get this one right, and everything could change. Do this the same old way with the same old stupidities, and we'll just keep circling endlessly around what the city could be.

Emanuel Kelly, the lead architect, said he was "flabbergasted" by the vehemence of the criticism, including the charges of secrecy. Roz McPher-son, the project manager, said the memorial was not intended to be a pre-cise reconstruction. Superintendent MacLeod said that the power of the site primarily comes from the human stories to be told about it. Historians Randall Miller and Gary Nash, involved with the project from the outset, both emphasized the importance of telling the story of slavery on the site and making sure the interpretive materials were as good as possible (Salis-bury: 2009b). Michael Coard called the criticisms sincere and well intended but fundamentally flawed. "Hyper-technical replication must sometimes give way to practical-minded necessity. If people can't access or see it, then what's the point?" He then charged that the critical historians "have focused on the inanimate bricks and mortar rather than the 316 Black men, women and children Washington held as slaves, especially the nine held here in Philadelphia . . . although the house matters, the people who were inside it matter more" (Coard 2009).

When the Oversight Committee met to consider the criticisms of the design, it had what was described in a press release a month later as "a spirited discussion." The committee's statement echoed Emanuel Kelly's explanation for rejecting the historians' concerns, emphasizing practical problems such as the reduced width of the busy sidewalk on Market Street by two feet, and the problems inherent to the placement of the memorial directly over the remains of the area where some of the enslaved Africans had slept. This would place the memorial so close to the Liberty Bell Center that it would present logistical challenges of access and compliance with the Americans with Disabilities Act and the fire code, among other things. The statement also noted that there were a number of points at which the eighteenth-century historical plans for the building and the architectural remains were at odds, which raised legitimate questions as to how much of the "original" design could even be known or discerned. Finally, "the majority of the committee agreed that the main purpose of the site is to tell the stories of the people who lived and toiled at the site, especially the enslaved Africans who lived the hypocrisy of slavery in a new nation built on the ideals of freedom for all men."[6]

While a decision had been reached, it took some time before it was made public and the divisions within the group remained so inflamed that members of the Oversight Committee agreed not to comment individually and publicly on the contentious issues (Salisbury 2009a), a policy that some of them continued even several years later, when I sought to interview them.

"The telling-the-story phase of the President's House project is just as important as the archaeological phase of the design phase," observed Karen Warrington (personal interview, January 11, 2011). In many ways, it proved to be the most contentious of all. The tension between history and commemoration dominated this phase of the controversy: To what extent was the President's House/Slavery Memorial site going to emphasize the early history of the republic and the founding of the Executive Branch of the government under Washington and Adams? And how much would focus on the story of enslavement at the site and throughout the country's first seventy-plus years and commemorate the enslaved? Could both be done adequately in the small space available?

In a microcosm, this conflict captures the incompatibilities in the complex, braided relationship between freedom and slavery that is present not only on this site but throughout the country's history. These tensions were considerable, and some of the people most involved in the project never fully accepted the final design that tried to address both the commemorative and historical goals in the text panels, images, and videos, or the process through which these were decided. Almost every person or group that participated felt passionately about the project, but clearly not for the same reasons, and acceptable compromises often proved to be elusive. Strong differences about the language to be used in the panels and the images to be displayed were hard to bridge. When one also considers the ongoing differences around the role of minority contractors, it looked to some as if the crucial fault line was racial, making any disagreements around the project's content even more complicated to settle. At several points in the process, the NPS and the Oversight Committee brought in public historians and other experts for meetings with the group when interpretive materials were discussed.

Clay Armbrister, Mayor Michael Nutter's newly appointed chief of staff, agreed to head up the Oversight Committee, as Joyce Wilkerson had done under Mayor Street. He was an experienced financial administrator in school systems before taking this job and reported that he was quickly struck with Wilkerson's commitment to the successful completion of the project. The first time he walked into her office, one long wall was lined with pictures of the site. Roz McPherson, whom the city had hired as the project manager, briefed him about the state of the project in detail, the personalities on the Oversight Committee, and issues on the table. Nonetheless, Armbrister made it clear to me that he had not been ready for the level of contentiousness he soon found in the group, as its members clearly had strong opinions and were not hesitant to express them (personal interview, February 17, 2011).

Meanwhile Rabinowitz's group continued to work on the interpretive materials and after a while held few face-to-face meetings with the Oversight Committee, as differences in the committee over his materials grew more contentious. Differences between Rabinowitz and the Oversight

Committee were increasingly strong and despite what he perceived as clear requests for major changes, his revisions failed to come close to meeting what the Committee sought. Rabinowitz later told me that he wished there had been a facilitator to manage the increasingly unproductive interactions (personal interview, February 25, 2011). He also said he was sensitive to the Park Service's concerns and did not want to provide materials that they would find politically problematic or interpretive content for which visitors would blast them. He worried that those wanting the story to focus primarily on the history of slavery and race failed to consider that "this is a small project and possibly can't bear the weight of all that anguish" (Salisbury: 2009c).

It became clear that differences among the members of the Oversight Committee remained strong on philosophical and sometimes racial lines. Warrington told the *Philadelphia Tribune*, "It's shaping up as a true battle" that continued to pit those wanting to emphasize the story of slavery and the enslaved people who lived in the house against those who wanted more emphasis on the narrow political context of the early U.S. government and the two presidents. Rather, she said, "it should be a site for learning and healing" (Mayes 2009). Stephan Salisbury reported not just that the group was deadlocked but that the materials that Rabinowitz had prepared were problematic for a number of reasons and satisfied few on the oversight committee. McPherson feared that they would be too Eurocentric: "You can't have whites write the Black experience" (Salisbury: 2009c). Despite calls for a public meeting to discuss the situation from members of Generations Unlimited, there was little desire to hold one, given the contentious and not very successful public meetings in the past. In late 2009 six African American consultant scholars were called in to make suggestions about how to rework the interpretive materials.

In December, the Oversight Committee called for a pause in the process to review the work of the previous two months and asked for a postponement of the opening of the site from July 2010 to sometime in the fall, despite the pressure to finish the project. This resulted in the decision that it would be best to change the interpretive team to one that would provide more compelling materials, and the committee issued a press release explaining its decision.[7] It was clear that the group wanted more focus on the story of enslavement in the house and more expressive language in the panels describing slavery and that they needed more time to accomplish these goals.

In my conversations with some Oversight Committee members I was told that many felt Rabinowitz had provided too much text, using very flat language. Furthermore, many were concerned that he focused too much attention on details about the two presidential administrations and too little on enslavement in the early United States. Rabinowitz conceded that what he had provided to date was not his best work but that he was willing to continue to make revisions. His goal, he told me, was to integrate the story of the house's urban neighborhood, with that of the executive mansion, the early presidency, the enslaved Africans, the city's large free Black population, the complexity of race relations in the house, and the hierarchical nature of American society in the country's early years (personal interview, February 25, 2011). Looking at the materials he prepared, I could see that all these topics were introduced, but they were barely interconnected and not well developed.

Rabinowitz clearly felt very alone and misunderstood, and he cast blame in many directions—on members of the Oversight Committee, on the NPS, which took no responsibility for the project's content, on the historians who were silent in crucial meetings, on the polarized racial politics of Philadelphia, and on the city's inferiority complex, which he said had also played a role. He was clearly frustrated that others did not appreciate the limits on what could be done that was consistent with INHP's historical mission, in a small space, that would be accessible to the public twenty-four hours a day, seven days a week. He was very critical of the decision to make the archaeological findings the focal point of the site. He noted that the dig, which had attracted so much attention from the public, found nothing significant that could be tied to Washington or to the enslaved people who lived there. Similarly, he characterized the fuss over the bow window as silly, saying that the model for the one in the White House in Washington, D.C., came from a house in Virginia, and not this one.[8]

When I examined the interpretive materials that Rabinowitz had produced, working with Joe Nicholson of UJMN Architects and Designers in Philadelphia, I understood why their content was so problematic to the Oversight Committee. Since 2002, when Congress called on the NPS "to appropriately commemorate the slaves who toiled in the house of President George Washington when he lived in the first 'White House' in Philadelphia" (Salisbury 2002a), it was clear to many that the story of slavery was to be the most important part of the new site. All of the public meetings, discussions, and fund-raising focused on it.

However, as the Rabinowitz team prepared their interpretive materials, their emphasis was quite different from what most of the Oversight Committee, the city, and the Congressional committee recommended in 2002. There was too little that explained slavery at the time, and the language that was there did not communicate its anguish, although people visiting the site would have known little about slavery there. At the same time, the brief references to many of their materials on the executive branch and the political debates in the late eighteenth century would likely be inaccessible to most visitors coming to the site, especially since so many would arrive there on their way to see the Liberty Bell and Independence Hall, knowing little to nothing beforehand about the President's House or enslavement in it. It is hard not to conclude that Rabinowitz emphasized historical details,[9] while most of the members of the Oversight Committee wanted some of this to be included but with a much more significant commemorative component, using a language that would recognize slavery at the site of the country's founding and acknowledge its pain for the enslaved and their descendants.

The Rabinowitz team's research and materials did provide the basis for some of the revised panels that were ultimately adopted, such as those about free Blacks in the city, and the arrival of refugees from the Haitian Revolution after it began in 1791. But a majority of their text panels were discarded, as were some of their proposed images. The themes of their different panels were not particularly connected to each other, and they were insufficiently focused on the people living and working in the house, despite the team's stated goal of identifying the multiple social divisions among the thirty or so people inhabiting and working there. Questions posed to visitors at the end of some panels seemed simplistic and forced. One of the proposed panels entitled "Liberty for whom? Liberty for what?" juxtaposed two paintings, but seemed quite diffuse, while another focusing on hierarchy and privilege used an 1861 painting named *Lady Washington's Reception Day*, an imagined rendition of life in the house seventy years earlier. It is not obvious, however, what purpose it served, given both the limited space available and its dubious resemblance to how the Washingtons lived in Philadelphia. The Oversight Committee had been very explicit that the existence of slavery in the house and in the city was the highest priority for the site.

Relations between the Oversight Committee and Rabinowitz were probably exacerbated by Rabinowitz's statements that communicated that he was the expert in this area, that the Committee's agenda was inappropriate, and that they needed to follow his decisions because of his years of experience. This did not promote constructive dialogue or a constructive solution.

Eisterhold Associates of Kansas City, a firm that had previously worked on a number of projects involving African American history, was then hired, and the revised interpretive panels they produced were put on display for public comment in April 2010 at the park's Visitor Center. The most noticeable change was that the question of slavery in the house, the city, and the country received more focus. More emotion is communicated in the text and images, and they provide more direct connections between slavery and politics of the period. Because the physical structure of the site was already set, the amount of material to be hung on the brick walls and the amount of text did not significantly change: there were still four major text panels with images as well as a number of smaller ones. The themes for the five videos remained unchanged, although their text was not available to the public or to the Oversight Committee for review. At the same time, in addition, Eisterhold also proposed a set of sixteen black-and-white drawings, most of which featured the enslaved individuals on a panel labeled "Life Under Slavery: Storyboards," none of which were used in the final design. Some members of the public complained that the enslaved individuals looked too well dressed and even happy in the proposed displays.[10]

Judging from the dozens of comments on the forms completed at the Visitor Center and the several hundred sent in by e-mail, many, but not all, people who viewed the new text panels and images liked them. Some people wanted to know more about slavery and the lives of the individuals at the site. Others said they wanted to know more about the founding of the republic and requested more details about John Adams, Martha Washington, and Abigail Adams. Many people simply wrote about how glad they were to see the story of slavery told. A good percentage of those writing were African Americans and members of ATAC. Many expressed strong emotions about the upcoming opening. A few were angry, saying that there was too much attention to slavery. Some people wrote several paragraphs suggesting modifications in the proposed text or correcting what they saw as mistakes or points that they found vague. McPherson wanted the project to move forward and hoped the Oversight Committee, working on a tight schedule, would hold a public meeting the next month, after which they could make a final decision on the content.

The public meeting to discuss the Eisterhold interpretive materials in early May 2010 was raucous, and there was no substantive discussion of the interpretive materials—in fact no one offered any nuanced comments at all. Some attendees loudly argued that Washington was still portrayed too positively, that the pain and suffering of slavery was not portrayed sufficiently, that the enslaved Africans were seen as too contented and happy, and finally that minority contractors were not getting enough of the construction work. Critics of the project, led by Charles Blockson and Sacaree Rhodes, interrupted from the outset over the use of a white general contractor and the presentation of the Black experience. Rhodes loudly demanded to know "Where is the rape? Where is the brutality?" and others called it a house of horrors and a house of bondage. Others criticized the video presentations (Salisbury 2010a). The sharply clashing visions of what should and should not be presented made a straightforward discussion of the proposed exhibits impossible in a large public meeting. For example, Blockson questioned the basic premises of the project, asking, "Why are we honoring that house of bondage? Do Jews rebuild concentration camps?" And historian and school curriculum designer Edward Robinson called for references to the African ancestors of the enslaved: "We are descendants of world-class literacy and science. That must be incorporated into the exhibits" (Washington 2010).

Further discussions and modifications in the interpretive materials continued over the next several months. In late July Mayor Nutter and Park Superintendent Cynthia MacLeod met with the designers and reviewed what all hoped would be the final interpretive materials. They made small modifications in the organization of parts of the four long rectangular panels displayed in April and edited some of the headers and text. In addition, there were now sixteen colored paintings on glass with two to five sentences on each, describing an event or person associated with the house. These glass panels were added by the Oversight Committee after the Eisterhold materials were discussed at the public meeting and were not part of the earlier designs.[11] The panels represented what the Oversight Committee viewed as an appropriate compromise between an emphasis on George Washington and the Executive Branch of the government in its first years and the memorial to the enslaved people who lived and worked in the house. Clearly not everyone agrees that the right balance was reached. Nor is there any obvious consensus among the public and reviewers that the site is as interesting or engaging as it could be. But why should this be surprising given the controversial history of race in

Figure 9. President's House/Slavery Memorial is in the foreground, in front of the entrance to the Liberty Bell Center. Behind it in the next block is Independence Hall.

the United States and its virtual absence from so much of the country's public commemorative landscape such as museums or memorial sites until very recently?

The large panel visitors first see in the Entry Hall on their left when entering the house through the front door on Market Street, "The Executive Branch," briefly describes the new government (Figure 9). It identifies some important executive decisions from the 1790s, such as the Jay Treaty with Britain, the establishment of the First National Bank of the United States, the Alien and Sedition Acts, and the settlement of the Northwest Territories, driving the Indian populations farther west. Next to it six painted glass panels describe related issues from the period, such as the rise of abolitionist sentiment, the mobilization of opposition to the Jay Treaty, and the 1793 Fugitive Slave Act that Washington signed in the house. On the opposite side of this wall are five more panels showing scenes of life during Washington's term, including Ona Judge, "I Am Free Now," refugees from the Haitian Revolution, and the yellow fever epidemic, which shows Washington moving out of the city and a contrasting representation of death carts, with a description of how free Blacks in the city cared for the sick and buried the dead.

The panel in what is identified as the Steward's Room, "The House and the People Who Worked and Lived in It," provides a time line of the house, a description of its ground plan and architecture, an overview of the kinds of people associated with the house, the different categories of labor utilized in it, and slavery in the house. It includes an explanation of how Washington avoided the requirement of Pennsylvania's Gradual Abolition Act that said enslaved persons from other states who resided in Pennsylvania for at least six months could petition for their freedom (assuming that they knew about this provision); Washington moved the enslaved out of and then back into the state regularly so that with one exception they were never in it for an uninterrupted six-month period. Next to it is a painted glass panel showing Ona Judge overhearing Martha Washington saying that she planned to give her to one of her granddaughters as a wedding present.

The large panel in the area above the house's original kitchen, "The Dirty Business of Slavery" (Figure 10), shows a world map with the pattern of slave trade in the Americas, a description of the slave economy, numbers and details about slavery in the country and region, and a slavery time line. This is the panel that I have seen visitors read the most carefully. Next to it is a painted glass panel with a poignant quote from Washington, expressing the fear that, seeing so many free Blacks around them in the city, his enslaved Africans might try to escape. "The idea of freedom might be too great a temptation for them to resist. At any rate, it might, if they conceived they had a right to it, make them insolent in a State of Slavery."

The final large panel, "Life Under Slavery" (Figure 11), is above the Wash House toward the back. It describes the capture in Africa of the future slaves, the intentional brutality experienced by the enslaved on many plantations, resistance, slavery in Philadelphia, and the movement from African to African American culture. On the right the second half of the panel asks the question "How Did Enslaved People Become Free?" It describes the law, self-emancipation (referring to people who purchased their own freedom or ran away), refuge in churches, organization, and eventual emancipation following the Civil War.

The five video clips focus on Africans—enslaved and free—in late eighteenth-century Philadelphia.[12] Two of the five focus on Ona Judge and Hercules—the two enslaved Africans who were in Philadelphia and escaped

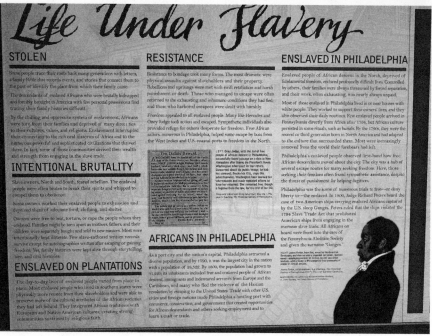

Figures 10 and 11. These two text panels, "The Dirty Business of Slavery" and "Life Under Slavery," on the inner walls of the President's House/Slavery Memorial site offer details about the slave system and the lives of enslaved people in both the North and South.

during Washington's years as President. The video portrays Judge first in the President's House as a young woman and then in New Hampshire, recounting the story of her life as an older woman. She tells how in her years in the city, she made the acquaintance of free Africans who helped her get to the ship that took her to freedom in New Hampshire, where she married, had three children, and died in 1848. She recounts how for several years, Washington tried to recapture her using the 1793 Fugitive Slave Law, and how abolitionists in New Hampshire helped her avoid capture. Being free was worth all the trials and tribulations she experienced, and in the video she expresses no regrets about her decision or any love for her former owner. Hercules was Washington's master chef, and the video featuring him is set in the house's kitchen where he prepared the meals for the household. He is shown in the kitchen with his son Richmond. Richard Allen, who has already purchased his freedom from Benjamin Chew and is working as a chimney sweep, pays him a visit. They chat for a while, and then we learn more about Hercules and his son.

The video on the granite wall on the east side of the house, above the underground passageway from the kitchen, provides brief biographies of the nine enslaved men and women. It is narrated by an actor portraying Christopher Sheels, Washington's enslaved attendant, who was reported to be the only one of the nine who could read and write at the time. A video shown in what was believed to be below Washington's second-floor office features the Reverend Richard Allen and the Reverend Absalom Jones, two free Blacks in Philadelphia who founded Black churches in the city in the 1790s. They called on the country to end slavery upon Washington's death in 1799, which mirrored Washington's gesture in his will, freeing the people he had enslaved. The video in the State Dining Room describes the yellow fever epidemic in the city that forced Washington to flee to Germantown, just outside the city at the time, for the summer of 1794, and the revolution in Haiti (then Saint-Domingue) sparked by a revolt of the enslaved there that both brought refugees to Philadelphia and led many whites in the young United States to fear slave insurrections.

On December 15, 2010, a sunny but frigid day, the "President's House: Freedom and Slavery in the Making of a New Nation" officially opened following a well-attended public ribbon-cutting ceremony that featured many public officials and almost all of the key players in the eight-year battle over the site's creation in attendance (Figure 12). There were stirring

Figure 12. The opening ceremony for the President's House/Slavery Memorial, December 15, 2010, Michael Coard, leader of Avenging the Ancestors Coalition, addresses the assembled crowd.

words about a new opportunity for having real dialogue about race in the country and a packed audience eager to look firsthand at the product of eight years of contentious discussions, despite the freezing weather (Miller 2010; Salisbury 2010b).

Soon after the official ceremony ended, ATAC organized its own celebration fifty yards away from the house site to mark the occasion to avenge and remember the ancestors. People carried Black liberation flags and signs with the names of the nine who had been enslaved at the President's House and posters declaring "*Real* American History Begins Today" and "Free at Last, Free at Last, Thank God Almighty, They're Free at Last." The celebration began with a libation to remember the ancestors at the end of which the speakers called out the names of the nine enslaved by Washington. Michael Coard gave a speech in which he celebrated the establishment of the commemorative site and reviewed the history of ATAC's struggle to get the memorial built and the rationale for the emphasizing the story of slavery at the site. The group was in a very celebratory mood—with good reason. Several groups of young people performed songs and dances that were much appreciated by the crowd of two hundred or so in the icy, windy weather.

Reviews of the "President's House: Freedom and Slavery in the Making of a New Nation" were distinctly mixed after it opened. Some were glad that it had been built and told the story of slavery in the country through the account of the nine enslaved people in the house, even if they had concerns that it was not done as well as they would have hoped. Others questioned the architecture of the site and suggested important ways that it was too fragmented and unintegrated to engage, let alone excite, visitors. Finally, others raised questions about the site's interpretive materials: some thought there was too much text for most visitors. Others objected to the balance between attention to enslavement, on the one hand, and the early years of the American Republic, on the other. On this issue, people differed greatly in terms of what should have been done differently, with some finding the material on Washington and Adams boring, and others wanting much more on their administrations, and the Presidents' wives, Martha and Abigail. Then there were those who wanted to know much more about the lives of the nine enslaved Africans, both before they came to Philadelphia and afterward, as well as people who wanted a more extended discussion of slavery in the city, region, and country.

Having visited the President's House/Slavery Memorial a number of times since the opening, I found that most visitors walk through or around it on their way to see the Liberty Bell.

Even before entering the President's House/Slavery Memorial, a visitor can't help but notice the large glass vitrine in the middle of it, so many people head over to see what it is. Looking down, people can see parts of the exposed foundations that are visible below. Small panels next to the glass on three sides explain some of what they are seeing and how archaeology was used in the research on the house site.[13] At the same time, to appreciate the emotional power of the place, the visitor needs to connect with and feel the story about life in the house over 230 years ago and what they are seeing underground to grasp its powerful meaning. Only a small number of people I have seen there actually do this—slowly reading the panels next to the vitrine and then staring at the remains below and reflecting on what they see. Most only look briefly, probably because it is unclear what they are seeing. Then they quickly move through the exhibit, often barely stopping, since they are usually on their way to see the Liberty Bell, and perhaps did not even know about the President's House/Slavery Memorial when they first entered it. The visible remains below are very modest, and without understanding the connections between the physical remains and how the enslaved worked in the house, most visitors wander away fairly quickly. During the dig in 2007, the archaeologists speaking to people on the platform were able to provide interpretation, but there is no such interlocutor for visitors now that the site is open.

Aden (2015) argues, and I think he is correct, that some of this haste and inattention is because of the absence of signage to direct people through the site. The open structure with entrances on all four sides is confusing, and visitors get no clear indication of what exactly it is or what is the best way to visit it. The architect Emanuel Kelly told me that having multiple ingress to the house was meant to convey a structure that had many people coming and going, who would have used it in very different ways, depending on who they were and what they were there to do. However, this is certainly not communicated in any coherent way to visitors, and I doubt that many people understand the very subtle message or its symbolism. On the outside of a granite wall on the eastern wall the names of the nine enslaved Africans are engraved, and an adjacent television monitor streams a video of biographical information on each of them. It is simple and effective in my view (Figure 13). However, because the wall faces away from the rest of the exhibit, it is easy for visitors not to see it at all, so many people never know it exists. A site map to direct visitors would help a lot.

INHP rangers are rarely present to explain the site; nor is there any written material distributed about it, either at the Visitor Center or on the site itself.[14] When people do enter the site, they rarely read the panels from start to finish; nor do they watch the videos in their entirety. One thing that is clearly missing for visitors is any written material that might explain what they are seeing or that they can take home with them to reflect upon what they saw. The Park Service had a short handout at the Visitor Center available for a brief time, when the site first opened, but it was never reprinted. What's more, it mainly focused on the Executive Branch of the government in the 1790s. Also missing is a small single-page map to depict the site's outline and what a visitor might see there. This is especially

Figure 13. The memorial wall with names of the nine enslaved. On the left side is a television monitor that offers a short biography of each of the enslaved people whom Washington brought to the house. The flowers were placed there as part of the Juneteenth celebration in 2016.

important given the different places where someone could enter the house, since there is almost never a person available who can offer an overview of the site. Having park rangers and docents available to talk to visitors and provide background on the story of the house and slavery in it would help meet many of these needs as well, but to date they are not available either.

After looking at the archaeological remains, some visitors watch one or more of the videos on the monitors hung on the walls at five locations. Each video is about five to seven minutes long, and my sense is that many people watch parts of some of the videos but far fewer watch one or more from start to finish. The one that features Ona Judge and tells the story of her escape from the house and her life in New Hampshire where she lived until 1848 is probably the most effective one. A few people read the larger panels with text or at least part of them, but when I have watched visitors, almost none systematically read all of them.

Similarly, the Slavery Memorial, tucked in the back of the site, is easy to miss, and it is not at all clear that it sits symbolically above the slave quarters, where some of the enslaved slept (Figure 14). It was made using glass, metal, and wood. On the outside are the names of the ethnic groups from which enslaved people in the United States originated, along with the names of today's independent countries that were their homelands. On the inside, walls feature inspiring quotations from Maya Angelou, Frederick Douglass, the Sankofa sign (Figure 15) along with the phrase, "Go back to the past to build the future." The memorial is tall and deliberately feels cramped inside, to evoke the small quarters in which slaves were forced to live. People seem to look at it from the outside, but only a few actually enter it to reflect on the memorial's meaning. Again, an explanation from either a booklet or ranger would certainly help.[15]

Although the Park Service was supposed to take over the site from the city once it was opened in 2010, the transfer was delayed until the end of 2015 because of ongoing problems with the site. The original monitors, neatly tucked into brick walls, malfunctioned owing to Philadelphia's temperatures in winter and summer. In the first summer monitors overheated, and it was clear they could not be fixed. These were replaced with monitors from a different vendor, which hung outside the brick wall to help with cooling, but many people then complained about their ugly positioning. They worked somewhat better but one or more still regularly shut down due to problems with the computer controlling the system. As a result, the city agreed to buy a new set of monitors that were installed in late 2015.

Significant water problems in and around the vitrine arose from faulty design and construction. If not corrected, pooling water and leaks in and around the original building's foundations would lead to significant deterioration. The water leaks caused the vitrine to fog up, making it hard for visitors to see the foundation stones below. A number of repairs were made to the paving tiles around it, a leaking hatch door, replaced joints in the panels of the vitrine that needed to be sealed and resealed, a faulty surface drain, and a poorly functioning humidity monitoring system in the foundation area. In addition, a belowground drain in the original design was never installed.

The Park Service is very concerned about deterioration of the foundations, which they are charged with preserving and protecting, to the point where they had discussions about filling the foundation area with sand to

Figure 14. The Slavery Memorial shows many of the names of the ethnic communities in West Africa from which the enslaved in the colonies and, later, states came.

protect it from further damage (Salisbury 2011, 2012a, 2012b, 2014c). At one point, the NPS put sand over some parts of the foundation, including sections of the bay window, that were especially vulnerable. By mid-2015, the repairs apparently were working and the sand was removed. The city said that some of these problems were the architect's responsibility, but Kelly/Maiello disagreed. To finally resolve the problems, the city used money in the site's maintenance fund, in the hope that the NPS would finally take full control over the site's management, which they agreed to do, in light of the progress made (Salisbury 2015).

A last problem I observed in since 2016 is that, at least on busy summer days, the NPS has people waiting to see the Liberty Bell line up on the west

Figure 15. A quotation from Frederick Douglass inside the memorial.

side of the President's House/Slavery Memorial, so visitors are unable to walk all the way around the vitrine to see the exposed foundations, looking down from the west side. In addition, people who are not in line to see the Liberty Bell are unable to read the inscriptions on the west side of the memorial or enter it from that side. Somehow, the de facto use of what is a historical and memorial site as a passageway seems very inappropriate.

The panels at the President's House/Slavery Memorial contain a great deal of text and five videos that tell the specifics about enslavement at the house and in the city. The noise from all the videos means that there is virtually no quiet space where a visitor can sit and reflect on what they have learned, and no help is provided to lead people through it. My sense is that there is a sensory overload for many visitors, who have trouble digesting the information presented there. One key way to improve historical sites is by providing spaces where visitors can quietly reflect on what they see and hear, although there is more than one way to do this successfully.

Visitors need more help to understand what is on this small site, and its diffuse organization in part causes most of them to move through it quickly. If more information about it were available in a small booklet that people could read at the time and take home with them, they would probably digest the site more fully and better appreciate what they had seen. However, at present, there is no takeaway material about the President's House/Slavery Memorial. Even the books for children about Ona Judge that were for sale for a while at the INHP Visitor Center bookshop are no longer available.

The President's House/Slavery Memorial located the story of slavery squarely across from the entrance that visitors use to see the Liberty Bell, and the proximity of the two emphasizes the problematic reality of the contradictory stories of slavery and liberty in the founding and early development of the United States. People who stumble upon it on their way to see the Liberty Bell, the park's main tourist attraction, can learn something about the presence of slavery in the city and region at that time. The site still needs significant improvement, but it does tell the complex, braided history of slavery and liberty in the country, as NPS chief historian Dwight Pitacithley hoped for in his 2002 memo. At the same time, this site needs revisions and upgrades to meet this challenge going forward, including simple things, such as the replacement of panels that have badly faded in the bright sun in only a few years.

The story of enslavement told at the President's House/Slavery Memorial remains poorly integrated into what is presented in other parts of Independence National Historical Park. Park rangers are now more likely to mention enslavement in places such as Independence Hall or on the mall while giving tours, but there still is lingering discomfort for some in how to connect it to the uplifting story of liberty. While the National Park Service has had a policy of greater inclusion of the stories of minority communities in its sites, its actual implementation is still a work in progress, as it is in many other parts of American society.

Visitors to the President's House/Slavery Memorial need clearer indications of what they are seeing and more structured directions to move through the site. Visitors do not easily grasp the house's layout, and the different parts of the narrative they are seeing and hearing are disconnected. Critical to the lack of guidance is that the Slave Memorial at the rear of the site is a puzzle to most people. It is not clearly explained and the reason why it located there is obscure. All of this could be handled by providing a map, good signs, park rangers, docents, or handouts, but visitors on their own too often simply and quickly give up. Finally, there needs to be a more explicit effort to connect the story of enslavement to the narrative of liberty that is told next door.

The rediscovery of enslavement at President Washington's home in Philadelphia led to an eight-year process that finally came to an end with the opening of the President's House/Slavery Memorial to visitors at IHNP. Some people remained very unhappy with the final design and its displays. Be that as it may, for the first time the site did present the story of enslavement in Philadelphia and other parts of the North. It raised questions about how that story could and should be told and remembered. In the short time since the site's opening, there has already been a flurry of new discoveries of sites of slavery in cities, towns, and hamlets throughout the region. It clearly stimulated questions about forgotten histories and collective memory recovery.

The inclusion of the story of slavery at the President's House/Slavery Memorial and its prominence on the National Mall in Washington at the newly opened National Museum of African American History and Culture are long overdue and significant additions to public history on the country's two most sacred landscapes. Memory recovery of enslavement throughout the thirteen colonies and original states has advanced. As the narratives about enslavement in Philadelphia and other parts of the North have spread, ritual expressions and enactments tied to them have increased, and their visibility on the commemorative, public landscape has risen. Yet far more needs to be done to accelerate this process.

The publicity given to one site of Northern slavery, such as the President's House/Slavery Memorial or the African Burial Ground in New York, often galvanizes interest in identifying and publicizing other sites. Awareness today of the existence and extent of enslavement in the North is far greater than a few decades ago, as is popular interest in learning about it. The story of the President's House forced the city of Philadelphia, the National Park Service, and people in other parts of the country to consider why slavery remains both highly contentious and worthy of serious attention. These sites are certainly a piece in the recovery of the collective memories of Northern slavery but not the end of the work. Histories of enslavement in the various colonies and, later, the states need to be infused into school textbooks and educational videos across the country.

Efforts to make the country's slave past more visible and better understood offer a serious challenge. For decades, the issue of slavery was never broached at IHNP, because to do so would have threatened the focus on American freedom and liberty and how they were achieved there. At the same time, making the story meaningful when it has long been forgotten and there are few readily available ways to communicate it in persuasive, emotionally challenging ways in a country where race is still highly charged and hard to talk about is challenging. Confusion about how to present and talk about race is not necessarily a bad thing, however. Similarly, we need to learn what is and what is not effective with the diverse public in this country. The idea that we can get this just right immediately is very naive. Mistakes, however, are opportunities for learning, and the large number of sites in the North that are broaching their past histories of enslavement offers opportunities to learn how to do this meaningfully and effectively.

In addition, important lessons can be learned from the President's House/Slavery Memorial story that should help communities do this. One is that effective mobilization of community action made a huge difference. As Michael Coard has observed more than once, the combination of activists in the streets and academics in the offices was hard to resist and eventually led to the decision to tell the story of the enslaved Africans in the context of American liberty and the country's founding. At the same time, we might take away some lessons about how to tell these stories about the past even more effectively in the future.

How to share stories effectively on public, historical sites is always challenging, largely because of the diversity of visitors' knowledge, interests, and backgrounds. Some know a great deal about a topic, while others may know next to nothing, so how can a site be meaningful for both groups? A good exhibit makes powerful links for a wide range of people by offering personal connections to which visitors can relate. Not all public history sites get this right from the outset—in fact, most do not, as perfection on a first try at anything is rare—so it is crucial that the people managing one learn what is and what is not working for visitors. This was certainly a stated goal for the NPS administrators at INHP, but there is little evidence that it has taken place to date, for there have been no significant changes or updates to the presentations at the President's House/Slavery Memorial since it opened.

Visible places and objects in the public and commemorative landscape are critical for the development, retention, and transmission of collective memory. Narratives about people and events and rituals marking them are emotionally compelling, and locating people or events in specific places or viewing objects associated with them greatly strengthens memory development and retention. Consider, for example, sacred sites in Jerusalem such as the Haram al-Sharif for Muslims, the Western Wall for Jews, the Church of the Holy Sepulchre for Christians, and the many people who for centuries have made pilgrimages to them. Or think about the power of relics associated with historical figures or sacred (religious or secular) places. These examples do not mean that physical markers of memory are all that matter to connect the past and present, but as a form of "official history" they greatly enhance memories.

The story of the enslavement at the President's House/Slavery Memorial in Philadelphia illustrates the linkage between the presence of visible public landscapes and objects, on the one hand, and recovered memories, on the other. While the archaeological dig in Philadelphia at the house where Washington had kept the nine enslaved Africans did not turn up specific objects clearly associated with them, it did reveal the outline of places in the house in which the enslaved lived and worked that are now part of Independence National Historical Park's commemorative landscape. The passageway between the kitchen and the front of the house where they walked with the Washingtons' food evokes powerful feelings for many people of what slavery must have entailed, but especially for African Americans, in much the same way that walking on the Via Dolorosa in Jerusalem or visiting the Church of the Nativity in Bethlehem is powerful for Christians.

The President's House/Slavery Memorial demonstrates both collective forgetting and the recovery of a long-ignored and forgotten story. Initially it seemed quite straightforward, until tensions rose and it became very complex. Its manifest content—the story's actual details—is clearly interesting to many people, but what is more significant is the latent content, meaning what it reveals about race and identify in the United States in the early twenty-first century, the deep feelings the story released, the emotional connections and pain it evoked across time and space, and the awareness of how partial our understanding of the past sometimes is. In short, the story is not only about the culturally constructed nature of collective memory; it also invites us to explore collective forgetting and to examine the process of recovering long-forgotten collective experiences and memories.

Chapter 6

The Bench by the Side of the Road

> *There is no place you or I can go, to think about or not to think about, to summon*
> *the presences of, or recollect the absences of slaves. . . . There is no suitable*
> *memorial or plaque or wreath or wall or park or skyscraper lobby. There's no*
> *300-foot tower. There's no small bench by the road. There is not even a tree*
> *scored, an initial that I can visit or you can visit in Charleston or Savannah or*
> *New York or Providence or, better still, on the banks of the Mississippi. And*
> *because such a place doesn't exist . . . the book had to.*
> —Toni Morrison (1989), discussing *Beloved*

The absence of visible markers on the public landscape facilitates collective forgetting. Buildings and other manmade features of a society's physical landscape are often connectors—or what Volkan (1988) calls linking objects—that help people recall past events and individuals years later. After a time, what is actually recalled or remembered is not the events or people themselves, but the stories told about them, transmitted across generations. Earlier I wrote that a society's commemorative landscapes communicate and frame social and political messages about public places imbued with emotional significance that can express a society's core values and honor its heroes through images, objects, and other expressive representations (Cosgrove 1998). As Confino (2011: 41) points out, "One's memory, like one's most intimate dreams, originates from the symbols, landscape, and past that are shared by a given society . . . embedded in a specific cultural, social, and political context."

The presence of physical markers and the ability to name them, especially on commemorative sites, can generate narratives that transmit collective memories, as well as alter them, over time. O'Brien (2010) argues that English settlers in New England asserted their claim to the land in part with monuments and commemorations. Yet in much of the North, there have been few visible signs of the historical presence of African Americans on the landscape. This "is symptomatic of a larger neglect of the Black presence in the North, a neglect that serves northern misrepresentations of the causes and cures of racism" (Paynter 1994: 52). The public and commemorative landscape in the South is similar in that only a few monuments, memorials, and museums focus on acknowledging the presence of African Americans or their history of slavery. At the same time, the recognition of a Black presence and history on the South's landscape, both explicitly and implicitly, has grown significantly in the past decades. Such sites, along with ceremonies and rituals held on them, can reinforce group identity and enhance the power of a group's narrative.

Inclusion and exclusion can be effectively expressed through the expansion or restriction of a society's public and commemorative landscape. Exclusion of groups, as has been the case for enslaved and free Blacks, is an obvious denial of belonging—a form of distancing and forgetting. In contrast, a more inclusive landscape can powerfully communicate shared connections and a common stake in society. Think about sites such as the National Mall in Washington or Independence National Historical Park in Philadelphia in terms of their many years of exclusion of African Americans. The Martin Luther King Jr. National Memorial on the Washington Mall, for example, was only completed in 2011, and the Smithsonian's National Museum of African American History and Culture opened in 2016.

In the late 1980s when Toni Morrison's *Beloved* was first published, there were few, if any, sites on the country's public, commemorative landscape where one could contemplate its slave past. This has changed somewhat in the three decades since then, and one small reason is the Toni Morrison Society's Bench by the Road Project, started in 2006 to mark her seventy-fifth birthday.[1] Its goal is to mark important outdoor locations in African American history and place specially crafted benches with an inscription to explain their significance. The first one was located at Sullivan's Island near Charleston, South Carolina, and home of Fort Moultrie, the point of entry into North America for about 40 percent of the enslaved Africans who entered the United States (Lee 2008). Now it is part of a National Park site. Through 2017, the bench project has placed twenty other benches in the South, North, and overseas.

The argument in this chapter builds on Connerton's (2009) analysis of collective forgetting, which emphasizes the importance of place familiarity to remembrance. Conversely, its absence easily leads to forgetting. He argues that when places themselves change through deterioration, destruction, or modernization and development, their ability to evoke memories declines. This also occurs when geographic mobility is high, since people no longer are near the places associated with their earlier memories—not just those of their youth, but also those of previous generations transmitted orally or through pictures and objects tied to place. As I puzzled about the dynamics of collective memory and forgetting, I realized how hard it is to imagine what slavery in the North must have looked like. Where were the "plantations" where the enslaved lived? What kind of work did they do? Where were they bought and sold? What were their families like? No places I had ever been in the North, or that I learned about as a child, or that I knew about when I began this project, gave me any good answers to these questions. Apparently, there is a paradox here. While the South has sites galore where slavery could be remembered, it has not been publicly discussed in most until recently. In contrast, in the North, people don't have a wrong image; they simply, at least until recently, have no image or awareness at all.[2]

The South's landscape is filled with plantations[3] and other sites, including monuments, museums, historical markers, battlefields, former slave markets, flags, parade uniforms, and more that are visibly associated with and evoke enslavement. Active heritage groups and many festivals also remind participants of the region's slave past. Even after slavery legally ended with the passage of the Thirteenth Amendment, many former slaves and their descendants continued to live as sharecroppers on the plantations where they had been enslaved for the simple reason that they had no alternative. In addition, there is no lack of books, films, paintings, folktales, newspaper articles, and magazines that communicate images—both positive and negative—of the antebellum period.[4]

The challenge there is how to recount enslavement in ways that are accurate and not only from the perspective of the slavery's supporters. Many Southern places of enslavement, including some tourist sites today that previously did not explicitly discuss slavery, are now more prominently and openly addressing it. However, there is a good deal of variation in how this is done and what exactly is presented. For example, sites that focus on the Black experience typically retell the past and slavery very differently (Eichstedt and Small 2002, esp. chap. 8).

Even when a landscape has not changed, what is told about it can shift rather dramatically. Tours at Thomas Jefferson's former plantation, Monticello, once had little to say about the more than six hundred enslaved people who had lived and worked there in his lifetime. Sally Hemings, the enslaved woman who was the mother of six of his children, was not mentioned on tours. However, visits to Monticello are very different today. Its former slave quarters on Mulberry Row were recently excavated, a good deal of research on the enslaved and their descendants has been conducted, and tours have been reoriented to place more emphasis on the people who lived and worked at Monticello and focus less exclusively on Jefferson and the house he designed and lived in. Today, a tour includes "Slavery at Monticello," showing a reconstructed slave cabin, places where the skilled craftsmen and women worked, and the reconstructed work and sleeping spaces under the main house and adjacent to it. The research over the past thirty years allows the tour guides to tell visitors a good deal about the lives of individual enslaved people who had lived and toiled there, to describe their families, and, in some cases, to offer significant details about their descendants, including those alive today.[5] Being able to walk through the physical spaces occupied by the enslaved accompanied by detailed narratives is a compelling combination for visitors.

When Eichstedt and Small (2002) visited Washington's Mount Vernon plantation in the late 1990s, they termed the tour's treatment of the enslaved as "segregated," noting that in the mansion tour, the enslaved were invariably described as servants, if they were mentioned at all, and little information was provided about them beyond the separate slave life tour. Often, tasks were talked about in the passive voice, to avoid having to say who was actually doing the work being described. A good deal has clearly changed since then, judging by the tour I took in 2015. The visit through the mansion uses the term "enslaved" (and not servants) regularly, and the presentation is more balanced in describing the Washingtons than the 1990s tours that Eichstedt and Small described. At the same time, the fact that Washington chose to free those he had enslaved upon Martha's death is mentioned several times, and it is also noted that he is the only one of the Founding fathers who did this.

The "Slave Life at Mount Vernon" tour attracts far fewer people than the tour of the main house. In addition, it is only offered once a day (in contrast to the "Slavery at Monticello" tour, which attracts many visitors, enough to be offered hourly and sometimes more often than that. This tour is built around the work done in the different buildings surrounding the commons in front of the main house. Most of those enslaved at Mount Vernon lived and worked on the outlying farms, and those who lived near the mansion were more highly skilled and worked on a trade or inside the house. One learns, too, that in 1781, during the Revolution, seventeen enslaved people (fourteen men and three women) fled to a British ship anchored nearby in the Potomac River and that, after the war ended, seven of them returned.

At Mount Vernon the "House of Families" near the plantation's mansion where some enslaved lived was torn down in the late 1780s. A later excavation of the site did yield a number of objects that provide details of how the enslaved lived. Likewise, the restoration of some slave cabins among the outbuildings helps the tour guide explain where the enslaved lived and the work they did.[6] For example, visitors are told about Washington's abandonment of tobacco as a cash crop in the 1760s and his conversion to more profitable grain crops, which were far less labor intensive. At that time, most of the fieldworkers were women, whereas the men learned the various crafts that produced additional income for Mount Vernon. Family relationships, leisure time, and earning opportunities for the enslaved also existed. However, in contrast to Monticello, relatively few details were presented about specfic enslaved individuals or their descendants. This shifted somewhat in 2016 when a new exhibit in the visitor center provided more details about enslavement at Mount Vernon and brief profiles of nineteen of the enslaved individuals.[7] There is also an ongoing excavation on Mount Vernon's Black burying ground containing the remains of a number of enslaved people. However, there is no identification of the specific individuals interred there, and the goal is to not disturb the burials but to dig down no more than six to eight inches to learn more about how many burials are there and how they are aligned.[8]

In Richmond, Virginia, walking tours visit a number of sites of slavery in the city, many of which were established by the Richmond City Council Slave Trail Commission. Since 1998 these tours have included the docks where in the nineteenth century enslaved people were shipped to the Deep South to be sold to work on cotton plantations. In its work to date, the commission has established seventeen slave trail markers and has begun planning a Richmond National Slavery Museum.[9] In North Carolina, Virginia, Louisiana, South Carolina, and other states tourists and local residents can visit plantations where the former slave cabins are now part of the tour and the lives of the enslaved are described, sometimes in great detail.[10]

This is not to suggest that all or even a majority of Southern plantations or other sites of slavery treat the lives of the enslaved treat the lives of the enslaved extensively or accurately. But widespread change has happened since the late 1990s, when Eichstedt and Small (2002) studied the representations of slavery in 122 plantation museums in Virginia, Louisiana, and Georgia as well as twenty African American sites to analyze counternarratives of race and enslavement. They coded each plantation tour based on how it described enslavement. The vast majority (85 percent) were seen as engaging in either "symbolic annihilation" or "trivialization and deflection." In other words, enslavement was not dealt with at all or was treated only very little. A small minority of sites actually incorporated stories of enslavement into their wider presentations or were at least taking steps to do this. While Eichstedt and Small (2002: 9) emphasize how narratives "generally valorize and normalize white elite behaviors and mask the participation of these white individuals in the institution of slavery," it was certainly clear to visitors that slavery was an integral part of the plantation system, no matter how it was portrayed. Eichstedt and Small also found a few plantations that were more forthright in their discussion of slavery, challenging the dominant Southern narrative and emphasizing resistance, resilience, and the dignity of the struggle against it (2002: 233).

The number of sites doing this kind of interpretation seems to have increased in the two decades since their research. The five sites I visited in and around Charleston, South Carolina, in 2014 did focus on slavery, and when I asked how long each site had been doing this, they all told me the shift was relatively recent, in the previous ten to fifteen years. The most detailed and powerful account of enslavement was in the Old Slave Mart Museum in downtown Charleston, a city-operated museum that opened in 2007. It is in a building that was once part of a larger complex in which slave auctions were held in the late 1850s, after the city banned outdoor sales of slaves.[11] On its first floor a powerful account of the working of the slave trade starts with the role that the building played in it, effectively using pictures and objects such as shackles, combined with explanatory text panels. On its second floor, the exhibit describes African American experiences from the end of the Civil War through the civil rights movement. In addition, the staff is very knowledgeable and readily answers questions and elaborates on points made in the exhibits.

I also visited Drayton Hall Plantation, Boone Hall Plantation, and Magnolia Plantation, all near Charleston, and the Aiken Rhett House in the city's downtown. All included something about the enslaved people on their tours, but in different ways and to different degrees, and have been doing this since the 1990s or early 2000s. Plantation tours invariably focus on the large houses in which the slave owners and their families lived and on their grounds and gardens. On the tours of each one I was assured that the owners all treated the enslaved well, were reluctant to break up families by selling individual family members and in some cases even helped the enslaved learn to read and write (a claim I found dubious). Generally, many pieces of period furniture and other objects reveal the lavish lifestyle of the plantation owners. In contrast, the slave quarters that I visited were very minimal dwellings, often shared by many people. In two of them—at Boone Hall and the Aiken Rhett House—the housing for the enslaved was made of brick, while at the Magnolia Plantation and Stagville Plantation, outside Durham, North Carolina, they were wood.[12] On all the plantations African Americans remained on the property and worked as sharecroppers after the Civil War, sometimes well into the twentieth century.

Boone Hall dates from 1691.[13] The layout of the plantation—its huge trees, the many buildings, and the grandeur of the main house—is striking. Its economy was based on fruit, grain, bricks made from the mud in the nearby creek, and, later, cotton. Eight of the former slave quarters on "Slave Street" located near the mansion house were living quarters for the enslaved people who worked inside the main house and have recently been restored (Figure 16). However, the plantation once had many other slave quarters that no longer exist, closer to the fields in which the enslaved worked. By 1860 there were probably two hundred to three hundred enslaved people on this planation. A self-guided tour of each of the restored cabins offers detailed explanations of slave life, demonstrations of crafts the enslaved practiced, and videos and panels on Black history, including the civil rights movement and Black achievements in the post–Civil War period. Also, on the day I visited, a docent was present to answer questions about Black life on the plantation.

In 1750 Magnolia Plantation had about 140 enslaved people who grew rice (named "Carolina gold" because of its value). Before beginning the tour, visitors to Magnolia Plantation and Gardens can view a short film about the plantation[14] that devotes a few minutes to a discussion of the lives of the enslaved people who lived and worked there and their relationship to the slave owners, the latter depicted as benevolent and the former as loyal.

Figure 16. The restored slave cabins along Slave Street near the mansion at Boone Hall Plantation outside Charleston, South Carolina. These were for the enslaved who worked in the big house. There were other cabins near the fields where the enslaved field hands lived.

At the same time, it is clear that their very work was hard, despite the use of what was described as the less harsh "task" (as opposed to gang) system common to the region. Under the task system each individual was given a job to complete each day. Once completed, the individuals could work in a personal garden or on a craft. This gave the enslaved some time to raise crops or engage in crafts and allowed them to produce goods they could sell. The gang system, which became common on cotton plantations in the nineteenth century, had a foreman and gang leader who directed all of those working in the fields throughout the day and maintained a rapid pace that all needed to match or be punished physically (Baptist 2014).

At Magnolia, there is a separate tour of the restored slave cabins, located about a half mile from the main house, to which guides drive visitors on a small open-air tram The almost hour-long tour, offered a number of times a day, includes a group of recently restored wooden cabins that were once housing for the enslaved and then used by sharecroppers until just a few decades ago (Figure 17).[15] Each cabin contains furnishings and information panels about different periods ranging from the 1850s to the 1970s. The

Figure 17. One of the half dozen restored slave cabins at Magnolia Plantation near Charleston, South Carolina. Most of the enslaved workers living in these cabins grew rice at one time.

displays include profiles of specific individuals who lived in each cabin and a few vignettes about their lives. The guide explained the daily and seasonal work routines and the danger of disease for those raising rice in the mosquito-infested lowlands. She was very engaged and knowledgeable and thoughtfully answered many questions from our group.

Drayton Hall Plantation, not far from Magnolia, whose main house dates from the 1730s, has been owned and run by the National Trust for Historic Preservation since the 1970s.[16] The main house was never modernized and contains almost no furniture. Visiting it, one can learn a great deal about the architecture and values of the early slaveholding class in the region. An integral part of the tour includes a one-hour presentation entitled "Connections: From Africa to America," which emphasizes how African practices and traditions still can be seen in the region today. Small groups of visitors hear a detailed presentation of the plantation's history with an emphasis on how the enslaved lived and worked. The guide's presentation explains the technology of rice farming and how Africans from the Guinea coast who knew a good deal about rice production were especially sought by Low Country slave owners. Their specific knowledge and experience were critical to the success of the rice plantations that dated from the end of the late seventeenth century and prospered for more than 125 years.

A burying ground on the plantation dating from the 1790s contains the remains of at least forty enslaved and free Blacks (Figure 18). It was dedicated in 2010 as a sacred site and is one of the older African American burying grounds still in use in the United States. After the Civil War, "the cemetery was at the heart of a community of families—of small frame houses with swept dirt yards, vegetable gardens, outbuildings, and fields. In keeping with the wishes of Richmond Bowens, a descendant of the enslaved at Drayton Hall, the cemetery has been 'left natural,' not manicured or planted with grass or decorative shrubs. As he said, 'Leave 'em rest.' Mr. Bowens was born at Drayton Hall in 1908, lived and worked at Drayton Hall on and off for over 50 years, including as gatekeeper and oral historian, and was buried here in 1998."

As significant for collective memory as the Southern plantations are books and films portraying Southern slavery. Most famously, *Gone with the Wind* created for many people who had never even been in the South an image of plantation life that relied on loyal slaves who were well treated by their white owners. Nowhere in either the book or the film does one learn about the life of the enslaved in terms of work demands, the possibility of being separated from family members, harsh punishments, the struggle for survival, and physical and emotional deprivation.

The South has a good number of "Faithful Slave and Mammy" memorials and plaques (Shackel 2003: chap. 3), such as the one in Mebane, North Carolina.[17] One is also part of the large Confederate Memorial at Arlington National Cemetery, constructed in 1914 after a ten-year campaign by the United Daughters of the Confederacy (Cox 2003, McElya 2007: 116) (Figure 19). It includes images of a loyal "faithful mammy" and an enslaved Black man accompanying his owner to war. A Northern example is the one in Great Barrington, Rhode Island, installed in 1903.[18] In 1922, there was a campaign to place "a monument to the faithful colored mammies of the South" near the just opened Lincoln Memorial on the Washington Mall (McElya 2007: 116). Early the next year, the Senate passed a bill granting the request, but the House never brought the bill to the floor following a flood of protests in the next few months (McElya 2003: 203). Savage (1997: 155–61) suggests that these monuments are more about nostalgic sentiments for the region's former lifestyle than slavery itself. I am not persuaded that the distinction is so clear. How can we separate the two?

Figure 18. The entrance to Drayton Hall's Black Burying Ground where the sign on the arch reads, "Leave 'em rest."

In the North, few places on its landscape or other physical reminders clearly mark the region's long history of enslavement from the early seventeenth century until its demise with the passage of the Thirteenth Amendment to the Constitution. Nor is there much public recognition in the North that slavery was a significant feature of the economy of colonial America and a

Figure 19. An enslaved woman holds a white child up to its white father for a goodbye kiss as he heads off to war. This is one of a number of "Faithful Mammy" images found throughout the former Confederate states in the decades after the Civil War. Confederate monument, Arlington National Cemetery.

driver of its prosperity before the Civil War, despite work of historians and others who have made this argument. For many decades, when slavery was publicly marked and discussed in the North, it was almost invariably in reference to Northern abolitionist activity. Northerners have been much more comfortable emphasizing those who struggled for freedom than their own history of slavery. As a result, Underground Railroad sites are frequently identified and celebrated, while nearby sites of slavery are ignored or discussed far less.

One reason is that slavery looked very different in the North than it did in the South, where large plantations remained even after enslavement ended. In the North, most slaveholders owned a small number of people—most often one or two. Few needed to build separate quarters, and in cities there was often little space for such additions in any case, unless they were temporary structures in yards. Rather, housing for the enslaved was generally not as distinctive as in the South, for they most often lived in the owner's house, in the attic, back rooms, a kitchen, or basement spaces.

Although there were plantations with up to twenty enslaved Africans in eastern Rhode Island in the Narragansett region, Fitts (1996, 1998) reports that probate records from the eighteenth century show that most enslaved people lived in the main plantation house and that few had separate quarters. We might say that the spaces of bondage and liberty in the North blurred more than in the South, while the relations among the people remained clear. Even in New York, which had more enslaved Africans than any other Northern colony, in the city and on farms on Long Island and in the Hudson River Valley, I have found only a few extant references to where the enslaved lived. One is the Pieter Claesen Wyckoff House in Brooklyn's Canarsie section, where a house dating to 1652 is said to be New York's oldest building. Wyckoff was a Dutch settler who first farmed the surrounding land. While there was no evidence that he enslaved people, by the 1740s enslaved people lived with his great-grandson in the expanded house. There were more on this family farm in the first two decades of the nineteenth century, even as slavery in New York was ending. In 1819, however, Abraham Wyckoff entered into an indenture contract for a young Black boy, which shows the family's ongoing commitment to continuing their labor practices in a revised form (Sawyer 2005: 54–55).

In 2001, researchers described the Lott House in the Marine Park section of Brooklyn as the "first known slave dwelling in what would become New York City" (Staples 2001). The building began as a modest three-room eighteenth-century farmhouse but is now an eighteen-room structure. The Lott family owned twelve enslaved people in 1803, the last of whom was freed in 1820. Recent research discovered two small, low attic rooms where at least some of the enslaved lived, and corncobs, found under their floorboards, were arranged in a shape that "suggests a cosmogram, a symbol known to anthropologists as a West African depiction of the cosmos" (Staples 2001).[19]

John Vlach (2005) tells us that slave labor worked the land for the most part in New York's upstate countryside, originally settled by the Dutch (cf. White 1991; Groth 2017). Some farms had between thirty and sixty enslaved persons, although most had fewer. Vlach includes a picture taken in 1936 of the Mabee House, a small, simple slave cabin in Rotterdam Junction, New York, near Schenectady. Clearly, the house had been maintained and probably upgraded. He says this house in the picture was typical of slave quarters on the larger early Dutch plantations, that he obtained at the Library of Congress (2005: 72–73). The Dutch continued to dominate as landowners in rural New York in the Hudson River Valley and on Long Island, and in northeast New Jersey even after 1664, when New York became an English colony. The rich farmlands relied on enslaved labor for decades, but this story was not well known, even though the practice was very common. In recent years, greater interest in the history of enslavement in the Hudson River Valley has led to scholarly research as well as tours and exhibits (Armstead 2003; Groth 2003, 2017). There is also more local interest in this aspect of the region's history (Levine 2017).

In 2010 Joseph McGill launched the Slave Dwelling Project, which publicizes and hopes to preserve places where enslaved people slept.[20] Each year McGill overnights at places where former slaves slept to stress the value of the sites' preservation. He posts on his blog about each visit and almost always gets publicity in local newspapers. Initially visiting sites in the South, by now he and his colleagues have slept in every Northern state that were originally part of the thirteen colonies except New Jersey. Among other sites, McGill and others have slept in the Bevier-Elting House on Huguenot Street, in New Paltz, New York, where the practice of enslavement was quite common in the eighteenth century. Built in 1698, the Bevier-Elting House is one of two houses in which enslaved people lived in this historic area. In 1790, the town's population was 2,309, and 77 slave owners there possessed 302 slaves, an average of just about four slaves per owner, with enslaved people composing 13 percent of the town's population. The Bevier-Elting House had a very low basement, where McGill's group slept in September 2016. As part of his visit there, he spent time at the local university speaking to a number of groups, and students were among those who joined him at the house sleepover.[21]

In 1984 historian Mac Griswold (2013) stumbled upon Sylvester Manor's gardens and house on Shelter Island, at the eastern end of Long Island, while she and a friend were out for a summer ride in a dinghy. No one was home, but she learned who lived there and wrote to the owners—a descendant of Nathaniel Sylvester and his wife. She explained that she was a landscape historian and was intrigued by what she had seen on her short walk around the grounds. They invited her to visit and gave her a tour of the house and the grounds. The owner, Andrew Fiske, was especially interested in history and had carefully organized the house's extensive papers. Griswold was more than a little intrigued when Fiske showed her the "slave stairs" by which the enslaved climbed to their quarters in the attic. He told her about the Quaker family's history, including the existence of enslaved people who had lived and worked there, growing food that was raised on the plantation and sold, destined to feed the enslaved people growing sugarcane in the Caribbean. Soon Griswold was engaged in a long-term research project, going through the archives at the house, and when Andrew Fiske died in 1996, his wife Alice remained committed to the project. In fact, Alice expanded it to include archaeological excavations, for which Katherine Hayes was the project's field superintendent. In the end, Griswold and Hayes and their team learned a great deal about the social and economic organization of this plantation on which enslaved Africans, local Indians, and the family worked and lived.

Hayes's archaeological research and Griswold's analysis of family papers at Sylvester Manor found that many enslaved Africans had lived in a separate building near the main house from the middle of the seventeenth century (Hayes 2013). It appears that the building was torn down in the 1730s when a larger main house was built. Slavery at Sylvester Manor, however, continued until 1820, and at least some of the enslaved were housed in the attic of the newer, larger house, making it easy for later occupants to forget about enslavement that existed there decades earlier.

> For the Sylvesters and their descendants, the materials excluded from memory included the very structure of the plantation itself, in which such a diversity of people lived and worked . . . Indeed, historical narratives arise from the willingness or desire of communities to remember or forget. . . . Unearthing discarded evidence allows us not only to recover excluded histories but to investigate *how* and possibly *why* they are excluded . . . Forgetting is both complex and critically constitutive of memory and heritage. . . . Forgetting can be commanded by offering amnesty (linked to amnesia). . . . [while] the very course of modernity, rupturing associations with tradition and dispersing people from familiar places, has been a strain of forgetting on a massive social scale. (Hayes: 2013: 5–6)

Hayes (2013) added that none of this is accidental as "popular histories reproduce the 'invisibility' of enslaved Africans in Northern colonies, of Indians in settings of modernity, or of the pluralistic communities forged between them" (9). By the eighteenth century, later generations of Sylvesters sought to situate themselves in a more elite class by casting off earlier associations with provisioning and commerce, which promoted their "for-getting" about the earlier enslavement on their plantation. Her exploration of the Sylvester plantation emphasizes "the many subtle and complex ways that history is forgotten" in a setting now shaped by modern sensibilities (15). By 1884, the commemorative landscape of the plantation "situated the histories of Europeans, Africans, and Indians literally at a distance from one another and marked each group in its own temporally secluded realm" (16). Hayes points out, "History, like memory, is a construction of associations. . . . But narratives may also be written to sever certain associations, especially if they either raise uncomfortable questions or are linked to infa-mous events. . . . [Thus] the taint of racial prejudices or support of slavery was deflected by either ignoring the practice of slavery in Northern colonies or claiming the distance of time from when the 'last slave,' who very often conveniently disappeared into the mists of history, was freed" (121–22).

In the summer of 2015, Joseph McGill visited three houses where slaves once lived on eastern Long Island, including Sylvester Manor, where he slept in the mansion's attic that is accessed through twisting "slave stairs" (Schuessler 2015; McGill 2015a). The other two were Joseph Lloyd Manor in Huntington, the former home of Jupiter Hammon, who in 1760 became the first published Black poet in the country; and the Thomas Halsey Homestead in Southampton, built in 1648 and home to enslaved people at various points in its history (Schuessler 2015).

McGill has stayed twice at Cliveden in Philadelphia—once in 2011 and again in 2015 (Figure 20). Benjamin Chew, the Attorney General and the Chief Justice of the Supreme Court of Pennsylvania before the Revolution, built this large mansion as a summer home in the 1760s, and seven genera-tions of his descendants lived there until 1972, when the National Trust for Historic Preservation acquired it. For a long time, Cliveden offered visitors a traditional house tour that emphasized its architecture, its history, its grounds, and its furniture. However, when David Young became the new Executive Director in 1994, its orientation shifted radically. Recognizing that the mansion was located in an almost entirely African American com-munity that saw itself as having no shared interests with Cliveden, Young worked hard to shift the program and build local ties.

Until recently, it was not widely known that the Chews had significant investments in slave plantations in Maryland and Delaware and that some of these enslaved people were brought to Philadelphia to work at Cliveden and at the family's downtown house. Cliveden reflected the great wealth of

Figure 20. Cliveden was a mid-eighteenth-century mansion built by the wealthy Chew family. James Smith is seated on the house's front steps in this 1860s photo. Once a family slave, he was freed in the 1820s and continued working for the family for the rest of his life. (Courtesy of the Pennsylvania Historical Society)

the Chew family, much of which is directly attributable to the labor of the enslaved (Seitz 2014). It is not known with certainty where or how many enslaved people lived there over time, because they were often moved between the Chew homes in the city and the plantations, depending on who was present at different times. Young told me that the best estimate is that as many as sixteen to twenty-five enslaved people lived at Cliveden at peak times, over a span of years from 1768 until 1831.

With grants from the Pew Foundation, the staff at Cliveden were able to research the extensive family records stored in the Pennsylvania Historical Society, where they learned details about the Chew's long connection to enslavement. The staff at Cliveden soon developed new exhibits and public presentations that discussed race in the context of the American Revolution, the Battle of Germantown that took place on its grounds, and details about the Chews' Delaware and Maryland plantations. In June in recent years, Cliveden has presented a play, *Liberty to Go and See*, based on a partnership between Cliveden, the Young Philadelphia Playwrights, and the New Freedom Theater. It features episodes of daily life and work in the house, and it tells the experience of the enslaved, indentured, and family members through performances in various rooms throughout the house. The play presents a good deal of information about the enslaved and family and includes a follow-up discussion between the actors and the audience, all of which is very effective in using the site to depict its history of slavery. When Cliveden decided to restore the house's 1767 kitchen, a local Black Boy Scout troop participated in the work.

Cliveden hosted "Kitchen Conversations," presentations and discussions related to race, the history of the house, and the local community a few years ago, in addition to regular public talks. McGill gave one such talk about his project on each of his visits. He explained that because some of the enslaved worked as cooks, McGill slept in the kitchen on his first stay there, in recognition of the fact that often the enslaved "lived where they worked." In 2015, he slept in the attic, another place where the enslaved had slept in the house (McGill 2015b).

In Greenwich, Connecticut, in 2012 McGill slept in the attic of the 1730s Bush-Holley House along with three members of "Coming to the Table," a project to discuss the legacy of slavery that has brings the descendants of former enslaved people together with descendants of former slave owners—one of whom was the descendant of both a slave owner and his enslaved woman. Late in the eighteenth century, this was the home of ten enslaved people who were listed in David Bush's will and inventory when he died in 1797. McGill said this was the first time he had ever spent the night with descendants of former slave owners and the discussions among them were moving. When he asked the two men whose ancestors were slave owners whether they were feeling like outcasts for revealing their family's history, it was clear that even in the face of possible ridicule, they would not cease discussing this part of their family's past (McGill n.d.).

On a 2015 visit to Rhode Island for a conference McGill had the opportunity to sleep in the slave quarters of Smith's Castle in North Kingstown, Rhode Island, which was a large plantation in the Narragansett area of the state in the seventeenth and eighteenth centuries. In 1757, when its owner, Daniel Updike died, his inventory included eighteen enslaved people. By 1800 two remained (Dunay 2014).[22]

McGill slept at the Royall House and Slave Quarters in Medford, Massachusetts, which is said to be the only remaining freestanding eighteenth-century slave quarters in the North, in 2013. He spent two nights with different groups of people, including Tufts University students, Civil War reenactors, and descendants of both former enslaved people and enslavers. The blog posts by McGill and several others communicated the intense emotion of the experience and the meaningful conversations that took place in the slave quarters and at the public discussions he attended (McGill 2014). What particularly interested me was how many people were surprised when he told them he planned to sleep in slave dwellings in the North. Most had no awareness that Northern slavery ever existed.

The Royall House and Slave Quarters museum (Figures 21 and 22) is located on what was originally called Ten Hills Farm, which John Winthrop, the first governor of Massachusetts Bay Colony, settled in 1630 (Manegold 2010). A later owner, Isaac Royall Sr., the son of a carpenter in Maine, grew very wealthy through both the lucrative slave trade and his sugar plantation in Antigua, worked by many enslaved Africans, where he lived for almost forty years in the early eighteenth century. When conditions there deteriorated and many whites felt threatened by potential slave rebellions, he moved his family back to New England in 1737 to Ten Hills Farm, which was then more than five hundred acres. Royall had purchased it five years earlier, and it housed the largest number of enslaved people from the colony. In preparation for his return, next to the main house Royall built the separate slave quarters, where many of the twenty enslaved Africans that he brought from Antigua lived. Royall died two years later and his son Isaac Jr. took over the farm. He married well and with his wife soon owned six homes in New England, all of which had enslaved people on the premises. As many as sixty-four were known to have been working in these homes, and many more still in Antigua (Chan 2007: 6; Manegold 2010: 190). Royall's wealth later funded Harvard's Law School's endowment and its first professorship of law, and his portrait still hangs in the Law School.[23]

A 1990s archaeological dig on the remaining ground of the former Ten Hills Farm unearthed many objects used by both the Royall family and the enslaved people who lived there. However, the archaeological research was only able to provide some general details about how the enslaved lived and worked. Using available archival records, including Royall family documents and census and probate records, Chan (2007) learned that the

Figure 21. Isaac Royall's mansion, which was once the home of John Winthrop, the first governor of the Massachusetts Bay Colony.

turnover of the enslaved people there was considerable over time, supporting other findings that in the North the enslaved were often unable to live in the same place or with the same owners for extended periods. She reports that three-quarters of the Royalls' sixty-four known enslaved people spent fewer than ten years with them (Chan 2007: 147). The enslaved tended to sleep where they worked, including in the Royall home, in the slave quarters, and at times in the barns and other structures on the large farm.

Today the Royalls' home and slave quarters are open for visits and school trips.[24] The slave quarters consists of two sections—the brick one that Royall, Sr. had built in the 1730s before his return, which contains a summer kitchen with a huge fireplace downstairs, and a sleeping area upstairs. There is also and a larger wooden section that Isaac Royall Jr. added a few years later. Today it contains panels that explain the archaeological excavation and cases displaying a few of the many artifacts that were uncovered there. The buildings were once part of the very large farm, with fruit trees, gardens, and a summer gazebo/cottage, at a time when the Mystic River was much nearer than it is today.

Figure 22. The brick portion of the slave quarters (*left*) was built by Isaac Royall near his mansion upon moving there from Antigua in 1737. His son Isaac Jr. added the addition (*right*) a few years later.

On our tour there, the guide took us through the slave quarters and main house and integrated the story of slavery into the entire tour rather than compartmentalizing it. However, not a great deal is known about the individual enslaved people who lived and worked there beyond their names, sex, and approximate ages. One exception is a woman named Belinda who had been enslaved on Royall's farm in Medford for almost fifty years. She went to court in 1783 and submitted a petition asking that a pension be paid from the Royall estate to support her and her infirm daughter. It was granted, and she returned to the court four years later to ask for additional support, which was also granted. No more is known, however, of the fate of Belinda or her daughter (Chan 2007: 1–3). Finkenbine (2007), who quotes her petition, says that some people mistakenly saw it as a plea for freedom, which it was not; rather, he said, the petition should be seen as an early appeal for reparations that outlined her suffering in bondage from the time of her capture in Africa and the wealth she

Figure 23. Marker installed by the Pennsylvania Historical and Museum Commission in 1991 at Front and Market Streets in Philadelphia, just a short distance from the Delaware River where slaving ships sometimes landed and slave auctions were conducted.

helped Royall accumulate through her decades of unpaid work (see also Ragovin 2002).

While in some cases, such as Sylvester Manor, the houses on the large farms still exist, they are not commonly viewed as sites of slavery any more than are old townhouses in Philadelphia, New York, or Boston. In each of these cities, however, a recent development is the installation of a historical marker to identify the location of a prominent slave market in the city. Philadelphia was the first to do this, in 1991 (Figure 23); New York followed suit and placed a marker at Wall and Water Streets, near the East River, in 2015.

For many years, New Yorkers knew little about slavery in their city or state. This began to change dramatically in the early 1990s with the rediscovery and excavation of the African Burial Ground in Lower Manhattan (see Introduction), and the "Slavery in New York" exhibit at the New-York Historical Society in 2005 and 2006. Recently, the National Park Service developed a tour that focuses on the role of enslaved and free Blacks in New York's earliest years.[25] One can take the tour with a ranger or listen to downloadable MP3 recordings of a presentation at the tour's seven stops. At each stop the guide describes New York's early history of slavery, beginning in 1626, soon after the arrival of the Dutch.

In 1664, the British captured the city and renamed it New York. British rule was more severe than the Dutch, and slavery was further institutionalized. A slave market was established at Wall and Water Streets near the East River in the eighteenth century, during which time as many as 20 percent of the city's population was enslaved and 40 percent of the households owned one or more people. The NPS tour explains that between 1700 and 1776, 6,800 enslaved Africans were brought into New York, 2,800 of whom were from the West Indies. The guide underscored that, with the large number of enslaved people, the local economy was directly and indirectly tied to the slave trade.

The tour continues in City Hall Park, the site of New York's eighteenth-century commons, where the Dutch first introduced the three-day Pinkster celebration in which Africans participated and began incorporating their own cultural traditions in song, dance, and sports. By the late eighteenth and early nineteenth centuries it was seen as more of an African than a Dutch event. There was even a "king" for the festival, generally an enslaved man who was honored with symbolic power over the slave community.[26] In 1766 the free Blacks in the city, though small in number, formed the John Street Methodist Church, the oldest Methodist congregation in North America, in a response to the continuing discrimination against Blacks in white churches, including the refusal to allow Blacks to take communion before whites. The tour ends at the African Burial Ground with the story of its creation, use, and rediscovery and with Rodney Leon's memorial.

Philadelphia has no comparable comprehensive tour of its sites of slavery. The city's African American History Museum's permanent exhibit, entitled "Audacious Freedom: African Americans in Philadelphia, 1776–1876," provides little information about the more than one-hundred-year span when slavery was common in the city. Nor does it report that slavery existed in Pennsylvania as late as 1845, or give any of the details of the severe harassment, discrimination, and brutal attacks that were almost a daily reality for free Blacks in nineteenth-century Philadelphia. The portraits and stories of Black heroes presented in this exhibit may also give the false impression that resistance was common and often effective for the enslaved.

In Boston, although enslaved people were owned or "rented" from their owners by many middle- and upper-class families during the colonial period, learning about the almost 150 years of slavery is not easy, even on historical tours and at museums, despite the fact that historians have carefully documented it. Writing in the mid-1990s, Paynter found an absence of the African American experience on the state's historical sites in contrast to what is said about people of European origin. "The overwhelming and erroneous impression conveyed is that Afro-Americans are absent from Massachusetts history" (Paynter 1994: 51). He notes that there are very few African American sites in Boston on the National Register of Historic Places and some of these sites commemorate the abolitionist activities of whites. When I visited in 2015, little had changed. For example, the National Park Service's Black Heritage Trail tour only focuses on the city's free Black community in the early nineteenth century, taking visitors through the North Slope of Beacon Hill, which was an African American neighborhood at the time. The tour begins at the Massachusetts Fifty-Fourth Regiment Memorial on the Boston Common.[27] It stops at buildings that were sites of important African Americans and/or events in the pre–Civil War period. Almost all the buildings are private homes today, so the guide can only stand on the street outside to talk about the events that took place and people who lived there.

On our tour, only two sentences were devoted to the 140-year history of slavery in the Massachusetts colony, and perhaps they were offered only because I had earlier asked the guide why he said nothing about slavery—as opposed to the post-1800 history of free Blacks in Massachusetts—on a tour called the Black Heritage Trail. He said that most enslaved Blacks lived more in the North End of Boston during their enslavement and that few buildings are left from the period when they were enslaved, so it would be hard to do a tour there. This reluctance to discuss history in the absence of physical evidence—a "need for artifacts" mentality—contributes to the erasure of slavery from collective memory in the North. This pattern, begun long ago in Boston and other places, emphasizes the region's role in the story of freedom and liberty while excluding accounts of local slavery. His explanation seemed highly dubious since on the tour he was leading, we never went inside any of the homes he was showing us and talking about. Certainly, a tour that emphasizes free Blacks mobilizing to oppose Southern slavery is much easier to tell and less embarrassing to white or Black people. While a story of resistance may be more reassuring, the reality is that it is too simplistic and limited. It conforms to "the North is different" story, with its emphasis on abolition and the Underground Railroad, and ignores the era of slavery in which many "distinguished" New Englanders played a leading role and built their fortunes.

Similarly, Boston's nearby Museum of African American History, also an NPS site, had the same partial and limited account of Blacks in Boston with basically nothing about Black life in the area before 1800, other than the mention of the participation of Black patriots such as Crispus Attucks in the American Revolution. The emphasis again was on local opposition to Southern slavery in the nineteenth century, Black Bostonians' fight against the 1850 Fugitive Slave Law, and their involvement in the Underground Railroad. The museum was shamefully silent about the earlier 140 years of enslavement. A simple time line, a map showing some of the sites of slave markets, descriptions of slave traders in the colony would be easy to display with small information panels. There is also nothing about the widespread anti-Black sentiment in the nineteenth century, including the rise of support for the American Colonization Society that wanted to return Blacks to Africa, the highly restrictive laws aimed at controlling the movement and behavior of free Blacks, and the outlandish racist stereotypes of Blacks commonly presented in the nineteenth-century press. Apparently, the museum and the NPS continue to believe that if the story of enslavement is emphasized in Boston, it will confuse people who want to understand the city's role in the achievement of American liberty—just the kind of dilemma that initially characterized the conflict over the President's House/Slavery Memorial in Philadelphia.

One possible sign of change in Boston is the Boston Middle Passage Remembrance Ceremony, held in August 2015 at Faneuil Hall as part of the International Day for the Remembrance of the Slave Trade and Its Abolition. As part of this recognition of Boston's early participation in the slave trade a historical marker will be placed in a location where it was likely the ship carrying the first enslaved Africans to the city docked in 1638 (Seelye 2015; Smith 2015).

Tiny Rhode Island was the leading American colony in terms of its participation in the slave trade. Merchants from its cities sent out ships that brought many thousands of people from Africa to the Western Hemisphere from the late seventeenth century until sometime in the first half of the nineteenth century. The voyages continued despite U.S. prohibitions on them in 1794 and 1800, and the official end of the importation of enslaved Africans in 1808. Illegal slaving voyages continued well into the nineteenth century.[28] As pointed out earlier, most of the enslaved people they purchased in Africa to be sold did not end up in the North. It was not just the slave-trading merchants themselves who were involved in the slave trade, since to hedge the costs of the voyages they regularly sold shares in them to local people who looked forward to the prospect of getting rich on the trade (Lin 2002).

For many years, little was said about slavery in Rhode Island. However, this began to change around 2000. The story of Brown University's examination of the role of the Brown family in the slave trade is now well known (see Chapter 2) and shows that, not unlike the case of other early American Ivy League universities, slave traders and slave owners were among its earliest benefactors and administrators (Brown University Steering Committee on Slavery and Justice 2006; Wilder 2013). One outgrowth of the Brown Committee's recommendations was the development of a publicly available school curriculum on the history of slavery.[29] Another has been an increase over the last decade in Rhode Island sites that tell their history of slavery.[30]

As a result of the 2006 report, Brown University, in conjunction with the city of Providence and the state, created a commission to recommend what might be done to memorialize slavery in the region and consider how to best do this (Brown University 2009). It pointed out that there has been some public recognition of the state's intimate involvement with slavery and that "Bristol and Newport's preserved waterfronts, houses, offices, and warehouses played a significant part in the slave trade. The Negro Burying Ground in Newport is perhaps the clearest reminder of the slaves who lived in the state" (Brown University 2009: 5–6). In 2014, the university dedicated the installation of sculptor Martin Puryear's memorial in a prominent location of the campus.[31] Other prominent universities have been much slower to take even this modest a step.

John Brown, his father, and his three brothers were eighteenth-century slave traders. However, John's three brothers ceased participating in the trade by the time of the American Revolution, and one of them, his brother Moses, became a Quaker and soon headed Rhode Island's Abolition Society (Rappleye 2006). He engaged in a series of very prominent public exchanges with John about the morality of slavery and slave trading. John Brown, however, remained a libertarian and continued to defend slavery and the slave trade and even voted against legislation to limit it as a member of the

U.S. House of Representatives in 1800. This largely explains why he was the first Rhode Islander tried for violating the 1794 Federal Slave Trade Act, which banned the participation of Americans in the trade of humans to or from any foreign country. John Brown made a fortune in his day from his various activities as a merchant and built a mansion atop a hill in East Providence in 1786 that his descendants donated to the Rhode Island Historical Society in 1941. Now restored, the house is a popular tour site that focuses on architecture and its impressive furniture collection.

In 2001 the Historical Society received a letter complaining that the object-oriented tour ignored Brown's involvement as a slave trader and owner, except for a brief reference in an introductory video to the mansion tour, and demanding a plan to incorporate the story of enslavement into the interpretation of the house (Melish 2009: 107). The committee soon appointed to address the issue was divided. Some saw the site as a "house of slavery" and wanted objects associated with the slave trade as part of its presentation, while others argued that Brown was more a man of this times, and slave trading and slaveholding were not central to his economic activities.

The outcome of the deliberations a short pamphlet, "Rhode Island and the Slave Trade," now sold in the building's bookshop,[32] a bronze plaque posted on the house that mentions Brown's involvement in the slave trade, and house's inclusion as an African American site in the city. On my visit in 2015 there was a longer presentation about Brown's participation in the slave trade at the outset of the tour, in a room that was once the carriage house behind the main building. There also were exhibits in the rear of the house that explained straightforwardly the Brown family's slave-trading activities and the involvement of many other Rhode Islanders in them as well. Additionally, a small temporary exhibit called "Women of Note" focused on thirty Black women from Rhode Island. The docent who led our tour began in the back of the house and told us a good deal about Brown and the slave trade and his efforts—legal and illegal—to continue engaging in it. She also told us about the division within his family over the issue.

However, once the house tour itself began, nothing more was said about enslavement and no objects in the house tour itself were associated with slavery or the slave trade. Rather, the focus was entirely on furniture, wallpaper, pictures, and various objects, and by far the most important focus of discussion was George Washington's visit to the house for tea in 1789, to mark that the state had finally ratified the Constitution—the last to do so. The docent pointed out the chair where Washington presumably sat.[33] The disconnect in content between the two parts of the tour was striking, although the guide was quite comfortable in each and not at all hesitant to talk about Brown as a slave trader in the first part.

Other Rhode Island sites include Newport's Brick Market Museum. It is not very large, but its second-floor exhibit provides an overview of the city's volatile economic past, including the importance of slave trading and slavery in its early history, and surveys the development of the city through objects, photos, and information panels. Slavery was well integrated into the exhibits and the narrative: one text panel reported that half of eighteenth-century Newport families owned slaves, most of whom came from the West Indies. There were also suggestions that slavery here was different from in the South and that since many of the enslaved were highly skilled, some were able to purchase their freedom by working as sailors or in other skilled jobs. Clearly the implication was that enslavement in Newport was not the painful, brutal experience that it was on Southern plantations. Panels also showed the recent work of local schoolchildren, who had learned about Newport's slave past.

Bristol, Rhode Island, was the most active American city in the slave trade between 1725 and 1807 (Coughtry 1981: 25; Johnson 2014: 15). It was also the home of the notorious James DeWolf, who with his family sent many ships to Africa and the Caribbean, even in the years when the slave trade was illegal in both Rhode Island and the United States. DeWolf, like Brown, continued to strongly support the idea of slavery and the slave trade after it had lost a great deal of support in the North following the American Revolution. DeWolf, who became the mastermind behind his family business operations, began conducting slaving voyages soon after the Revolution ended, when he was twenty-one. He was involved in at least 103 trips before 1807 and other undocumented ones after 1808, when it was no longer legal (Johnson 2014: 46).

DeWolf served in the Rhode Island legislature for nearly forty years and part of a term in the U.S. Senate, and he used his political connections to great advantage to promote his trading activities. Among the best known was getting President Thomas Jefferson to name DeWolf's brother-in-law as the customs collector for Bristol in 1803, so DeWolf would not have to deal with the Newport customs collector—a strong abolitionist whom

President John Adams had appointed. By the early nineteenth century DeWolf's vertical empire included distilleries that produced rum to purchase slaves in Africa, insurance companies to protect against possible losses on voyages, a bank, and plantations in Cuba, where enslaved workers grew sugarcane and produced molasses. Some claim that he was the wealthiest man in America at one point, and in 1812 he owned more ships than the American navy. The family's slave trading built the economy of Bristol, just as the slave trade in Newport had, earlier, built that city's fortunes. People in the town worked in all parts of the shipbuilding business, in the distillery, and for his other enterprises, and many purchased shares in slaving voyages as well.

Today in Bristol, there are many markers of DeWolf's earlier activity, including the DeWolf Tavern, built in 1818 as a warehouse on the water along the DeWolf Wharf. Its walls are partially made from African granite that came to Bristol as ballast on some of the ships to stabilize them on their return journeys. Handouts given to visitors, signs on the walls, and the people working at the tavern describe DeWolf's slave-trading activities. Linden Place is a magnificent mansion that James's nephew George built in 1810.[34] In 1988, the state of Rhode Island purchased it, a nonprofit organization restored it, and it now offers daily tours. DeWolf was clearly willing to do whatever it took—legal or illegal—as a merchant and politician, and his story with many of its warts is well recounted on the house tour. The guide when I visited made it clear that this was a family affair and that most of his male relatives—first his brothers and then his sons and nephews—were involved in slave-trading activities.

In 2001 ten DeWolf family descendants convened to explore their family's slave-trading and slaveholding past through trips to Bristol, Ghana, and Cuba, and they shared what they learned in the PBS video *Traces of the Trade* and the book *Inheriting the Trade: A Northern Family Confronts Its Legacy as the Largest Slave-Trading Dynasty in U.S. History* (DeWolf 2008). Katrina Browne, the descendant who organized the group, had earlier written to some two hundred of her relatives to invite their participation, but only sixty responded, and nine agreed to participate with her. When the group first met in Bristol, they discussed their reactions to learning about the slave-trading history of their ancestors and why most of them had no previous knowledge of it. Browne notes at one point that it was "in plain view" but no one saw it. As with most other Northerners, they did not want to see or understand the family's slave-trading past until the recent generation.

This chapter is rooted in the idea that collective memories have a far better chance to persist when they are associated with or made visible on prominent commemorative and public landscapes. How this is done can vary greatly: in concrete ways with explicit images, text, buildings, or statues, or indirectly through abstract, evocative signs or symbols. The key is a physical setting or something on it to remind us of the people or events associated with the site or the events it is designed to remember.

One way memories are sustained on particular, sometimes sacred, sites is through ceremonies and rituals that are periodically held there. Some will follow a particular calendar on special days; others will be more spontaneous and responsive to local needs. These ceremonies or rituals can take a wide range of forms involving music, recitations of particular texts, or physical embodiments; they may require specialists who conduct the events, such as religious figures or political leaders, but many do not. Some of these ceremonies can only occur on particular sites, while others are performed in many places but still have special emotional meaning to people no matter where they take place.

Even when sites are designed to remind people about past events or individuals, they often lose the power to do this effectively. For example, statues or historical markers of long-forgotten heroes or events outlive the significance of those they commemorate. Only some have a long existence in the memories and narratives of communities, for the memorial's importance needs to be periodically reinforced by emphasizing its connections to what is happening at the present time. This reminds us again that the needs of the present often shape the past that we remember or forget. How this is done can vary widely, but sustaining memories for long periods of time is far more difficult without some kind of presence on a community's public or commemorative landscape.

Chapter 7

Burial Grounds as Sites of Memory Recovery

> *Because white Northerners excluded Black corpses from their burial grounds the*
> *graveyard became the first truly African-American institution in the Northern*
> *colonies, and perhaps in mainland North America.*
> > —Ira Berlin, *Many Thousands Gone: The First Two Centuries*
> > *of Slavery in North America*

Landscapes and objects link the past and the present. The specific details of a woman carrying a flag, or a man wearing a military uniform, riding a horse, are not as important as the ways that we understand these representations. We create meaning and draw lessons from inanimate objects to which we attribute great emotional power. This perspective illuminates the significance for African Americans of rediscovered or recently cleaned burial grounds in the North. It took me a while to recognize and understand the significance of the burial ground for African Americans as a symbol of the 246 years of enslavement in the United States, and to realize its power as a source for memory recovery in many other places, ranging from Portsmouth, New Hampshire, to the Deep South. Rediscovered and memorialized in different ways, burial grounds can foster connections to the hidden and forgotten past of enslaved and free Blacks that many never imagined. However, the process of doing this is not always easy or quick, as the story of the African Burial Ground in New York makes clear. To explore this dynamic here I first describe the presence, rediscovery, and emotional power of Black burial grounds in the North, and then examine in greater detail two recent conflicts in Philadelphia over the recognition and memorialization of former Black burial grounds.

Despite the near invisibility of slavery in the North and the dearth of commemorative or public sites that acknowledge it, burial grounds throughout the North contain evidence that Black people had lived and died in the region for a long time, and available written records sometimes document that many of them were enslaved for part or all of their lives. The sites themselves, however, are often obscure and unknown. Older Black burial sites are often unmarked in the region; others are literally buried—covered over by buildings or roads that conceal the site—while others still are now parks or playgrounds that hide their former stories. Documentary evidence about them is often only available in dusty archives and municipal offices, if it exists at all. Too often today no one knows that they once existed.[1] There are seldom good records of the boundaries of the burial ground or the names of the people who were interred in them. Furthermore, when their presence is discovered, controversy and difficulty often ensue in trying to commemorate the site. Galland (2007) describes the battle to mark Love Cemetery in East Texas, which local Blacks had used perhaps as long ago as 1830, but that a timber company more recently acquired. When in recent years, descendants of those buried there sought access to clean and preserve the grounds to honor and remember their ancestors, the timber company refused.

Undeniably, however, these discoveries—when made—have deep emotional significance for African Americans and some whites as well. They inspire researchers, such as Terry Buckalew, to learn the names of many of those buried on the rediscovered sites and something about who they were and how they lived. They link contemporaries to a heretofore lost past; they validate accounts of enslavement; and they are proof of a Black presence centuries ago. If nothing else, they simply say, "We were here, too."

Burying grounds, as cemeteries were called before the mid-nineteenth century by both Blacks and whites, existed from the earliest days of the colonial period, but only more affluent families installed burial markers. Sometimes rural properties with enough land would have family burial plots. Graveyards, specifically, are burial areas close to churches. Potter's fields were land on which poor people were often buried in unmarked graves. In many parts of colonial North America—especially in New England—there were Common Burying Grounds in which a town or village's residents were buried. However, it seems true that no matter where burials took place, except perhaps for some potter's fields, white and Black people were segregated in death, as they were in life. Sometimes there would be separate burying grounds for each; in other cases, a burying ground would have one section for whites and another for Blacks, enslaved and free.

In many Northern villages, towns, and cities, starting in the early colonial period, Blacks were buried in potter's fields or on their owner's land, often in unmarked graves. By the beginning of the eighteenth century, many places passed laws making it illegal to bury Blacks on public land inside a settlement's limits. In Philadelphia, as Blacks formed churches in the late eighteenth century, some were buried in the churches' often very small graveyards. Over time, churches moved or closed and many of these burial sites—not clearly identified as such—were later built over. In some places in the North, enslaved and free Blacks were buried in separate sections of white cemeteries, mostly in unmarked graves. Later many of these sites were used for other purposes, which sometimes disturbed the remains, and their existence was gradually forgotten. There is not a single, simple answer to why or how this happened, often because the stories are rooted in particular local histories and events. But a good starting point is that Blacks at the time had little or no power and only meager resources to do anything differently to remember their ancestors.

For example, when a late seventeenth-century law prohibited Black burials inside New York's walls, a burial ground was designated just beyond the walls that is now known as the African Burial Ground (see Introduction). Over the years, memories of its existence faded and then disappeared. Only when the federal government was required to do an archaeological excavation before building a new federal General Services Administration office building in Lower Manhattan were old maps consulted that showed a "Negros Burial Ground" on the site. The required archaeological dig surprisingly found remains existed for 15,000 to 20,000 people, most of whom were enslaved at the time of their death. Most of the burials were undisturbed, and researchers learned a great deal about how these people lived and died at the time from the 419 burials that were removed and later reinterred in a memorial on the site.

These often-forgotten burial grounds offer a place to rediscover enslaved people in the North, going back to the earliest days of the colonial period. We only know some of their locations at the present time, but their rediscovery is now taking place not only in the North, the focus of this work, but also in the South. In Pennsylvania, a group called the Hallowed

Grounds Project is dedicated to the discovery and preservation of African American cemeteries in the state. They host an annual conference that includes people working on preservation throughout Pennsylvania, state officials such as those in agencies doing preservation, and invited speakers who are documenting historical sites. There is also a statewide Historic Preservation Office, a clearinghouse for projects that also approves applications for historical markers. Representatives from these state agencies often attend the Hallowed Grounds meetings and are available to provide help and advice.

Sandra Arnold, a graduate student at Brown University, recently established a website for a burial database of enslaved Americans, which is intended to be a user-generated source of sites throughout the country.[2] She realized that learning about a rediscovered burial ground often sparks an interest in tracking down the names and identities of people buried there. While this is not always easy or possible, it has been a way for African Americans to gain a deeper sense of their earlier history. Last, but not of least importance, for many Blacks these discoveries offer an emotionally meaningful way to connect to the ancestors and to recover their own links to the past, although, as we will see, discovery of a past burying ground, followed by demands for its public recognition and memorialization, is often a source of intense controversy.

Portsmouth, New Hampshire, a small port city (and capital in the colonial period), had the largest enslaved and free Black population in the colony. Little was known about Black life there, when Valerie Cunningham was a young African American girl, with an after-school job in the town library in the 1960s. She started wondering about Black people in colonial Portsmouth, since she had never seen any references to them in New England in the school books she had read (Sammons and Cunningham 2004: 1). For over thirty years, often on visits home to the small city, Cunningham followed the steps to learning the history of Blacks that she learned from Greene's ([1942] 1969) early pathbreaking book *The Negro in Colonial New England*. She interviewed older members of the African American community to learn the oral history they had heard when they were younger, examined town and church records, old newspapers, and other local publications, and found lost references to people and events that no one alive remembered. She wrote short biographical blurbs and stories for every Black person in the city for whom she found anything at all. Eventually she

Figure 24. A gravestone in what was once the Langdon family's Burying Ground near Portsmouth, New Hampshire, for what is believed to be the family's enslaved workers from the seventeenth and eighteenth centuries.

got together with New Hampshire public historian Mark Sammons, and the two of them produced *Black Portsmouth: Three Centuries of African-American Heritage*, a book that tells the story of Black people in the city from colonial times to the present (Sammons and Cunningham 2004).

They report that in the early city, Blacks were buried in different places than white people. These included a Negro Burial Ground[3] that was used from the late seventeenth or early eighteenth century until the 1790s, when there was pressure to use adjoining land for commercial purposes. Some Black burials took place in a back corner of Portsmouth's North Burying Ground, consistent with the "common regional practice of spatial segregation within a mostly white public burial ground" (Sammons and Cunningham 2004: 60). They also describe the large Langdon family farm just outside Portsmouth, on which enslaved people had "a small and ancient burial ground with toppled walls and inscribed burial markers (Figure 24). Oral tradition says the burial ground was for the Langdon family's enslaved people. . . . The family record of slave ownership makes it probable that these are indeed the burial markers of those farmworkers" (41).

In 2003, as Sammons and Cunningham were completing their book, the city was working on a water and sewer project on Chestnut Street in an older section of Portsmouth when a backhoe operator unearthed a coffin on the eastern edge of what was once called the "Negro Burial Ground" (Sammons and Cunningham 2004: 210). Within a few days, eight more burials were unearthed and five additional ones were identified. Roadwork was halted and archaeologists soon were called in to help determine who had been buried there. They concluded the people were of African origin. The following year the City Council appointed a committee to determine how best to honor those buried there. Over the next four years, there were a series of studies, the selection of a project team, public forums, and finally the approval of a design in October 2008, along with additional archaeological work. Fund-raising efforts began in early 2009, and included $100,000 from the small city toward the construction of the African Burying Ground Memorial Park (McDermott 2014). By mid-2014 $1.2 million had been raised, and work began in mid-August following a consecration ceremony led by Chief Oscar Ogugua Mokeme, a native Nigerian and director of the Museum of African Culture in nearby Portland, Maine. It included a libation that mixed three waters—rain, ocean, and spring water—to which community members added a pinch of salt. The libation was poured over the ground, and the names of those thought to be among the interred were read (Dandurant 2014).

The block on Chestnut Street is now closed to vehicle traffic, and the memorial (Figure 25) includes a vault at one end with the reinterred remains of the eight individuals disinterred in 2003 (Figure 26). The other end of the memorial features a granite wall with two figures, a man representing the first African enslaved in Portsmouth in 1645 on one side, and a woman representing Mother Africa, on the other. Their hands reach toward each other but are not quite touching. Between them etched on the ground and connecting the two ends of the memorial are the words from the 1779 petition to the New Hampshire legislature from twenty Portsmouth slaves asking for their freedom. It was not acted upon until 2013 (Chapter 2; Macalaster 2013).

The memorial's two-day opening ceremony began on May 21, 2015, with an all-night vigil in the New Hope Baptist Church. Those in attendance sat, sang, and kept the ancestors company before their remains were reinterred in new coffins made using wood from Nigeria. The following morning the memorial site was packed for the ceremony, which began with

Figure 25. The sign to one of the two entrances to the African Burying Ground in Portsmouth, New Hampshire.

a talk by sculptor Jerome Matthews of Savannah, explaining his goals for the project, the design and objects on the site, and his collaboration with the middle school students who designed the tiles on it, based on Ghanaian Kente cloth designs. The eight coffins were carried to the crypt one by one—and each was solemnly lowered into the crypt in the reburial ceremony. Afterward, Chief Mokeme performed a consecration ritual, first praying in Ibo and then translating his words into English. He sprinkled African ashes and sand on the caskets and then poured water as a libation over them. Finally, there was a commemoration at the Portsmouth Middle School with short talks and music with many references to the ancestors and what they had faced and the acts of present-day Portsmouth in remembering their suffering.[4]

Many of New England's cities and towns had African (or "Negro") Burying Grounds located at the edge of their Common Burying Grounds that were used in the colonial period and often well into the nineteenth century. Many, and probably most, of those interred remain unidentified and unmarked today. One striking exception is found in Newport, Rhode Island, where "God's Little Acre," as the Black section of the Common Burying Ground is known, contains the remains of almost three hundred enslaved and free Blacks (Figure 27). The exact number is not easy to know,

Figure 26. The remains of eight people were found under Portsmouth's Chestnut Street in 2003 and then reinterred in a ceremony in the crypt (located below the circle where visitors have placed flowers) at this African Burying Ground.

since often poor families could not pay for stone burial markers of which there are a good number. Newport claims to have the oldest and largest markers of enslaved and free Africans in colonial America, with gravestones dating as far back as 1720.[5] After the 1830s there were some burials of non-Blacks in the section too—but apparently not many. While it is distinct from the area for white burials, it is not walled off or labeled as separate. The burying ground is still kept as part of the public landscape, and many of the gravestones are maintained or even replaced as needed.[6]

Other burying grounds in small and large colonial-era rural areas, towns, and cities in Connecticut, Massachusetts, New Jersey, Pennsylvania, New York (e.g., Cruson 2007) were forgotten and only recently rediscovered. In the years since I began this project, many news stories have reported on Black burying grounds in the North that were either unknown at all or overgrown to the point where none of the gravesites could be recognized. For many, records suggest they could be the resting place for

Figure 27. "God's Little Acre" was the section of Newport, Rhode Island's Common Burying Ground reserved for enslaved and free Black people, beginning in the early 1700s.

both African Americans who were enslaved and others who were free. One such location is Schuyler Flatts, the Albany home of General Philip Schuyler, a Revolutionary War hero and the father-in-law of Alexander Hamilton. In 2005, a backhoe operator working on a construction project uncovered a skull, and soon the burials of fourteen people were found. Research shows that they were of African origin, although one of the women also had Indian ancestors. The state researchers said their bodies showed signs of arthritis, stress, and strong muscles. A Schuyler Flatts Burial Ground Project formed and in 2016, the fourteen, whose names are not known, were placed in pine coffins decorated with the Sankofa sign (a Ghanaian Akan image that literally means learning from the past to build the future) and reburied in a section of the St. Agnes Cemetery that over-looks the Hudson River, where wealthy families are buried (Grondahl 2015; Hill 2016).

In Philadelphia, a 2013 archaeological report provided a description of some forty-three African American burial sites described as potter's fields, almshouses, and church and Burial Grounds known to have been opened between 1780 and 1849. While some of these were not entirely unknown, it is fair to say that few people had any idea that they once existed. The report also makes it clear that "the known research regarding Black ceme-teries in Philadelphia . . . should not be considered exhaustive or compre-hensive, as much more documentation needs to be researched and collected" (Mooney and Morrell 2013: Appendix C.1). Very few of the sites are still burying grounds. In some, the report states that the older burials are believed to be still intact, and in other cases the human remains were significantly disturbed or moved when churches were either sold, moved, or closed prior to new construction on the site. In many, the remains were moved to the Lebanon or Olive Cemeteries, both of which opened in the late 1840s; Lebanon was closed in 1899 and Olive in 1923. Burials from both were transferred to Eden Cemetery in nearby Collingdale, which opened in 1902 and is now the most significant African American cemetery in the region.

Burials from two nineteenth-century church graveyards of the Philadelphia First African Baptist Churches (the church split in 1816) were excavated between 1983 and 1990, after they were rediscovered during a major construction project in the city. During the dig, the archaeological team set up an observation platform overlooking the site, where the public could stand, view the dig itself, and talk to a member of the archaeological team about their work. The remains were then examined carefully at the Smithsonian Institution in Washington. The research showed that 40 percent of the burials were young people; the average age of females was thirty-nine, and males, forty-five; people's bones showed the effects of poor diets and hard work; and some of the burials showed the survival of African traditions, such as the placement of plates on the stomachs or shoes on the coffins. The remains were reinterred at Eden Cemetery in Collingdale. Yamin (2008: 100–119) describes the process that John Milner Associates undertook before they began their work. They consulted with the city's Historical Commission, members of the descendant congregation, and the African American Museum located nearby to explain what they planned to do and why they thought this was the best way to proceed, and they promised to keep them appraised throughout the process—which they did (Robinson 1988; Yamin 2008: 103–5).[7]

Black communities express strong emotions when informed about these rediscoveries and have worked to create meaningful ceremonies and appropriate memorial markers for them. The language used to discuss these sites and the people buried at them are a powerful reminder to many of the trials and tribulations that their ancestors, first brought here as slaves, endured and survived. This emotion is both joyous, surrounding the rediscovery of the remains, and terribly painful, thinking about the ancestors' suffering and agony. The past and the ancestors are not an abstraction. For many the tangible, literal remains lead to a search for the recovery of their own personal forgotten past. This search is less about the challenge of identifying one's own family genealogy and more about the reinforcement of a collective identity, which can come up against significant white resistance when there are demands to mark newly discovered burial grounds as sacred. To illustrate this crucial point, I turn to two recent examples from Philadelphia that followed on the heels of the conflict over how to mark enslavement at the President's House/ Slavery Memorial in Independence National Historical Park. Intense controversies developed in both cases about how to honor ancestral remains in the rediscovered burying grounds. These disputes, both of which became quite intense at times, led me to better appreciate the power of place generally and, more specifically, how Burying Grounds today serve as important sites of memory recovery where written and other historical records are only partially available (Rollason 2016)

The first conflict involves a potter's field in what is now the Germantown section of the city. Quakers purchased land in 1750s to be used as a burying ground for "Strangers, Negroes and Mulattoes as Die in any part of Germantown forever" (Stackhouse 2003: 26). The earliest recorded burials were in 1755, and the site's use as a burying ground might have continued until 1916 (Mooney and Morell 2013: Appendix A.3). In his 2003 article on the Germantown potter's field, Stackhouse (2003) reports that local boys once played baseball there and used headstones as bases. The headstone of a John Brown who had died in 1874 was a makeshift home plate. Burials diminished in number by the beginning of the twentieth century, and the field soon became a dump filled with trash and broken glass. The property was made into a playground in 1920, and boys from the Wissahickon Boys Club, a Black club, were among those who used it.

Germantown was first settled by Europeans in 1686, with a good number of German Quakers. While some Quakers in the city and region were slave owners, a minority of voices in the group opposed slavery, and by the time of the American Revolution, these voices came to dominate the sect and those who chose to maintain their slaves were forced to leave the group. As more and more free Blacks lived in the region, a number settled in and around Germantown, and there is at least one well-known Underground Railroad "station" in the area. Accounts suggest that whites and Blacks lived together more easily in Germantown than in other parts of the city (O'Grady 1981). Black churches and other organized groups developed in the late nineteenth century, and the Black population in Germantown increased during the twentieth century and became a majority in the 1960s. There was some informal integration, but mostly separate white and Black institutions (O'Grady 1981).

In 1952, the Philadelphia Housing Authority (PHA) decided to build a sixteen-story public housing project on the block with the burial ground, and construction began the following spring. At the time, people reported that the work uncovered not only tombstones but also human remains, some of which were found years later. At the time there was no thought, let alone a requirement, that PHA first needed to conduct an archaeological study of the area that would be disturbed by the construction. Not only did the use of heavy building equipment destroy many of the remains, but a subsequent modern playground paved over a portion of the former burial ground, showing the city's total lack of interest in how the site had been used in the past.[8]

By 2010, the building, like many other high-rise public housing build-ings in Philadelphia and other cities, had become a dysfunctional eyesore. The PHA decided to tear it down and hired an architectural firm to provide a possible plan for the site that would consist of low-rise buildings; how-ever, the plan did not include any historical or archaeological work. It called for new housing on all four sides of the block with parking and some green space in the center, which was over the burying ground. People in the local community protested both the decision and the process by which it was made, which did not include local community involvement. Clearly, they felt unheard by the city's housing authority. The community emphasized that they wanted a voice in the decisions about what would be built, where it would be built, and who would live in the new housing.

Second, and even more contentious, was the demand from the newly formed Northwest Neighbors of Germantown and other local groups that neither the new housing nor the parking lot be built over the former burial ground, which was at odds with the PHA proposal. The Northwest Neigh-bors attended public meetings, threatened lawsuits, and emphasized that the plans for the site had to protect the remains of the ancestors and that nothing should be built over them. They made it clear that to honor ances-tors, the former burial ground should be recognized as a sacred site and that the hallowed ground be marked and undisturbed. In the process, they built a coalition of public and local groups that supported their position.

Finally, there was the question of the status of the playground located over the burials that dated back to the 1920s,. Could another location for it be found nearby to meet the needs of the children in the area? The housing authority defended its plan for a while and at one point tried to mobilize community voices from those people who were not concerned about the historical nature of the site. However, PHA soon realized that its proposal would not pass muster of a Section 106 review of the project, as specified in the 1966 National Historic Preservation Act, which requires an archaeological review of any site of possible historical significance involving federal funds—in this case from the U.S. Department of Housing and Urban Development (HUD).

As a result, PHA changed course and in early 2012 announced it would not knowingly build over any human remains. However, because of PHA's earlier actions, there was still significant skepticism about whether the research it was now willing to conduct would actually be done properly. PHA then undertook an initial archaeological study in the spring of 2012, using "ground truthing" radar in areas that were believed to have been outside the original boundaries of the burying ground to make sure they contained no human remains.[9] It revealed "anomalies beneath the surface in three locations . . . that are similar in size to both an adult interment and a child's interment" (Mosbrucker 2012). There was agreement that these results would require an archaeological dig.

In September 2012, the city's zoning board held a hearing to consider PHA's new project proposal for the site. However, the Northwest Neighbors, led by Lisa Hopkins, spearheaded an effort by various groups to argue that this was premature, given PHA's history on the site. They demanded that no new housing be built until the historical and archaeological study research was completed, to ensure the absence of human remains, and that the site of the former burial ground be preserved as a memorial park with no housing on it (Coard 2012). Hopkins stressed that unlike the earlier project this one should listen to the ancestors and not dishonor them. PHA responded that the process was still open and that it had applied to HUD to obtain a waiver for the Section 106 review for the project, despite the fact that the review was indisputably called for in the National Historic Preservation Act. Hopkins and others suggested that the burying ground could and should be listed in the National Register of Historic Places. As the controversy escalated, the number of interested parties increased and now included the Pennsylvania Historical and Museum Commission and the Philadelphia Preservation Alliance. They made recommendations as part of the discussions between HUD, the Northwest Neighbors, and other community groups. HUD then denied the immediate waiver and a Section 106 review was ordered.

In late October 2012, it was announced that there would be an excavation on the site that would examine the three areas outside what were believed to be the original boundaries of the burial ground to further investigate the anomalies that had been identified in the spring. The next month, the zoning board approved the plan for the new housing, which could be built after the archaeological work was completed. Weary of the delays in December, the PHA head Michael Johns attended a public meeting to discuss the future of the site and suggested that perhaps it would be best simply to refurbish the existing tower rather than to tear it down and build new units on the site, if the plan to build the new homes did not work. Predictably, this deliberately provocative act only raised tensions and failed to advance a viable solution.

The archaeological dig began in late winter 2013 and focused on the areas where the anomalies were found by the ground truthing radar. As the PHA continued to float the possible option of rehabilitating the old and now empty building, Lisa Hopkins of the Northwest Neighbors was firm that her coalition wanted recognition of the burial ground as sacred and that they did not oppose new housing on land that contained no human remains. However, there were as yet no plans for replacing the playground that had formerly existed over the burial site and moving it to another part of the neighborhood.

By late March 2013, the initial results of the archaeological study showed that there were no human remains next to the high-rise tower that was still standing or in the other areas where PHA planned to put up the new housing on the three sides of the site (Quinn 2013b). The final report completed in May was sent to HUD and the National Park Service's State Historic Preservation Office. Its findings were also of interest to the more than a dozen local, city, and state groups and organizations that had so far expressed an interest in the future of the site.[10] Although a local architect, who was a former board member of the Germantown Historical Association, presented three alternative designs to the PHA proposal—two of which included a playground—PHA declared that it would proceed with its own design, which already had zoning approval (Quinn 2013a).

Late in 2013 a programmatic agreement arising from the negotiations following the Section 106 review was signed. It involved HUD, the PHA, the State Historic Preservation Office, and the Advisory Council on Historic Preservation and was signed by twenty interested local groups, city officials, agencies of the city, state, and federal government. The agreement spelled out the details of how the project would proceed. It included provisions for the implosion of the high-rise building, additional archaeological work in some areas of the site, the presence of archaeological monitors to work carefully with the contractors to ensure that any human remains uncovered would be brought to the attention of the State Historical Preservation Office and the Advisory Council on Historic Preservation. It stipulated that there would be "no activities which might disturb or damage the remains until all parties have determined whether excavation is necessary and/or desirable." Remains that might be uncovered may be disinterred and stored for reburial at a later time and "will be treated with the highest level of integrity and sensitivity."[11] Last, the agreement specified that no new buildings would be constructed within the known boundaries of the potter's field and that that area would be returned to a green space upon completion of the construction.

Ten months later, the implosion of the empty tower took place early on a quiet Saturday morning, following a libation ceremony organized to honor the ancestors buried in the potter's field decades earlier. Ron McCoy, an ATAC member who presided over the ceremony, said, "I'm going to pour libations for the ancestors. We don't know who's here, but we know they're ours" (Lubrano 2014). Michael Coard wondered, "How many places in Philadelphia can you say that white people, Jewish or any other folk were buried at a location and people just forgot about it, built a city structure over it. Today we see an end to the desecration of our ancestors and the beginning of their consecration" (Lee 2014). Within six weeks the three-story-high rubble had been cleared from the site and soon thereafter the new construction began. People began to move into the new housing in late 2015. A meeting involving the community, the Philadelphia Housing Authority, and HUD in December 2015 discussed remaining issues. The work on the new buildings did turn up some artifacts of interest that will be placed either in the planned community center or in the Germantown Historical Society. Grass is to be planted over the Burying Ground. An application also has been submitted to the Philadelphia Historic Neighborhood Commission to place a historical marker on the Burying Ground that will recognize Black soldiers buried there who died nearby in the Battle of Germantown in October 1777, as well as the Wissahickon Boys Club.

Some people in Philadelphia were taken aback at the intensity of feelings displayed in the conflict over Germantown's potter's field. The city housing authority officials were not ready for the strong, organized opposition to PHA's initial plan to tear down the old high-rise building and to construct new public housing on Queen Lane without conducting any prior research or consulting the local community. Similarly, the intense emotion expressed over the need to recognize the Bethel Burying Ground in South Philadelphia in 2013 caught the local community and city officials by surprise. This is particularly curious in the aftermath of the recent conflicts over the President's House/ Slavery Memorial and the Germantown potter's field. The demands to mark the Bethel Burying Ground was motivated by the need to recognize the African American past in Philadelphia and the need to honor ancestors some of whom had been enslaved in the city in its early years. The conflict that developed included a wide range of actors and focused, in part, on who had the ultimate authority to make decisions about the future of the site. It is once again an example of a failure to recognize the strong identities and collective memories of the participants.

One of the largest potter's fields used during the eighteenth century in Philadelphia was located in a portion of Washington Square that Blacks at the time called Congo Square, less than two blocks south of Independence Hall. After independence, and for more than a decade, a group of free Black leaders, which included Richard Allen and Absalom Jones, petitioned to fence off and lease the Negro portion of the field, but the city never approved these requests. In 1794 the city decided to end burials on the square altogether (Buckalew 2015). There are reports that some of those buried in Washington Square were reinterred in the newly founded St. Thomas Church and later moved to Lebanon and then later to Eden Cemeteries.

By 1800 Philadelphia did not permit Black burials inside the city except in a handful Black churches' graveyards. But these had very limited space. In 1810, the Mother Bethel AME Church, founded and led by the once enslaved Richard Allen, purchased vacant land a short distance away, just south of what were then the city limits, to use as a burying ground. Allen felt it was important to provide burial aid as part of the church's mission, not only to its own members and their families, but also for poor Black nonmembers who could not afford the cost of burials. The Bethel Burying Ground (BBG) was used until 1864 when the small space—about a third of an acre—was full with burials stacked on top of each other, to a depth of eighteen or twenty feet. The church needed money, so a few years later they agreed to rent the land above the burials to a man who wanted to store his sugar refinery's wagons on the land, with the proviso that the burials not be disturbed.

Before long it was evident that the renter and probably others were using the site as a garbage dump, and people described its condition as shameful (Buckalew 2012: 7). The lease was soon ended, and a wall was built around the burying ground in 1873. By 1885 the church needed money to pay the mortgage on its latest building, and over the next few years it worked out an agreement to sell the site to the city for a generous payment of $10,000 in 1889. The lot was described in the press as rubbish strewn and a place where neighborhood children played until the city cleaned and improved it a decade later, transforming it into a school garden for a few years and then into the still-extant Weccacoe playground in the early twentieth century (Buckalew 2012: 12–15).[12] The burial ground lies under about a third of the present playground, and a deteriorating community center building built in 1925 sits over some of the burials.

Memory of the burial ground in the city faded over time and few remembered it, until historian and researcher Terry Buckalew found a reference to it while working on a project for a television series on the history of Blacks in the nineteenth-century city. He was interested in its location and its years of use, so he began to do some research. In 2011, he shared his findings with Rev. Mark Tyler of the Mother Bethel AME Church. Tyler said he had had no knowledge of the burying ground and was quite interested in Buckalew's findings, which were mainly based on city records, books on the famous church, and newspaper reports, since church records, including burial records from the time, had been lost and perhaps destroyed. Buckalew thought the site was important, and he spent laborious hours in the city records office. To date he has identified the names of almost 2,500 of the people buried there and often their gender, age, and their parents or children.

One is Ignatius Beck, who was a free Black illegally captured in Pennsylvania and taken south and then sold back into slavery. After being used to build the U.S. Capitol he escaped and returned to Philadelphia, where he

founded the Free Produce Society of Philadelphia that spearheaded boy-
cotts against any products made using slave labor. By 2014 Buckalew developed a website that he often updates with events, including burials, that
occurred on the same date at the Burying Ground.[13] He often posts items
about those buried on the site, including biographical information he has
learned about them, on the anniversary of their interment. In 2013 Buckalew asked the Philadelphia Historical Commission to include Bethel Burying Ground on the Philadelphia Register of Historic Places. Tyler supported
the historical recognition of the site, but was critical of Buckalew for pre-
paring the proposal without what he considered sufficient consultation with
the church. Tyler had the view that, as the onetime owner of the land, the
church should have had a privileged role in the process.

Buckalew's request was granted in a few weeks, which meant that the
Historical Commission would have jurisdiction over future construction
on the site (Salisbury 2013a, 2013d). An important consequence of this
designation was its relevance for the local neighborhood association, the
Queen Village Neighbors Association and the Friends of Weccacoe Park,
who were among those who had earlier submitted a proposal for a "green"
renovation of the playground and had received $535,000 from the state and
the city for their project. The historical designation meant that any changes
to the Burying Ground part of the playground would require prior approval
from the Historical Commission.

Unanswered was how the historical designation might affect the renovation that the community very much wanted to see go forward. Over the next
few years this would turn out to be highly contentious, since the parties
interested in the site often strongly differed in their conception of appropriate
commemoration. While there was widespread agreement that none of the
burials should be disturbed, emotions ran high over other issues. The land
belonged to the city, but Mayor Michael Nutter and his administration were
more than a little reluctant to make any decision that might produce a strong
reaction from either the local community, Mother Bethel, or those who
wanted a clear recognition of the historical significance of the Burying
Ground. Some, including the recently formed Friends of Bethel Burying
Ground, thought that the land over the burials should be fenced in, the community center moved, and an appropriate memorial placed on the site. At
the other extreme were those who felt that a grassy area with a historical
marker and perhaps a bench would be sufficient, but that the land above the
burials could still be part of the playground and house the community center.

Archaeological test excavations and ground-penetrating radar taken in July 2013 uncovered at least one headstone, confirmed that the Burying Ground covered about a third of the playground site, and marked its limits so that playground renovation could proceed and not disturb the burials (McDuffie 2013; Salisbury 2013c).[14] The researchers estimated that there were at least five thousand people interred there—far more than was previously believed. One concern was that the utility lines—sewer, water, and electrical—required for the playground renovation might disturb the burials. In addition, because the city's large water lines in the nearby streets were over 175 years old, Buckalew and others were concerned that they were unreliable and if one broke, as many older pipes in the city have in recent years, it would flood the burial ground, possibly creating sinkholes, and human remains would soon be floating down local streets. Third, there was a danger from the water pipes over the burials running to the community center building.

Tyler again asserted that Mother Bethel had a special responsibility, because the Church had once owned the Burying Ground. For a time, both the city and local community groups accepted this and deferred to Tyler. They said they could accept whatever Mother Bethel preferred. Others disagreed. Michael Coard and ATAC were increasingly explicit that a historical marker on the site alone was insufficient; rather, the key issue was a strong need to honor and remember the city's ancestors—meaning the first generations of Blacks, enslaved and free. When Tyler continued to privilege his church as the direct descendants of those buried in the cemetery, ATAC jumped into the fray and formed a committee called "NOT over Our Dead Bodies" to protect ancestral and historical memory. Coard declared the city's Parks and Recreation Department "racially insensitive" and called for people to attend a public meeting Mother Bethel organized, asking, "Are you going to avenge them by doing what they [the ancestors] ask?" (Salisbury 2013b; also Ceil Keller e-mail, November 24, 2013). Coard made it clear that he was ready to challenge the city and its renovation plans, saying, "A fun-and-games children's playground and a solemn and hallowed cemetery cannot coexist and will not coexist at least not without a loud, public, confrontation, and sustained holy war" (Salisbury 2013b).

The public meeting at Mother Bethel took place on the day of a severe snow and ice storm in the city, and many people who tried to attend, Coard and myself included, were unable to get there. People were angry that Tyler did not reschedule it, despite requests to do so. At the meeting, he circulated a letter he had solicited from five of Richard and Sarah Allen's descendants that basically approved his proposal for no disturbance to the burials, permitting the playground renovation including the area above the burials, registration of the burying ground as a National Historic Landmark, and a commemoration that marked the site as historically significant and included the name of every person interred there.

Soon a new group, the Friends of Bethel Burying Ground Coalition (FBBGC), formed and led by former Philadelphia mayor Ed Rendell's former Managing Director Joe Certaine.[15] The group strongly articulated Certaine's argument that the city should make the decisions about the site since it owned the land, not local interested parties. They called for a moratorium on construction plans and asked for an engineering study to precede any work. "This is public property," said Certaine, "and some people are trying to treat it as though it were not" (Salisbury 2014b). Congressman Bob Brady, the head of the Democratic Party in the city, in whose district the burying ground is located, sent a letter to Mayor Nutter supporting the Friends of Bethel Burying Ground Coalition's request and emphasizing the city's responsibility for the site. "I am asking the City to rethink its current renovation plans while taking into consideration the national historic importance of the property" (Salisbury 2014b).

Next, the FBBGC called a public meeting of interested persons at the city's African American Museum, at which Certaine and Buckalew reported on a recent meeting they had attended with the Mayor's Chief of Staff Everett Gillison and other city officials. They explained both their insistence that it was the city's responsibility to make a decision, since it owned the land and the reasons behind their demand for an engineering study of the site prior to any renovation of the playground (Salisbury 2014a). The group emphasized the need to move the ninety-year-old community center that sits right above the burials and to cap its electrical, water, and sewer pipes underneath. Certaine again strongly emphasized that the city was responsible for the site. He and others underscored that they were not interested in a dispute with Mother Bethel or the local community and hoped for a mutually agreeable solution. The group decided there was a need for a prayer and libation ceremony at the Burying Ground and hoped to hold one soon to remember the ancestors buried there. Finally, there was support for filing a proposal to have the Bethel Burying Ground declared a National Historic Site.

The Friends of Bethel Burying Ground Coalition met again two weeks later and it was reported that the city had agreed to halt all work on the playground and the community center for the time being and to talk further about next steps (Muhammad 2014). The meeting focused on many of the points made at the earlier one, and Certaine, who presided, spoke about a meeting with Gillison and other city officials two days earlier, at which the city representatives seemed to understand the group's demands more fully and offered some reassuring steps: The water department would undertake a study to determine how to best deal with the aging water main, and the Deputy Mayor for Environmental and Community Resources Michael DiBerardinis reassuringly said that he did not see anything in the Friends of Bethel Burying Ground Coalition's proposals that could not be accomplished. Certaine announced plans for a prayer vigil and libation to emphasize the sacred nature of the Burying Ground and the imperative to treat it differently than an ordinary site. "We need our energy and the ancestors need to know we have not forgotten them," he added. Tyler, who had been at the recent meeting with the city, was asked to officiate but, unexpectedly, he declined to participate. Plans were discussed for having African drummers present. In the end, however, the ceremony was postponed since there was a torrential downpour in the city on the scheduled day.

In early May 2014, Gillison, the Mayor's Chief of Staff, presided over a packed public meeting with several hundred people in attendance at the African American Museum to discuss plans for the site (Russ 2014). The Queen Village Neighbors Association and the Friends of Weccacoe Playground had mobilized their members, but so had the Bethel Burying Ground Coalition and ATAC. In addition, city officials attended, including the City Council member for the area, Mark Squilla. The standing-room crowd jammed into the large auditorium before the meeting even began. Gillison spoke for perhaps fifteen minutes, reviewing the history of the site and identifying key issues. These included the old water pipe on Queen Street, a mulch pile that was covering some of the burials, and the community center that he described as "temporarily resolved," meaning that the issue had not yet been addressed but would be. He reported that the city would address the water pipe issue by either shutting it if all houses in the area had water access through other existing pipes or replacing it. The archaeological firm that had done work on the site the previous summer would deal with the mulch pile. Gillison also promised that the meeting would be the first of many public meetings—but more than nineteen months later, when Gillison and Nutter left office in January 2016, this was still the only one that was held.

Tension increased in the room when Gillison opened the session for questions and comments. Young children spoke and said, basically, "Please don't take away my playground." Some of the newsletters from the neighborhood association as well as talk in the community had led people to believe that the entire playground was at risk and that some people were proposing to close it rather than to protect the section over the Burying Ground. A few voices said that worrying about an old burial ground was a waste of time and the city's money, when the city schools were under great financial stress. Gillison disagreed, saying that a city always has multiple issues that require attention.

Soon, common interests and alliances emerged. Some local residents spoke in favor of doing something that would teach people about the history of the site, and others felt that some kind of significant memorial would be a good idea. When people claimed that this one project was unique and placed a special burden on the neighborhood, Gillison pointed to the Queen Lane burying ground in Germantown. Others emphasized the need to remember and honor the ancestors, and Michael Coard, while thanking Gillison for calling the meeting, asked the group if five thousand people from any other ethnic group in the city were buried in a site, would there would be any prolonged conversation about what to do? Rather, he suggested, there needed to be a national monument on the site.

There had been a lot of constructive comments but few specific commitments other than to address the issue of the water pipes and to hold more meetings. In addition, an undercurrent of coded language masked some significant differences between the sides. Some neighborhood people resented "outsiders," meaning people from other parts of the city involved in what they saw as a local matter. There was also a clear racial dimension, as almost all the neighborhood people in attendance were white, while most of those who wanted a significant memorial for the site were African American. Finally, while almost no one said that the history of the site did not matter, the core of the differences had to do with the community center and whether it should or could be removed from its current location to another part of the playground. It was not clear that there was any common ground, and afterward Certaine articulated this to his allies when he complained about how the Queen Village groups that packed meetings and the lack of any commitment from Gillison to the Friends of Bethel Burying Ground Coalition's key points. Certaine was skeptical about what would happen next.

The next few months proved that Certaine's instincts following the meeting were on target. He reported in late September at a FBBGC meeting that Tyler had agreed in June to moving the community center building and sealing the utility lines, so long as this did not disturb any of the remains below. He agreed to talk to the local groups in the community to tell them that there should be no activity on top of the burials themselves once the center was moved and said he would participate in the libation ceremony now scheduled for the early fall. A few months later, however, he broke off communication with the coalition members and said he was working on other issues. Meanwhile Terry Buckalew spearheaded the submission of an application to have the Burying Ground recognized as a National Historic Site.

The Bethel Burying Ground Coalition's long-awaited libation ceremony to honor the ancestors buried on the site took place in October 2014. About one hundred people gathered a few blocks away and marched with a police escort to the Weccacoe Playground, where the hour-long ceremony was held. A number of people carried black, green, and red flags. Mwalimu Waset, who had done much of the organizing for the event, played the drum as people gathered and then managed the proceedings. In attendance were both men and women—older rather than younger—and only a handful of whites.

Ron McCoy led the processional and officiated at the ceremony. Waset spoke about the debt owed to the ancestors, the need to honor them and to pass the knowledge about them to the younger generation. Three different religious leaders spoke, as well as Certaine and Coard. McCoy's libation was longer than what he typically does at other events I've attended, but his tone and warmth were the same (Figure 28). Mama Gail, head of the Universal Love Ministries in the city, read from a notebook the names of some people buried there, and McCoy asked people in attendance to read aloud the names of people buried there from cards distributed earlier to the crowd. Terry Buckalew was recognized for his hard work to rediscover the burial ground and research the names of those buried there. As a whole, my sense was that the good turnout, the flags, the power of the site, and the thoughts expressed during the ceremony made the event very meaningful for those in attendance.

The religious leaders offered comments that came very much out of their own individual traditions and tied to the theme of honoring the people buried at the site in the nineteenth century (Figure 29). They also

Figures 28 and 29. Ron McCoy and Lisa Hopkins (top) leading the celebrants at a libation ceremony at the Bethel Burying Ground in Philadelphia in recognition of the more than five thousand Black people, both enslaved and free, who were buried there between 1820 and 1864. Nick Taliaferro and Mwalimu Waset address the attendees (bottom).

emphasized what the interred had gone through in their lives, their struggle for existence, and their resistance to the conditions of the times. Certaine and Coard spoke more about the specific demands for the site and what they would like to see happen. Certaine expressed a certain pessimism that much would happen very soon and suggested that the FBBGC needed to mobilize for the next year's mayoral election campaign and force the candidates to address the Bethel Burying Ground issue. He talked about the specific concern that the community center be rebuilt on the site of the present tennis court at the playground. Coard was more direct in explaining what it is about the center that most upset him—the bathrooms over the remains. "I don't want people pissing on the graves of my ancestors." As usual he was articulate and graphic, which was useful in focusing on the politics to express why the ceremony was needed in the first place.

As Philadelphia moved into an electoral campaign for a new Mayor in 2015, the issue of the Bethel Burying Ground's future went into a deep freeze. There were no more public meetings; no more discussions with the administration; and no decisions in response to the FBBGC's demands and the community's wish to move ahead with the playground renovations. The application to declare the Bethel Burying Ground a National Historic Site was submitted to the National Park Service, moved through its bureaucracy, and was finally approved in January 2016. In the city, the new mayor Jim Kenney and the city's managing director Michael DiBerardinis soon called a meeting of the interested parties and said that while the renovation of the playground would soon go forward, none of it would take place over the burials, that the work would be supervised by an archaeologist, that the National Historic Site status was a significant achievement, and that the mayor pledged his full commitment that the City of Philadelphia would work to ensure the protection and preservation of Bethel Burying Ground as a publicly owned historic site.

Another meeting was held in July 2016 with the city officials, but little was firmed up about plans for the site. The city did, however, agree to do a study of the condition of the community center building, which was completed but not released for months. Then, in April 2017, Michael Coard (2017) wrote a column in the *Philadelphia Tribune*, asking why the city was so slow to respond to the need to protect the Black burying ground when it had quickly reacted when a Jewish cemetery had recently been desecrated, Mayor Kenney called Coard a few days later, saying that the city was prepared to remove the old building from above the burials, mark off the area above the remains, and contribute $50,000 to launch the fund-raising for a memorial on the site. Since then, there has been another meeting where the city officials again committed to removing the building and putting an appropriate memorial on the site. To do this they said they soon formed a committee to oversee the process, including all the stakeholders, that would also be responsible for helping select a memorial from the designs they hoped to solicit from a national competition.

Archaeology is an important tool for exploration and recovery of the past. It can also become very political, as I learned in research I conducted about its use in the Old City of Jerusalem, which both Jews and Palestinians understood as ways to validate their own political claims while denying those of the other side (Ross 2007: chap. 6). The dig at the President's House/ Slavery Memorial site clearly had a political side to it as well, validating the shift of the narrative on the site from "this is where George Washington lived and worked while he was President" to "this is where George Washington held nine of his enslaved Africans who lived and worked here while Washington was President." For many people, it was no longer a "Washington slept here" story but a "Washington was a slave owner in Philadelphia" story that more than slightly tarnished his image and that of other slave-owning Founding Fathers.

A visible presence on the public landscape is a crucial way that collective memories are built, preserved, and transmitted. However, presence alone is not sufficient. For memories to matter, they must be sustained over time, meaning that the landscape and objects on it have to be described and interpreted in ways that establish emotional connections for people. Without narratives about a site and objects on it or ceremonies and ritual expressions, their emotional power will easily diminish and fade over time.

In the epigraph to this chapter Ira Berlin suggests that burying grounds or cemeteries were "the first truly African-American institution in the Northern colonies" (1998:62). He goes on to say that white slaveowners were uninterested in dealing with the deaths of the enslaved. In addition, separate areas for Black burials afforded the enslaved a measure of control over them, including the ceremonies and events that occurred on them. The African Burial Ground in New York, for example, was in a swampy area outside the city walls. The introductory video at the National Park Service's visitor center there reported that it provided a place where the enslaved could be together away from white supervision, where they could remember their ancestors and conduct ceremonies rooted in African traditions. It afforded them a small measure of control that joined the community together and could be conducted free of white control. In many ways, this pattern never ended, since Black and white burials in the past and today are only sometimes integrated.

Black burying grounds were public spaces associated with the enslaved, and later, free Blacks. They also were associated with rituals, music, prayer, and they became emotionally meaningful to the descendants of those interred in them. The intensity with which people have called for restoration of rediscovered burying grounds and ceremonies to remember the ancestors whose remains they contain well illustrates Berlin's point and the power they hold for African Americans today, even when the identities of the specific people in them are rarely known.

Chapter 8

Overcoming Collective Forgetting

Indeed, the last years of the twentieth century and the first years of the twenty-first have witnessed an extraordinary resurgence of popular interest in slavery, which has stimulated its study and provided the occasion for a rare conversation between historians and an interested public. Slavery has a greater presence in American life now than at any time since the Civil War ended.
— Ira Berlin, "American Slavery in History and Memory"

The history of race in the United States can easily be characterized as frequent episodes of collective forgetting. We forgot how many Blacks fought in the Revolution. And historians have described how post–Civil War reconciliation between whites in the North and South required "forgetting" about Black participation in the war and the fact that slavery was the primary cause of it (e.g., Linenthal 1993: Blight 2001). This forgetting certainly is connected to the segregation of and discrimination against African Americans in both regions afterward as well. It also "normalized" whiteness and treated any deviations from it as problematic.

There is surely no single, best explanation for how and why collective forgetting about enslavement in the North occurred. The six plausible explanations for its disappearance from American's popular understandings, discussed in Chapter 3, do not mean that no one in the region had any knowledge of Northern slavery after it ended. Certainly historians, both professional and amateur, knew and wrote about slavery throughout the North, as these chapters have described; also, some white families were aware of its practice among their ancestors, but most probably were not;[1] and some Black families in the region as well knew about the enslavement of their own ancestors or those of friends in the North. However, awareness was hardly public or widespread,[2] despite the existence of public records, including early censuses in the individual colonies and those for the country as a whole, starting in 1790, which reported the number of enslaved persons in each state and local community. Village, town, city, and probate records often contain information on enslaved people, as do family records and histories.

Collective forgetting involves an absence of widely shared, emotionally powerful narratives, meaningful ritual expressions and celebrations, and evocative objects in the public and commemorative landscape. All three are present in the South but have virtually disappeared in the North, which makes it especially difficult to maintain the collective memories of slavery in the region. Collective forgetting of complicated, emotionally powerful events such as Northern slavery rarely occurs in a simple way or for a single reason. It invariably involves multiple processes with certain ones important for different people. Often, several ways of forgetting reinforce each other, making it hard to disaggregate the distinct impact of each.

I argued earlier that the six different ways the collective forgetting occurred all played a role in the process and reinforced each other. Gradual attrition through loss of significance is common and widespread, because the salience of events typically diminishes with the passage of time. Destruction or modification of sites associated with collective memories matters a great deal, particularly in the transmission of memories across generations. Incentives for forgetting (or punishments for remembering) affect how memories disappear over time. They are related to, but not the same as, fear of painful memories or retribution and need to be identified separately from them. Powerful feelings of shame and/or guilt promote memory loss and especially in small, primary groups where the judgments of others can be particularly powerful. Last, the cognitive reframing of events alters their meaning over time as small groups shape not just what people think but also *what they think about.*

When we think about lost or forgotten collective memories, the question of recovering or reviving them is not often asked, especially for individuals. However, with collective memories the dynamics are often different. For example, in recent decades interest in details about the Civil War greatly increased following Ken Burns's PBS nine-episode documentary, first broadcast in 1990. Popular interest in the war surged after the series and resulted in a sharp rise in visits to Civil War battlefields and other sites, the purchase of objects associated with it, as well as participation in reenactments (Horwitz 1999).

Historian Ira Berlin (2004: 1266) wrote that "the long complicity of the North [meaning its own history of enslavement] must be unveiled." While I certainly agree that the story needs to be told much more widely than it has been, it is less clear to me that "complicity" is the best way to describe what took place, to the extent that it suggests the existence of a conscious, coordinated set of actions intended to deceive people. While complicity surely occurred in some instances, the evidence seems to point more to a widely shared set of often uncoordinated beliefs and actions over a long period that produced the disappearance of awareness of slavery from the region's collective memory.

Within a short period after abolition in the North there were few institutions, practices, and cultural expressions that transmitted the narrative of Northern slavery or provided visible displays of its earlier presence on the region's public and commemorative landscape. Only in recent years has there been a significant rise in popular reconsideration of slavery in both the North and South, as Berlin (2004: 1251) notes in the epigraph for this chapter. His assessment is very correct and directly speaks to the question of how collective memories once forgotten are recovered.

So, what happened that made the recovery of the collective memories of Northern enslavement begin and then build steam in recent years? Rather than pointing to a single moment or event crucial to this process, it is more useful to think about a series of partially related events that launched and slowly strengthened the memory recovery process.

First, following manumission in the North and the Civil War, the region supported segregation and racial discrimination, and the belief in Black inferiority was widely accepted. The North had little to no concern about Jim Crow and the blatantly unequal treatment of Blacks in the South after the war. African Americans received little government assistance. Booker T. Washington's emphasis on education, economic self-help, and individual advancement rather than direct political action helped lead to the rise of a small Black middle class and institutions such as Black colleges. By the second decade of the twentieth century W. E. B. DuBois and others saw this as insufficient, and when Woodrow Wilson adopted racist positions and policies as President from 1913 to 1921, Black organizations like the then recently formed NAACP and members of the Black clergy protested. However, precious few Northern whites expressed opposition, let alone outrage, at Wilson's actions, such as showing *The Birth of a Nation* at the White House, demoting Black civil servants, and resegregating government departments, agencies, and offices in the Capitol. Occasionally, Northerners protested lynchings in the South, but Southerners in Congress blocked all attempts to legislate against it. As Black emigration to the North increased during World War I and after, white resentment grew and anti-Black riots erupted in many Northern cities—communicating something short of a warm welcome (Francis 2014).

It took several more generations for a good number of politically atten-tive Northern whites to focus on the treatment of African Americans. What this meant in practice was a focus on the South, in effect repeating what took place in the first half of the nineteenth century, which was defining race as a Southern problem, and focusing on segregation's most visible manifestations—public schools, seating on public transportation, drinking fountains, poll taxes, lynching, public accommodations, and voting rights, all of which civil rights protesters highlighted. When police attacked non-violent demonstrators or when figures such as Orval Faubus, George Wallace, or Lester Maddox uttered hateful phrases while railing against integration of their states' schools, Northern white sympathy for Black demands rose, as did their support for federal civil rights legislation. But the relevance of the struggle for equal rights to the North itself was something few appreci-ated or understood (Sugrue 2008). The civil rights victories of the 1960s did not rectify the racial injustices in the country, yet by the end of the decade a majority of Northern whites told pollsters no more government action was needed—a stance that persists today. The victories, however, helped to create a number of changes in American society that did matter, even if they fell short of all that was required.

Second, the presence of more African American faces and voices in public life and their increased visibility in the media meant that Blacks began appearing in other than the Stepin Fetchit or minstrel roles, and sometimes even as dignified, smart, honorable people. African Americans in television and major films now appeared in some serious roles, and Black intellectuals, such as James Baldwin, appeared on TV talk shows. There were even occasional Black newscasters, newspaper columnists, and sports-casters. A part of the greater visibility of African Americans and their experiences was a slow increase in their presence in museum exhibits and inclusion in the interpretive programs at historical sites (Blakey 1994: 42).[3] There was probably also a significant decrease in the proportion of whites who thought about racial differences in biological and genetic terms and believed that Blacks would never be as intelligent or as capable as whites. There was some increase in Black hiring for middle-class jobs, a slow increase in Blacks admitted to elite colleges and universities, and more interaction between whites and Blacks, at least in public settings, although there is far less evidence of change in terms of personal friendships. Black politicians began getting elected to local, state, and even national offices, although they overwhelmingly get elected only in Black majority districts.[4] For example, while there were only six African Americans in the House of Representatives in 1968, forty-six held seats in 2017. The elections of Richard Hatcher as mayor of Gary, Indiana, and Carl Stokes as mayor of Cleveland in 1968 raised the possibility of Black successes in local elections and were soon followed others in a number of cities—often those with Black majority, or near majority, populations.

Third, the reorientation of many historians toward social history meant that the study of how ordinary Black and white people lived and worked increased exponentially. Combined with an increasing number of African Americans teaching and studying in major research universities was a rise in studies of both contemporary and historical African American life, including questions about slavery and the lives of the enslaved. These questions initially were asked more about plantation life in the South than in the North, and the old adage that "slaves did not read and write so we can't know much about their lives" was shown to be wildly amiss. Once researchers actually started digging, it turned out that often there was a good deal more useful information available than many had believed. Still, research about Black lives in the North during the period of enslavement remained modest and basically unknown to the general public.

The examples throughout this book show that there is no single route to memory recovery. In places long identified with slavery, some Southern plantations, managers, curators, or boards of directors have initiated projects since the 1990s to tell the public more about enslavement and to incorporate it into their tours. This often first requires additional research and then the reconstruction of previously existing buildings and additional personnel to expand presentations.

In the North, initial rediscovery of former sites of slavery has occurred in many different ways. At the African Burial Ground in New York, the requirement that the federal government needed to conduct an archaeological dig because the site might contain historically relevant objects led to the unexpected discovery of the intact African burials from the eighteenth century. In Philadelphia, historian Ed Lawler's interest and research into the location and the architectural history of the house where Washington and then Adams lived while they were president unexpectedly revealed that the first president had kept enslaved Africans at the site during his presidency. Although the National Park Service had known about this for three decades, it had never shared this knowledge until there was public mobilization. It took interested and engaged individuals, such as Valerie Cunningham in Portsmouth, New Hampshire, who over four decades collected the names and whatever additional information she could about all Black people who had lived there since 1645, searching through local archives to publish their stories. Then in 2003 in Portsmouth, city workers discovered burials and hit upon coffins under an old street while replacing water pipes. This led to archaeological work, municipal action, and fund-raising to build a memorial to those who had been interred there.

In Philadelphia, a local group in Germantown mobilized to protest public housing planned over the remains of people buried in a former potter's field. Another group organized to demand a memorial on the site of the Bethel Burying Ground in South Philadelphia that researcher Terry Buckalew rediscovered as part of a film project on the nineteenth-century city. Other sites have been rediscovered as part of archaeological and archival research in a variety of places. Once such discoveries occur, interest often increases, encouraging other people to ask questions about their own communities. When places such as the African Burial Ground or the President's House/ Slavery Memorial get a lot of attention, the discovery process can snowball, as has historical research and popular interest in slavery since the 1960s.

Rhode Island residents increasingly recognized that prominent families in the state had engaged in the slave trade, but only very recently have their homes or workplaces been identified as sites of slavery. Former Brown University president Ruth Simmons noted that these sites were "hidden in plain view," but no one made the connection publicly for decades. For changes to occur there needs to be active publicity about the discoveries—specific actions that foster the development of a narrative about the people or events involved and some kind of physical memorialization of them. In 2015, concerns about the slave past of venerable institutions such as Yale, Harvard, and Princeton led to protests and decisions, in Yale's case, to no longer call faculty living in dorms "masters" and to change the names of buildings. Harvard changed its law school insignia, as it was related to the legacy of the Isaac Royall family. His eighteenth-century slave trading and owning made the family so incredibly wealthy that he endowed the Harvard Law School and its most prestigious chair.[5]

Memory recovery for families and individuals often involves a good deal of archival and genealogical research. An interesting example is found in Marjorie Gomez O'Toole's (2016) study of the slave past of Little Compton, Rhode Island, where she is Managing Director of the town's historical society, recently completed her carefully researched and very thoughtful book detailing the lives of the enslaved and indentured people who had lived there. O'Toole (2016) offers several examples of reframing in her study of enslavement in Little Compton (see also Chapter 3). The small town sits east of Newport, the major port for slave-trading ships in the colonies in the eighteenth century. It had a significant percentage of enslaved people from the late seventeenth century until 1816. In 1755, "there were 130 Blacks living there, but by 1820 the number was down to 8. Newly free people did not stay long in Little Compton" (O'Toole 2016: 214).

O'Toole used a number of sources—detailed town records and probate records, wills, local diaries, letters, family manuscripts, and more than one hundred interviews with the descendants of families whose ancestors were slave owners, enslaved, and indentured people. She makes clear that in the earliest period, slavery included Indians, the original owners of the town's land, and soon after, a growing number of Blacks.

As slavery was ending in the North, some white Little Compton men and women decided to seek their fortunes in the slaveholding South, and at least two enslaved people found their way to Little Compton as free men and women (O'Toole 2016: 182). Arnold Gray, a white man who was born into one of the town's largest slave-owing families, moved to North Carolina in about 1817. Upon his death in 1857, he owned fourteen slaves and his estate passed them on to seven relatives in Little Compton. The Northern relatives decided to sell all of them and divide the money from the sales equally. However, a few months later, one of them, Willard Gray of Little Compton, decided to have the two assigned to him, "Benjamin and a baby girl named Moselle, freed and brought North to live under his protection instead. Upon Willard's death in 1874, it was said that he saw this decision as the most memorable event in his life" (192).

Moselle was about three when she arrived in Little Compton. She lived with Willard, his wife, and their adult son George, his wife Elizabeth, and their daughter Bessie, who was born in 1862. Moselle attended school for eight years and was the only person of color there at the time. She went to school through eighth grade, but her "position in the household stands in contrast to that of Bessie . . . [she] may have been treated kindly by the Grays, but she was not treated like a daughter" (O'Toole 2016: 230). It is clear that she was not seen as capable of the same level of education as the Gray's daughter, although they clearly were supportive and caring of her. At fourteen, she worked as a live-in domestic for a neighbor and several years later as a cook for the Grays.

At nineteen, Moselle had a child named Alice, and it was believed that the father was white. She continued to live with the Grays for several more years and the family doted on Alice. In the early 1880s, Moselle and Alice moved to Newport, where Moselle found domestic work with other Gray relatives and, later, as a laundress. Alice had three daughters, Alfaretta, Mabel, and Bessie Violet, although she never married. In 1911, Alice died of a severe infection at age thirty-four, and Moselle died from pneumonia the next year at fifty-six. O'Toole (2006) writes, that while Alice was alive, she received an envelope every month from Little Compton with money in it, and when she died, they stopped coming. Alfaretta married Milton Massey in 1923, and they raised a thriving family in the Newport area. Moselle's descendants today are numerous, and they hold regular reunions in Newport. They are now using DNA to learn more about their ancestors (239). Moselle's "life in the North was not easy. Freedom did not mean comfort and equality in late nineteenth-century New England. Moselle struggled; her daughters struggled. As hard as Moselle's life may have been, Willard's decision still resonates today with each new addition to the Massey family" (240).

Recovery of collective memories occurs when remembering is connected to and serves present needs and interests. For example, African American power and voice have been more effective since the 1960s and have been occasionally joined by more vocal white interest and support. This has raised issues and produced results that have led to somewhat greater inclusion of the African American story of enslavement in local narratives and changes in the public landscape. Usually this is not without conflict and contention, as the African Burial Ground and the President's House/Slavery Memorial stories clearly illustrate.

Explorations in film, television presentations, books, museum exhibits, historical tourism, genealogical research, and antiques have kindled people's interest in their pasts and facilitated collective memory. Two television events are thought to have had a particular impact. The first was *Roots*, a 1977 eight-episode television miniseries on ABC, based on Alex Haley's novel. It recounted the story of Kunta Kinte, a Mandinka warrior, which begins in the Gambia in West Africa in 1750. Kinte is captured, sold to slave traders, and brought to colonial America, where he is sold again. His story is one of enslavement and struggle against it for survival. Haley's narrative traces Kinte's descendants to 1870. A sequel that aired a few years later brought the story into the 1970s. The audience for the first series was huge and the show's episodes were viewed on more than 60 percent of the televisions in the country that were turned on during their airing. It is also important that the portrayal of enslavement in *Roots* greatly contrasts with what had been the dominant film portrayal of it in the previous three decades, *Gone with the Wind*.

The power of Haley's story is its personalization, connecting Kinte's family to his own, and inspiring many African Americans to learn more about their own family's past and origins. It seems more than likely that the uplifting parts of Kunta Kinte's narrative involving his own survival, his refusal to accept enslavement, and his struggle to do his best to avoid the same fate for his descendants provoked discussion and reflection for many African Americans. His story encouraged people to consider their own narratives, to dig more deeply into their own genealogies and histories, to have kindled an interest in the experiences of enslaved people in the towns and cities in older parts of the North and South, and to do their own research in local libraries and archives. They consulted newspapers, public records, and discussed memories with older people.[6] What narratives might have arisen from such considerations? In how many families and churches were the barriers about discussion of enslavement weakened or removed? How many people talked to their grandparents and older relatives about what they knew about their enslaved ancestors?[7] How many constructed and enlarged their own family narratives and attended family reunions as their interests in the past increased? How many built narratives that were partially based on research spurred by Haley's inspiration?

We can also ask about the impact on the development of ritual expressions and enactments that grew out of *Roots* and the discussions it produced. Did families develop local ritual events to mark what they knew or discovered about the ancestors in their own families or in the larger communities where they lived? What were some of the rituals that may have taken place regularly with other family or community members? What about tours in cities and towns in parts of the North that now have something to say about local enslavement? How many were encouraged to visit the places where their ancestors were enslaved, in some cases hoping to find where their remains are buried? How many decided to learn more about African history, including the region from which their ancestors might have originated?

The second television event was Ken Burns' nine-episode documentary *The Civil War*, which first aired on PBS in 1990 and a number of times thereafter. It too attracted a huge audience, kindled a renewed interest in the details of the war, and greatly expanded participation in reenactments of its battles (Horwitz 1999). Although the story of slavery is obviously central to the origin of the war and its aftermath, the series was particularly important in sparking Americans' interest in visiting historic sites such as Civil War battlefields. In most cases, however, as Horwitz (1999) observes, popular emphasis was more on the micro aspects of the war's battles, such as military tactics, weather, terrain, soldiers' clothing, and sleeping and eating arrangements, and less on the larger questions of the causes of the war and motives of the powerful people behind it.

For others, however, this original interest fed into an already emerging curiosity about history and family genealogies among both Black and white Americans. Interest in the Civil War also increased interest in the Black experience before and after it, which paralleled developments in academia more than a generation earlier, as more Blacks were trained as historians and social scientists, and the number of African American museums increased throughout the country.

After the 1960s there has been greater societal legitimation and integration of African American histories and experiences into the country's collective story, and we can see this in the narratives, ritual expressions, and symbolic landscapes in the North as well as the South. Parts of the media, public institutions such as museums, community activists, scholars, and ordinary citizens played important roles in this memory recovery. In a variety of ways each provided critical research and voices that increased awareness of the North's once central role in the slave trade, enslavement in the region, and the direct and indirect contributions of slave labor to the region's economic development. However, there is a good deal more to do, and schools in the North have been very slow to teach students about this part of the region's past, largely because teachers do not yet know much about it and because textbooks have only slowly been updated and revised.

Museums in the North (and South) began to offer exhibits on the once "hardly talked about" topic of slavery late in the twentieth century. In the North, historical markers slowly began to appear on a few sites of slavery, such as the plaque that New York erected in 2015 to mark the site of the city's slave market at the eastern end of Wall Street from 1711 to 1762. Archaeological excavations revealed evidence of earlier enslavement, often in places where there was no public memory of it having taken place, such as the African Burial Ground in New York, and other local burial grounds throughout the North, often forgotten for decades and even centuries, that hold the remains of both enslaved and free Blacks. Equally forgotten for so long was the story that President Washington brought enslaved Africans to his house in Philadelphia.

Visibility on the public landscape is especially vital in the development, retention, and transmission of collective memories. Public visibility sustains narratives and encourages further research to identify and celebrate places and events with large and small rituals. What is the causal sequence operating here? It is probably one in which there are reciprocal interactions rather than any one single pattern that initiates this process. In the examples analyzed here, it is interesting that often an account of the past emerges from the rediscovery of a specific place on which past events occurred or where there are buried objects tied to events.

This is certainly what happened in the case of the African Burial Ground in New York and in Philadelphia at the President's House/Slavery Memorial and the Bethel Burying Ground. The President's House/ Slavery Memorial site on Independence Mall is now used for some African American ritual events, such as parades, speeches, and festivals held on Juneteenth, a holiday that commemorates the June 19, 1865, announcement of the abolition of slavery in Texas, the last state to hear about it in the former Confederacy. Once the significance of a site and what took place on it is understood more broadly, and the narrative about it more widely shared, ceremonies develop around it, as do demands that the site be clearly marked so it can become an appropriate place for collective memories and shared rituals. It becomes critically important to those making these demands that the site associated with the memories be transformed into a "sacred space" in which the events that transpired on it and the people involved in them can be remembered and celebrated (Durkheim [1915] 1995).

Sites on the public landscape can become "linking objects" that connect people and events across time and space (Volkan 1988, 1997). Standing near, touching, or viewing a place where emotionally significant events once occurred or where people to whom one is connected in the past once lived, visited, or are buried enhances and reinforces a site's emotional significance and justifies memorializing it. Think of photographer John Dowell's story (Chapter 4) about the day when he was photographing the excavation of the foundations of the President's House. He looked at the uncovered passageway between the kitchen at the back of the house where Washington's enslaved Africans worked and the rooms at the front where they walked, carrying food back and forth, and began sobbing as he thought of the possibility that the enslaved people doing this work could have been his own ancestors. Places are powerful connectors, and when they are associated with stories or they hold objects—even very simple or incomplete ones such as fragments of foundations, day-to-day objects, or their remains—they can heighten the emotional power for those who hear or see them, whether they are encountered intentionally or accidentally.

Requests that arise for marking the public landscape often quickly intensify when they represent group and individual identities. Denied requests easily escalate into growing demands that are experienced as tests of group worth. When public officials say something such as "nothing can be done" or "we don't have the money," those making the initial demands can quickly not only feel a strong sense of rejection just of the specific request, but also experience it as group devaluation. Soon, rejections produce new players, as allies are mobilized to increase support. In this kind of spiral, groups that perceive disrespect increase their inclination to protest and in turn escalate their demands for substantive actions. Identity politics is about acknowledgment and recognition, as much as, or more than, the distribution of tangible resources or services. What we can learn is that while the ostensible issues at stake concern the past, making sense of why and how they engage powerful emotions in the present requires understanding the present-day needs and interests that drive individual and group demands and explain their emotional intensity.

Since they were first brought to North America, Blacks have always recognized and thought about their ancestors. In the early years this often took the form of retelling stories and traditions about Africa and their ancestors. Where possible, they continued to prepare and eat foods as they had done in Africa. Many linguistic, musical, religious, wedding, and funeral carryovers persisted in Black culture as well. However, access to public spaces where ceremonies and other traditions could be celebrated was generally severely restricted. Laws that made it illegal for enslaved or free Blacks to gather in large groups presented further challenges. But this did not mean that these cultural expressions of connectedness or the significance of the ancestors disappeared, and integration into American white culture was in no way complete. Much of what was needed to keep traditions and memories alive was done secretly (Greene [1942] 1969; Piersen 1988; Horton and Horton 1997).

What eventually happened is that Black communities in both the North and South developed their own social, cultural, and economic institutions, although it is important to add that in many towns and cities, except for the Black churches, whites often carefully monitored and controlled them. Public spaces in downtowns and white areas were virtually unavailable to Blacks as places to mark collective experiences and memories, even with something as simple as historical plaques. In 1838 in Philadelphia, when abolitionist supporters built Pennsylvania Hall in the center of the city and invited abolitionists to speak there, a white mob burned it to the ground. In the twentieth century, segregation in all parts of the country, but especially in the North, meant that few whites entered Black communities, while many white communities remained lily-white for many decades and still are (Sugrue 2008; Coates 2014). With few if any shared spaces and most public parts of towns and cities considered white (even when Blacks worked and shopped in them), memorials and monuments therein were almost entirely about white achievements, and museums displayed objects from white culture. Of course, there are some exceptions. In Philadelphia, for example, the "All Wars Memorial to Colored Soldiers and Sailors," originally built in 1934 and installed in a not very visible location in west Fairmount Park, was moved in 1994 to a small but prominent square on the prestigious Benjamin Franklin Parkway.

In both North and South, sculptures, memorials, monuments, and museums displaying African Americans have been few and far between in the country's public and commemorative landscapes. "Before 1860 there are no known images whatsoever of African Americans, slave or free, in marble or bronze" (Savage 1997: 16). After the Civil War, there were plans for African American memorials in a variety of places that never came to fruition. In addition, of the thousands of common soldier monuments that appeared in the North and South in cities and towns by the thousands, the soldiers portrayed in the monuments were invariably white (Savage 1997: 162), as "the marginalization of African Americans went hand in hand with the reconstruction of white America" (19). Despite the fact that more than 200,000 Blacks had served in the Union army and 36,847 died, "only three monuments in the nineteenth century depicted Blacks in military service, all appearing in the last decade of the century and none of them generic war memorials" (192).[8] Savage concludes, "At the most basic level the monuments were white because the American polity itself was structured as white" (191).

Memory recovery is assisted when older ritual expressions and enactments are revived or new ones invented. The story of the conflict over the President's House/Slavery Memorial in Independence National Historical Park is important because it made people far more aware of the narrative of slavery in the North and made access to it more visible on the country's commemorative landscape, where, previously, visitors learned nothing about slavery. While Washington was a resident of Virginia, the fact that he could bring enslaved people to Philadelphia when he was president shocked many people when the story became public in 2002. It also led some people to ask questions about whether the other Founding Fathers and members of Congress and Washington's administration who were slaveholders did this at the same time. It turns out they did.

The site recounts a good deal about President Washington and slavery in Pennsylvania and in the young country. In addition, ATAC initiated and presides over at least three recently created "ritual events" regularly held there. Their Annual Black Independence Day celebration dates from 2002 and takes place near, or at, the President's House/Slavery Memorial site on July 3 or 4 each year. It features short speeches from ATAC members and others who attend and wish to speak, which connects slavery on the site to current concerns. They retell the struggle to have the memorial built on the mall and commemorate the nine enslaved Africans who toiled at the house in the 1790s. There are also flag displays, featuring Black Liberation flags, African drumming, and a ritual walk to the memorial site itself. In the early years, these events put pressure on the Park Service and the city's elected officials to build an appropriate memorial. As the plans for the site developed, the concerns shifted to details about the designs, then to a celebration of the achievement of the memorial, and more recently to current issues such as incarceration and police violence.

"Hercules Freedom Day" is a second commemorative event that ATAC holds at the President's House/Slavery Memorial. It was first held on February 22, 2010, to mark the escape of the President's cook Hercules from Washington's Mount Vernon, Virginia, plantation on the President's sixty-fifth birthday, February 22, 1797. It was previously known that Hercules had escaped, but research by Mary Thompson, a Mount Vernon historian, and a long two-part article about Hercules and Washington in the *Philadelphia Inquirer* (LaBan 2010a, 2010b) revealed that the escape was not from Philadelphia as had long been presumed, but from Mount Vernon, where he had lived since the previous November after Washington had sent him back, fearing that he might try to escape.[9] In the ATAC ceremony, Michael Coard told of Hercules' escape, providing details about his life and the few reports of people seeing him in New York after his escape. Little is known about his life afterward. In his comments about Washington, Coard delivered the simple message that "everybody knows George Washington's birthday is today, but we celebrate it as Freedom Day for one of the 316 Black people he enslaved"; he added that "Washington may have been a great general, a great leader, and a great President, but what kind of man was he who would enslave others?"[10] A few months later, on May 21, 2010, Coard and ATAC held another gathering to mark the anniversary of the day twenty-three-year-old Ona Judge escaped in 1796 when she slipped out of Washington's Philadelphia residence while the President and his wife, Martha, were eating their dinner and soon was taken to a boat leaving for New Hampshire.

By 2013 ATAC no longer commemorated each of these events annually, but on August 19, 2014, supporters gathered at the memorial site to mark the anniversary of the day when enslaved Africans first arrived in British North America, landing in Jamestown, Virginia, in 1619. Following a short ceremony on Independence Mall, the group then marched down Market Street to Front Street to the historical marker outside what was once the

London Coffee House, which served as a slave market in the eighteenth century (see Figure 23). Here Africans arriving on boats in the Delaware River from the Caribbean or Africa would be auctioned for sale. Coard told the crowd of perhaps one hundred people the story of enslavement, the dangerous crossing of the Atlantic, and the pain and suffering the enslaved endured.

The story of the President's enslaved Africans in turn stimulated other stories. In 2007, the Interact Theater Company in Philadelphia put on a play, *A House with No Walls*, which focused on the controversy over the design of the still unbuilt memorial. During its month-long run, there was a panel discussion featuring people who had been involved in the project or who had covered it in the press, as well as post-performance discussions involving audience participation.

In 2011, Michelle Flamer, a solicitor who worked on the city contracts for the President's House/Slavery Memorial and a quilter, organized a three-month quilt exposition, "The President's House: Their Untold Stories in Quilts" (Figures 30–32). It was inspired by the story of the nine enslaved Africans. She invited quilters from around the country to read online about the story of the house, the Washingtons, and the enslaved and to submit a quilt inspired by what they felt. Quilters from around the country ranging from master quilters to young children, submitted dozens of quilts, forty-one of which were in the show that was presented at the National Constitution Center on Independence Mall, at the Park's Visitor Center, and at the African American Museum.

A third cultural expression rooted in the story of the enslaved Africans in 2012 inspired a pair of performances organized by Philadelphia dancer and choreographer Germaine Ingram, followed by panel discussions tied to the story of the President's House/Slavery Memorial. The two performances and panels were quite different in focus although both drew inspiration from the President's House story of slavery—the first was a discussion of contemporary political rhetoric and the legacy of slavery, while the second examined trauma and healing following the genocide in Rwanda.

Once a narrative becomes publicly available, it can inspire further exploration and discussion that can take a wide range of forms. Memory recovery is not a linear process. Once it begins and diffuses there are opportunities for new discussions, modifications, and further expansion of its meaning. In almost all of the examples cited in this book, the story of enslavement in the North has generated widespread shock and surprise, in great part because it was literally buried for so long. Once a compelling

Figures 30, 31, and 32. Three of the
more than forty-five quilts produced to
honor the memory of the nine enslaved
people George Washington brought to
live in his house in Philadelphia while
he was President in the 1790s. "Let
Freedom Ring" by Carolyn Crump
(*above*); "Tree of Life" by Rachel
D. K. Clark (*right*); and "Truth Be Told"
by Sauda A. Zahra (*below*).

narrative appears in the light of day, people often show great interest in it and wonder why they knew nothing about it earlier.

At the same time, despite the cumulative, snowballing process I have suggested, the recovery of memories of Northern slavery has been gradual. Shifts in narratives, ritual expressions and enactments, and visibility in the public and commemorative landscape should be seen as both indicators and causes of this modest change. The many examples discussed throughout this book are just a small number of the places and cases where this is occurring. At the same time, only a minority of whites and Blacks living in the North are now aware that there once was enslavement there for almost 250 years and that it took place in every colony and state in cities, towns, and rural areas.

Prestigious museum presentations, displays in the region's important public sites, and media presentations (especially those on PBS) about Northern slavery certainly are making a contribution to changing collective understanding and memories. Schools also have somewhat changed their approaches and have begun integrating the slavery and African American experience into school textbooks and courses largely because more African Americans are insisting that their stories need to be a significant part of the country's narratives. Sometimes, there is meaningful white support from elected officials, school administrators, and local media for doing this, which can expedite the process. No longer are African Americans simply resigned to accepting what others decide is appropriate for them to know and learn.

Narratives and rituals, such as solemn ceremonies, certainly are important in collective memory recovery and preservation. However, a key element of the argument here is that without visible prominent sites on the public landscape where there are things to see and even touch, the power of the events and the people remembered can be difficult to sustain. The site where displays are located might be where the earlier events actually took place, such as a battlefield (Gettysburg, Pearl Harbor, Little Big Horn) or where critical political events occurred (Independence Hall, Congress, the Edmund Pettus Bridge in Selma). Interestingly, however, this is not necessary. The powerful Vietnam Veterans Memorial on the Washington Mall and the Holocaust Museum, nearby, are located thousands of miles away from where the events they mark took place, and yet each has a sacred character and represents the events associated with it, despite their physical distance from them. It is also useful to acknowledge the very different ways that these two sites are linked to the events they mark: the Vietnam Veterans Memorial is a stark stone wall on which the names of the soldiers killed in the war are engraved; in contrast, the Holocaust Museum has very graphic photos, videos, and objects with which to recount the story of the Nazi genocide. There is no single way that a powerful historical memory can be communicated and transmitted effectively. At the same time, however, if there are no sites on the public landscape associated with certain events, it is far more difficult for collective memories of them to survive.

Alderman and Campbell's (2008) concept of symbolic excavation offers an excellent way to conclude my argument about memory recovery. What they suggest is the need to dig into our minds and our thoughts and feelings to connect with what took place in the past in both the North and South. To do this, they argue that, in recounting stories of enslavement, objects involved in it add to the power of landscapes through their ability to channel and control meanings. As they explain:

> Symbolic excavation of slavery, as a negotiated process of memory recovery and representation, is carried about both discursively and materially. . . . Material objects and relics play an important role in casting legitimacy and authenticity on certain historical interpretations, [and] symbolic excavation also requires a collecting of artifacts and the construction of physical places of memory for their display, interpretation, and conversion into meaningful historical narrative. . . . The excavation or reconstruction of the history of slavery relies on a direct engagement with the politics of collecting, interpreting, and representing artifacts [none of which is innocent or neutral]. . . . An artifact politics approach recognizes that there is a history of uneven racially biased efforts to collect and preserve artifacts and material traces by curators. Collections have long been used to aggrandize the reputation of white elites. . . . Material objects and relics, like the larger landscapes they form, are collections of signs and symbols that communicate a way of seeing the world and a vision of who ultimately matters socially (and who does not). (Alderman and Campbell 2008: 343–45)

Using narratives, ritual expressions and enactments, and visible public and commemorative landscapes, it should be possible for much of the long-forgotten story of the period of enslavement in the North to help people to understand what took place and to feel the power and pain it produced for hundreds of thousands of people. This pain includes not only the enslaved but also their descendants. It also makes clear that millions of people and their descendants profited greatly financially, accruing privilege and power from the work of those enslaved across many generations, simply because their skin was a different color.

Epilogue

A few months after it opened in September 2016, I visited the National Museum of African American History and Culture on the Mall in Washington, D.C., to see how it presented the story of slavery, and especially enslavement in the North, on this prominent site.[1] The museum itself was a long time in coming. First proposed in 1915 and then again after 1970, it was not authorized by Congress until 2003.[2] At the outset, the museum had no objects or artifacts to display. In some respects that was fortunate, because it meant that its curators would not be obligated to exhibit items that its parent institution, the Smithsonian, had in storage. Instead, curators traveled around the country, speaking to individuals and local groups and communities to request the donation of worthy objects. In the end, they wound up with over 33,000 artifacts, some quite unexpected. The result is a beautiful building whose architecture has to be appreciated in person and six floors of exhibits with many stunning displays.

Enslavement in the North is an important part of the first-floor gallery, "Slavery and Freedom, 1400–1877," which is packed with panels, pictures, drawings, maps, objects, and more. Although the gallery contains a great deal to see and digest, the information is communicated clearly and effectively. Visitors moved slowly through the gallery, and small groups of people shared their reactions quietly. Both Black and white adults and children as young as ten were attentive and engaged.

The exhibit entitled "The Making of the Atlantic World" focuses on the fifteenth to the eighteenth centuries and four early European slave-trading countries (Portugal, Spain, England, France) that bought people primarily from Africa's West Coast and sold them in the Caribbean, North and South America, as well as Europe. I suspect that few people seeing the exhibit had ever considered the Portuguese (or Danes, shown later) as colonizers and slave traders. Maps showing the routes of the slave ships accompany an introduction to the African peoples and cultures most affected by the slave trade. Names of slave ships that voyaged to North America appear on a wall next to a small, dark room devoted to the Middle Passage from Africa to the Americas and the transatlantic slave trade. This exhibit uses objects recovered by the Slave Wrecks Project and the tragic story of the *São José*, a Portuguese slave ship wrecked near the Cape of Good Hope in 1794. The ship was carrying more than four hundred slaves from Mozambique when it struck a rock and began to sink. The crew and some of those enslaved were able to make it safely to shore, but more than half of the enslaved people aboard died in the rough waters. Visitors hear actors reading the survivors' words as they walk through the room, where they can also see pieces of the *São José*.

The extensive space devoted to colonial North America, here meaning the area that became the United States, is organized around regional differences between the slave systems in the Chesapeake, the Low Country (the Carolinas), and the North. Among the topics presented are the development of a racialized definition of an enslaved person and the gradual adoption of laws exercising social control over both enslaved and free Blacks throughout the colonies. Panels, maps, pictures, and objects from each region include a time line, a description of the work the enslaved did there, and the basis of the region's economy. Displays also describe variations in agricultural practices and the presence of more urban Blacks in the North.

Focusing on the North as I went through this exhibit, I thought the curators did a fine job of providing a great deal of understandable information in a modest space. Perhaps future exhibits could expand on a few topics such as the high rates of slave sales in the North and the consequent obstacles to forming families and stable communities. A discussion about the central role that Northerners played in the slave trade includes the DeWolf family and its illegal activities after 1808. The Revolutionary period of the exhibit uses charts, maps, and profiles of individuals in Philadelphia and New York. One detailed street map shows where the enslaved lived in Philadelphia during the eighteenth century, and a panel recounts the story of Richard Allen and the founding of Mother Bethel Church. Pictures and a description of Lower Manhattan include an overview of the rediscovered African Burial Ground.

Two elements help exhibits communicate ideas effectively to visitors—objects that serve as connectors (both cognitive and emotional) to a theme being discussed, and personal stories about a few specific people. Both of these are generally in short supply—but not absent—with regard to Northern enslavement in the seventeenth and eighteenth centuries. Physical objects from the period that we can associate with the daily lives of enslaved people—their dwellings, their tools, or their clothing—are rare. Yet the descriptions and drawings in the displays are well chosen and evocative despite the scarcity of artifacts.

Stories about individual lives or expressions of what enslaved people thought or felt in their own words are similarly hard to turn up prior to the Revolutionary period. Frequently all we have are the accounts of whites—often slave owners recounting what the people they have enslaved are supposedly thinking or feeling. Even the few diaries or life stories available from people who had once been enslaved are invariably documents that were dictated to whites, and we cannot be sure of their accuracy. Yet connections to specific people are found in the profiles of once enslaved Northerners, including Venture Smith, Richard Allen, Phillis Wheatley, Elizabeth Freeman, and Belinda, with images and some details about each of their lives. I was sorry not to see a mention that the gradual abolition laws, passed in the Northern states in the two decades after the Revolution, worked to very slowly grant freedom but failed to address equal rights for Blacks. Visitors may notice generally much less about slavery in the North after 1800. However, exhibits focus on central issues: the connections between the Southern slave economy and the growing industries in the North in the text accompanying a picture of the huge Boott Mills factory in Lowell, Massachusetts, in 1835, a producer of "Negro cloth"; the financial links between Northern banks and Southern growers; the rise of abolitionism; and the tensions that led to the Civil War.

Most important, telling the story of slavery in this setting on the National Mall directly addresses a topic that once was only discussed using coded words such as "masters" and "servants" or even "workers," if it was talked about at all. The museum presents what was once a taboo topic effectively and powerfully. Its exhibits also show that the North was directly and indirectly involved in slavery and the slave economy. Confronting these truths is difficult—and yet may be healing—for the United States and its citizens. Telling this story in such a sacred location is a long-overdue step. The topic, however, is not exhausted by any means, and regional museums and memorials contain opportunities for the story to be continually retold to new generations.

Notes

Introduction

Note to epigraph: Comments by Ruffins, curator of African American history and culture in the Division of Home and Community Life at the Smithsonian's National Museum of American History, speaking at a program relating to the President's House project, Philadelphia, June 5, 2006.

1. While the focus of this book is on the Northern English colonies that became the United States in 1787, enslavement also existed in the Northwest Territories that became states between 1803 and 1858, despite the fact that it was not permitted by the Northwest Ordinance passed in 1787 under the Articles of Confederation (Harper 2003, Miles 2017).

2. Harriton House still stands and is open for visits run by the Harriton Foundation (http://www.harritonhouse.org/index.htm).

3. "Black at Bryn Mawr," http://blackatbrynmawr.blogs.brynmawr.edu/.

4. http://www.slavenorth.com/author.htm If Harper had searched scholarly journals he would have found a good deal written on this topic. It is also the case that search engines at that time were nowhere near as effective as they became just a few years later.

5. http://www.slavenorth.com/index.html.

6. https://www.washingtonpost.com/news/wonk/wp/2017/09/28/black-and-hispanic-families-are-making-more-money-but-they-still-lag-far-behind-whites/?utm_term = .de6b2e8df377.

7. http://www.pewresearch.org/fact-tank/2014/12/12/racial-wealth-gaps-great-recession/.

8. Griswold (2013) calls them "provisioning plantations," an appropriate description.

9. For elaboration of this argument and details about the wide range of economic contributions the enslaved made to the growth and development of the Northern economy, see McManus (1973, 2000); Nash (1988); Sammons and Cunningham (2004); Farrow, Lang, and Frank (2005); DeWolf (2008); Baptist (2014).

10. Melish (1998) also emphasizes that while Northerners took the lead in the abolitionist movement in the nineteenth century, it partially overlapped with the colonization movement that sought to return free Blacks to Africa. Especially early in the 1800s, abolitionists were not egalitarians and many supported gradual, not immediate, abolition (Gigantino 2015).

11. McPherson (1999) described an ethnic-racial argument that some Southern intellectuals raised to explain succession. It emphasized incompatibilities between Southern and Northern whites who, they explained, were descendants of different races. Southerners descended from the Normans while Northerners arose from the inferior Saxons whose differences in temperament and capability propelled secession. Also see Coates (2012) and Hanlon (2013).

12. Sometimes, of course, there are deliberate efforts to remove links to the past. Among these are a changing a symbolic landscape produced by removing or destroying buildings, statues and paintings of the former rulers, renaming cities or streets, and building new monuments,

memorials, and other markers of their presence on the landscape as in the desecration of sacred sites as had taken place in Bosnia in the 1990s and Israel since 1948 (Benvenisti 2000).

13. While this book is focused on the North, there are times when drawing on examples from the South is useful as a basis for comparison.

14. "Lives Bound Together: Slavery at George Washington's Mount Vernon," special exhibit, October 2016–September 2018, http://www.mountvernon.org/plan-your-visit/calendar/exhibi tions/lives-bound-together-slavery-at-george-washingtons-mount-vernon/?gclid = CKzx0s6G8 NMCFVVXDQodhfsB4A.

15. Some of the objects from the daily lives of the enslaved presented in the exhibit came from materials at Williamsburg, Virginia.

16. Starting with no objects whatsoever, which turned out to be a blessing in many ways, curators traveled to regions of slavery, solicited materials, and wound up with more than 33,000 objects, including some extraordinary ones such as Nat Turner's Bible.

17. African Burial Ground National Monument, http://www.nps.gov/afbg/index.htm; Slave Relic Museum, http://www.slaverelics.org/blog/; Lest We Forget Museum, http://lwfsm.com/.

18. While a group of New Yorkers call themselves the "Committee of the Descendants of the Afrikan Ancestral Burial Ground," I have not found any claims that they saw themselves as direct descendants of those who were interred on the site.

19. It is crucial to remember that what was considered to be a "large farm" in the seventeenth and eighteenth centuries is small in today's terms as there was little to no mechanization and agricultural work was done using draft animals and human labor.

20. The 419 individuals were reinterred a decade later. Some sources report the number removed from the site as 420 or 427. The story of the archaeological work and its findings can be found in various articles, books, theses, and in two videos: *The African Burial Ground: An American Discovery* (Kutz 1994), narrated by Ossie Davis and Ruby Dee; and *Slavery's Buried Past* (Kurtis 1996).

21. A widely reported story was that for years when medical students needed cadavers to study, they would often dig up remains from the African Burial Ground for this purpose (Ottley and Weatherby 1967: 80). There is evidence that this kind of theft also took place in Philadelphia (Rowan 2017).

22. The Akan are an ethnic group in Ghana.

23. The Sankofa symbol is an Akan image that literally means learning from the past to build the future.

Chapter 1

1. Another often cited distinction is the one Lewis (1975) makes between remembered, recovered and invented history and the social and political needs and conditions that underlie with each pattern.

2. Bodnar (1992) distinguishes between vernacular and official memory, which is similar but not quite the same distinction, while Assmann (1995) emphasizes communicative or everyday memory and collective (cultural) memory, which has a much longer time frame. Lowenthal (1998: 7) distinguishes between history and heritage, saying, "History seeks to convince by truth, and succumbs to falsehood. Heritage exaggerates and omits, candidly invents and frankly forgets, and thrives on ignorance and error."

3. Even here direct experiences vary. Some people served as combatants in the wars, while others lived through them but neither they nor their families were as directly involved as the soldiers or civilians involved in the war efforts.

4. In 2015, a mother and her daughter called attention to a geography textbook used in Texas schools that contained a "description of the Atlantic slave trade as bringing 'millions of

workers' to plantations in the American South." The publisher of the text, McGraw-Hill Education, acknowledged that the term "workers" was a misnomer and promised to provide stickers to the schools to paste over the offensive sentences (Fernandez and Hauser: October 5, 2015, Rockmore: October 21, 2015).

5. For once, African Americans felt vindicated when the trial showed that a white police officer who lied about evidence was not able to persuade a jury to convict a Black defendant. Emotionally this was more important to them than finding him guilty.

6. In recent years, there has been widespread protest against Columbus Day as the brutality with which he treated native peoples has become more widely known. Some cities no longer celebrate it or have changed the name to Indigenous Peoples Day.

7. See http://en.wikipedia.org/wiki/Juneteenth.

8. This is not to say that collective memories are the aggregate of individual memories, although in some instances this seems to be the case. The relationship between the two is far more complex; while sometimes individual memories aggregate in a way that leads to collective, shared memories, at other times the group has experiences that are expressed in shared narratives that become the basis for individual memories.

9. For example, Devine-Wright and Lyons (1997) found that emotions associated with historically sacred sites in Ireland differed across political groups in significant ways and clearly show that "places seem to act as cues for [alternative] social memories for different groups" (1997: 44). Social psychologists and some others often call these schemas.

10. Social psychologists and some others often call these schemas.

11. Previously I have described these as worldviews that prioritize and shape beliefs and actions, particularly in high stress, ambiguous situations such as ones with actual or threatened high conflict and violence (Ross 2007).

12. By "indirect personal experiences" I am referring to those recounted by a person close to an individual rather than the individual having those experiences him- or herself.

13. Lewis (1975: 45) notes that all societies have narratives about the past that take different forms, as well as commemorations to mark significant past events.

14. Examination of the ways that individual societies mark important holidays and festivals over time shows significant changes in many aspects, although most people continue to view these occasions as unchanging.

15. He also helpfully adds that "commemoration is not to be understood as inferior history; nor, for that matter, is history to be understood as an antidote to commemoration" (Schwartz 2000: 11). Rather they each work differently even if they are highly interdependent.

16. Winter and Sivan, in discussing spatial memories and war memorials, note that "those in mourning used them not only for ceremony, but also for a ritual of separation, wherein touching a name indicates not only what has been lost, but also what has not been lost" (1999: 38). Think of the Vietnam Veterans Memorial as a connector working in this fashion.

17. The fact that a handful of people ran into the streets in panic during and after Orson Welles's radio broadcast of "The War of the Worlds" in 1938 or that Germans seemed dazzled by films of Hitler's speeches promoted that idea (sometimes called inoculation theory) that exposure to messages insured their correct reception and intended effects. Only after many years of studies showing how contingent such effects were was this assumption discarded in the literature, but not by most of the public.

18. Framing perhaps matters a great deal here, and what happened after 9/11 can easily be contrasted with the bombing of the World Trade Center almost a decade earlier, which the authorities treated as a criminal act and brought the perpetrators to trial (Ross 2002).

19. Another short explanation is the notion that the lives of most Black people in the country have not mattered for centuries and this explains much of the absence of awareness of Northern enslavement. Without rejecting the basic premise, it is hardly a sufficient explanation,

especially for lack of awareness in the Black community owing to denial, suppression, or avoidance of a painful topic. In addition, if this explanation is so powerful, Southern enslavement should also be absent from our collective memories, and this is certainly not the case.

Chapter 2

1. For example, see how it has been treated on the Sons of the Confederacy websites at times, but the ones I read earlier are no longer posted.

2. Zilversmit (1967) reports that in the middle of the eighteenth-century half of the families in Kings County (Brooklyn) owned enslaved Blacks.

3. Hodges discusses the effects of this in New York and New Jersey in a chapter on the role of Blacks in the American Revolution (1999: 139–61; see also Hodges 1996).

4. This explanation does not address why Northern opinions would have shifted far more than those in the South, when it was Southern voices such as Jefferson's and Patrick Henry's that framed many of the strongest ideological appeals for independence.

5. Berlin's (1998) masterful analysis of slavery is organized around four regions, the Chesapeake, the Low Country, the North, and the Mississippi Valley, and considers significant differences as well as similarities across them all.

6. Wheatley was born in 1753 and died at age thirty-one in 1784; her published work at the time was widely acclaimed.

7. Although Venture Smith tells us he was born in Guinea in 1729 and brought to the colonies at age eight, Lovejoy (2010) says he was probably twelve when he arrived in Rhode Island.

8. John Livingston was a ne'er-do-well son of the successful New York Livingston family.

9. While this is found in the South as well, it is not my focus here. However, my sense that in the North agency and autonomy were far easier to express than in the South where life was often restricted to the large plantation on which one lived. Baptist (2014) certainly considers how agency operated in some of the most oppressive settings in the Delta region.

10. Both Sweet (2003) and Hardesty (2016) consider Samuel Sewall's 1700 essay *The Selling of Joseph* that opposed slavery while essentially concluding that it was Black opposition and subversion of the system that eventually ended the practice in New England. They, like Davis (2006: 127), also consider ways that Sewall's essay was quite equivocal on many key points and hardly widely accepted at the time.

11. For descriptions of how this operated at the local level, see the accounts in Leahy (2003), DeWolf (2008), Johnson (2014), Manegold (2010), and Melish (1998).

12. This kind of role reversal in which those on the bottom of the social order are briefly at the top in festivals is well theorized in Gluckman (1954).

13. See http://slavenorth.com/exclusion.htm.

14. Lepore (2005a: 58) reports somewhat different numbers—forty-three brought to trial, twenty-five convicted, of whom twenty were hanged and three burned at the stake.

15. Vermont was admitted as the fourteenth state a year after the census, in 1791.

16. See http://slavenorth.com/newhampshire.htm.

17. White (1991) says that the same was true in New York and persisted even longer.

18. See http://slavenorth.com/connecticut.htm.

19. See http://slavenorth.com/nyemancip.htm.

20. In New York, the payments lasted until 1812 after which time sales of enslaved people to the South, although illegal, were permitted, while in New Jersey judges needed to give permissions, which were easily obtained, for such sales (Hodges 1999: 191).

21. In Pennsylvania, this occurred when the state constitution was rewritten in 1837.

22. The film *Twelve Years a Slave*, released in 2013 and based on a nineteenth-century memoir, portrays such a case.

23. Colonization is a position Abraham Lincoln often endorsed, believing that while slavery was wrong, people of African descent were not capable of developing the skills that citizenship required.

24. While there were town histories around the turn of the twentieth century that mentioned it and an occasional monument such as the one to Barrington, Rhode Island's "Faithful Slaves" in 1903, there is little evidence that the story ever achieved a significant popular consciousness.

25. The memoirs of former enslaved people in the South have been very informative about slavery there. Some were written after 1865, while others were written earlier, generally by people who had managed to escape from the South. A critical resource is the Federal Writers' Project, part of the Works Project Administration (WPA), which conducted more than one thousand interviews with former enslaved people in the 1930s. These are available through Library of Congress; see http://memory.loc.gov/ammem/snhtml/snintro00.html for an overview of the project. Using some of these testimonies, Baptist explains how diverse documents permitted him to develop "vignettes told from the perspective of enslaved people [that] incorporate not only the specific content of the historical documents, but also details from other sources, as is the custom in evocative history." He writes, "By drawing upon a wide variety of sources, I attempt to provide a richer depiction of the landscape, work practices, and cultural practices of the time and a more intimate portrait of the enslaved African Americans whose experience is the center of this history. These sources include the testimony of other formerly enslaved people who went through virtually identical experiences" (Baptist 2014: 428). Baptist certainly succeeds as a writer in achieving his goals while clearly communicating his methodology.

26. As the Civil War approached, "American scholars constructed two ideological paths to a national reconciliation: positive defenses of slavery grounded in history, theology, and economics; and scientific attacks upon the humanity of the colored races that denied black people the moral status of persons and forced them into the moral sphere of brutes" (Wilder 2013: 239).

27. Two well-known examples are John C. Calhoun and Robert Livingston.

28. He later said he was sorry since he decided the image was important in maintaining an understanding of what slavery entailed.

29. See http://www.harvardandslavery.com/.

30. See Schuessler (2017). Much of what the report uncovered is now available on a superb website that the university built, https://slavery.princeton.edu/.

31. One building in which enslaved people in the North that has been upgraded and maintained in this way is the Royall plantation headquarters in Medford, Massachusetts (see Chapter 6, Figures 21 and 22).

32. These houses and other Northern sites of slavery are discussed at greater length in Chapter 6.

33. A recent archaeological survey in Philadelphia listed some forty Black burial grounds in or close to downtown dating from 1780 to 1849, most of which are totally unknown to people today, even those living near them (Mooney and Morrell 2013).

34. Wikipedia defines the term "potter's field" as "a place for the burial of unknown or indigent people." The expression derives from the Bible, referring to a field used for the extraction of potter's clay; such land, useless for agriculture, could be used as a burial site. The term comes from the New Testament (Matt. 27:7), which refers to the thirty pieces of silver Judas brought to the chief priests at the temple, who after consulting together, "bought with them the potter's field, to be a burying place for strangers" (http://en.wikipedia.org/wiki/Potter's_field).

35. See http://untappedcities.com/2013/07/12/surprise-what-nyc-former-cemeteries-are -now/.

36. Many never had any permanent stone markers of any kind.

37. Savage (1997: 31) recounts that "the sculptor, Henry Kirke Brown, was actually a Northern abolitionist, morally committed to making the figure of the 'Negro' visible in public sculpture."

38. The film *Ethnic Notions* (1986) shows the outrageous stereotypes that circulated in the country in later periods though theater, cartoon images, and films.

39. For example, in most cities schools were segregated and Black teachers could not teach white pupils. In 1931 Ruth Hayre was not hired by the Philadelphia public schools, which at that time did not hire Blacks to teach in either junior or senior high schools. However, in 1946 she became the city's first Black high school teacher and later became the first Black principal and first female president of the city's Board of Education.

40. For a fascinating account of the developing of *Roots* and the ways in which personalization is used as fact and fiction were intertwined in building compelling characters for the series, see Delmont (2016).

Chapter 3

1. Forgetting is a normal human process and is an important way that we set priorities as individuals and in communities. We would be overwhelmed if our individual and collective memories were flawless and nothing from the past were ever forgotten. As Vivian (2010) interestingly argues, forgetting is almost always seen as a failure, a loss, or a weakness rather than part of the normal change process, and in some cases, it is an especially helpful way for a society to address an issue that was previously intractable. In some situations, forgetting can be a socially beneficial action and "can play a positive, formative role in works of public memory" (Vivian 2010: 6). At the same time, we need to understand why particular forms of forgetting occur. It is foolish to simply dismiss collective forgetting as accidental or inevitable with the passage of time. Sometimes forgetting is useful for groups and individuals (Rieff 2016).

2. Philadelphia's Civil War Museum announced it would move to a new site by 2014. However, to date there are no specific plans in place. At the time of its closure, the museum was only open from 11 to 4:30 three days a week. By 2016 it was clear that the museum would not reopen, and their collection was transferred to Gettysburg, the National Constitution Center in Philadelphia, and the city's African American Museum, where the items are now displayed (Salisbury 2016). The Grand Army of the Republic Museum in Northeast Philadelphia is only open the first Sunday each month from 12 to 5.

3. I wish to thank Randall Miller for pointing out to me that while some websites and people argue that Blacks also served in the Confederate army, no reputable scholar shares the view that they were ever armed fighters and did anything more than serve as cooks, wagon drivers, or body servants.

4. Connerton's (2008) list of forms of forgetting is interesting by itself considering how little has been previously written on this topic, but not all the types are relevant here. The first two are "repressive erasure" and "prescriptive forgetting," which are tied to organized state action. Third is forgetting that is constitutive of the formation of a new identity. Fourth and fifth are "structural amnesia," meaning forgetting unimportant details over time, and "annulment," resulting from a surfeit of information as individuals can no longer store it. Sixth is "forgetting as planned obsolescence." Finally, his seventh is "forgetting as humiliated silence," which is often covert, unmarked, and unacknowledged. This is certainly related to the discussion of shame and guilt below as one potential explanation for forgetting Northern slavery, as I argue.

5. There are many parallels to the treatment of Vietnam War survivors and returning veterans in the United States.

6. These same mechanisms can operate on the individual level as well.

7. Halbwachs ([1950] 1997) emphasized the social nature of the process and makes it clear that he believes that without social support memories are not very likely to survive a long time.

8. Soldiers returning from war are often very reluctant to talk about their war experiences or to visit the places where they had served, even decades after they had been in battle. A BBC broadcast on the fiftieth anniversary of D-Day in 1994 reported that, of the British troops who had taken part in the invasion and survived, about a third had returned regularly to the site in Normandy, another third came back in 1994 for the first time, and the final third had never returned to the battlefield at Normandy. Since it was easy to get to the Normandy beach for people living in Britain, it is clear that the reason for not returning for most of them must have been the painful memories they did not wish to reexperience.

9. Political psychologist Vamik Volkan (1988, 1997) discusses this pattern extensively in his analysis of incomplete mourning—one in which "chosen traumas" are transmitted across generations, and the descending generations are burdened with the often impossible task of "resolving" the traumas that preceding ones could not overcome.

10. Even when the story of the massacre became widely accepted among whites, Kelman (2013) recounts that the white Order of the Indian Wars (OIW) met in nearby Colorado Springs, and its leader, Jerry Russell, strongly criticized the emerging story and the plans for the National Park Service site and the proposed memorial, while defending Chivington's actions in the battle. The struggle to create the historical site was complicated by confusion about its actual location and strong disagreements among the tribes about the actual role each had played there and what each wanted to be on the site (Kelman 2013).

11. Zerubavel (2006: 1–16) analyzes situations of silence in which people are aware of things that they cannot speak due to fear, shame, or embarrassment; while this is not the same as forgetting, over time it easily leads to it.

12. Interestingly, after Coates (2014) published his widely read article "The Need for Reparations," it received a great deal of favorable media attention, public discussion, and significant exchanges on a topic that had been very difficult, if not impossible, to engage in meaningful, thoughtful, and respectful interracial discussions for years.

13. When journalists and historians tried to read this editorial years later, they discovered that it had been cut out of the bound volumes of the paper, clearly by someone wanting to remove it from Tulsa's history and memory.

14. Franklin was the father of historian John Hope Franklin who spent most of his illustrious career at Duke University.

15. The History Channel film and *60 Minutes* reports are available at https://www.youtube.com/watch?v=LD3aw4-RJpE.

16. http://slavenorth.com/denial.htm.

17. *Finding Your Roots*, season 1, episode 4, https://www.youtube.com/watch?v=TpbU1DBdgmQ.

18. http://www.pbslearningmedia.org/resource/fyr14.socst.us.rebel/bold-act-of-rebellion/#.

19. Japan—and many of its citizens and politicians—has also shown strong denial following the war as seen in its refusal to acknowledge the killings and massacres it committed such as the Rape of Nanking in 1937 or the use of Korean women as sex slaves during the war. For a good comparison of these two cases, see Lind (2008).

20. A simple example is the exclusion of domestic and agricultural workers from Social Security, a deliberate move to exclude Blacks, a majority of whom worked in these areas in the South.

Chapter 4

1. Two examples are contestation over Muslim girls wearing headscarves in French public schools and the display of Confederate flags and monuments in the South.

2. The Liberty Bell was housed in Independence Hall until 1976 when it was moved to a separate glass pavilion a block away at the time of the Bicentennial for easier public viewing.

3. Understanding why and how people react to different symbols is an interesting question. Most powerful symbols, such as national flags and the Liberty Bell, are ambiguous and abstract, meaning that how they are viewed and understood is almost never immediately obvious when one only observes them. Rather, it is crucial to understand the dynamics by which symbols are used in specific contexts and by particular groups of people.

4. The Independence National Historical Park Annual Report for 2015 says that almost 2.3 million people visited the Liberty Bell in the previous year, while almost 700,000 visited Independence Hall.

5. See Linenthal's (1993) discussion of various challenges in what to present and how in five of the United States' most sacred sites. The discussion of Little Big Horn (formerly the Custer National Battlefield) is perhaps the most salient one for understanding the emotional intensity of divergent views involving inclusion and exclusion, what a site should commemorate, and how this should be done as popular and political ideas change.

6. In other words, the history of enslavement was not viewed as important enough to tell visitors about it.

7. Lawler's careful research in the archives and city records produced the best available account of the house's history available to date. He reports that it was built in 1768 by Mary Lawrence Masters, the widow of a former Philadelphia mayor. Her daughter, who was married to Richard Penn, the grandson of William Penn, moved into it four years later. During the American Revolution two British generals lived there from 1777 to 1778, Benedict Arnold, an American general at the time, lived there in 1778, and a French consul occupied it in 1779. There was a fire in the house in 1781, and the wealthy Robert Morris, a slave trader, arranged to purchase it. He received the deed in 1785. Morris invited Washington to live there while he was President as did John Adams while he was president. All the residents of the house prior to Adams were slaveholders (Coard 2010).

8. In Lawler's ninety-one-page article only one full paragraph discusses the enslaved residents of the house, while there are some additional passing references to where they resided and worked in it. Also see Lawler's (2005) update on the original article.

9. A group of German Quakers living outside Philadelphia signed a petition in 1688 opposing slavery, but most Quakers in the colony and in others did not support it at the time. The petition is now stored in Haverford College's Quaker and Special Collections.

10. Washington became a slave owner at age eleven when his father died and he inherited ten enslaved people. At the time of his death in 1799, 318 enslaved people lived at his Mount Vernon plantation. He owned "only" 123 of them, and the remainder were Martha's "dower slaves," meaning that they had belonged to her first husband, Daniel Parke Custis, and by his will to be passed on to his grandchildren when Martha died. Washington freed those he owned in his will, but Martha could not have done the same even if she had wished to do so (http://www.mountvernon.org/george-washington/slavery/ten-facts-about-washington-slavery/).

11. The NPS has made it clear that that it is working to make its sites around the country more inclusive for some time now, but achieving this is often difficult and sometimes resisted by long-time staffers.

12. See the exchange between Aikens and the Independence Hall Association that Lawler probably authored in April 2002, http://www.ushistory.org/presidentshouse/controversy/aikens2 .php and the reply to it http://www.ushistory.org/presidentshouse/controversy/iha2.php To get a sense of the intensity of the issue that attracted a great deal of interest especially from African Americans in the city, see, e.g., Moore (2002b); and Washington (2002).

13. This turned out to be the first of an annual event for ATAC to mark what they called Black Independence Day, which was typically held on July 3 or July 4 on Independence Mall.

14. This letter is no longer posted on the USHistory.org site that once had virtually all the articles and documents associated with this controversy. Some, but not most, are still there.

15. Perhaps this was because so many Americans think of slavery as it was practiced on large Southern plantations, which they may have visited or seen in photos or films, and assumed that there was always spatial separation of whites and Blacks in sleeping arrangements at the time.

16. See http://www.ushistory.org/presidentshouse/controversy/lawler1.php.

17. ATAC position paper, July 3, 2003 (emphasis in original). http://www.ushistory.org/presidentshouse/news/atac070303.htm.

18. A decade later Beckert (2014) published a book spelling out his argument in detail. A similar argument is found in Baptist (2014).

19. https://www.nps.gov/inde/upload/PH-Site-Meeting.pdf.

20. For the detailed comments, see the last section of the link cited in note 19.

21. Mary Bomar left the position in the city when she was named head of the National Park Service in Washington.

22. "Mayor Street and INHP Superintendent Reidenbach Announce Semi-finalists for President's House Commemorative Project," March 28, 2006 (updated in August 2006), http://www.phila.gov/presidentshouse/pdfs/Semi-Finalists%20Announced.final.revised%20to%205.pdf.

23. Both talks are available in audio recordings at http://www.ushistory.org/presidentshouse/news/ph060506.php.

24. For the designs and a discussion of them, see Aden (2015: 83–112); for more images of the proposals, see "President's House Design Competition Photo Gallery" at http://www.ushistory.org/presidentshouse/plans/designcomp.php.

25. After it was uncovered in the excavation, it was then reburied, which is standard archaeological practice.

26. A brief PBS video offers some good images of the archaeological excavation of the President's House site: "Experience: The President's House" (2009), http://video.whyy.org/video/1366127827/.

27. As Karen Warrington (2007), a member of the Oversight Committee, wrote, "These stories [of the enslaved] must be told because they inform all of us: those who are the descendants of the enslaved and those who benefited from the commerce of slavery."

28. For a book-length treatment of Judge's escape and her life as a free person in New Hampshire, see Dunbar (2017), who calls her Ona rather than by the more diminutive Oney.

29. Political psychologist Vamik Volkan (1988) uses the term "linking object" to refer to a physical object, often incomplete, that promotes an emotional connection between the past and present for people. Often its very ambiguity increases the power of such linking objects. For example, consider the way that the simplicity of the Vietnam Veterans Memorial in Washington elicits powerful feelings from people.

30. Pennsylvania Office of the Governor, "Pennsylvania Governor Rendell Recommends DRPA Funding for Completion of President's House Site," January 21, 2009, http://www.prnewswire.com/news-releases/pennsylvania-governor-rendell-recommends-drpa-funding-for-completion-of-presidents-house-site-61140217.html.

31. A great deal of the information on the nine enslaved Africans is taken from Lawler (2005: 390–400). For information about Ona Judge, see Dunbar (2017), while for Hercules, see LaBan (2010a and 2010b).

Chapter 5

1. Recall the tremendous controversy over the selection of Maya Lin's design for the Vietnam Veterans Memorial in Washington in the 1980s and the more recent intense conflict over the 9/11 Memorial and rebuilding the World Trade Center in New York (Greenspan 2013).

2. The IHA was founded in 1941 to spearhead the creation of Independence Historical National Park and was written into the park's enabling legislation as an independent group of citizens charged with overseeing and being consulted on matters concerning the park.

3. The details of each of these concerns are spelled out in "Issues Concerning the Physical Design of the President's House Commemoration Project," http://www.ushistory.org/presidents house/plans/designissues.php.

4. Presumably the research was Ed Lawler's, and it was Lawler who drafted the outraged memo.

5. The collection of comments, posted on USHistory.org, is no longer available at the website.

6. "President's House Oversight Committee Meets to Resolve Design Controversy," press release, October 9, 2009, http://www.phila.gov/presidentshouse/pdfs/PH_OC_Resolution_ Release_100809.pdf.

7. "President's House Exhibit Concepts Under Revision," press release, December 23, 2009, http://www.phila.gov/presidentshouse/pdfs/President's%20House%20Release%20122309.pdf.

8. See Rabinowitz (2016: 308–11) for his reflections on his experience on this project.

9. Some details were far more esoteric than what most people cared about or could easily put in context.

10. For the Eisterhold panels and text, see "Exhibit Plan for the President's House Exhibition (April 2010)," http://www.ushistory.org/presentshouse/plans/eisterhold/index.php.

11. Aden (2015) reports that McPherson told him that adding the color on the panels was seen as a way to make the site more attractive.

12. Louis Massiah of Scribe Video Center produced them, and novelist Lorene Cary wrote the scripts.

13. One striking absence, which probably matters given how people often approach this part of the site first, is that none of the three small panels make any direct connection to the space we are seeing below and the life of enslaved Africans in the house. For example, none of them mention that the underground passageway leading from the kitchen to the Washingtons' living quarters is where the enslaved people probably walked to carry the food to the President's dining room.

14. A few times I have seen NPS rangers on the site. When I have asked them questions, I often found them to be ill-informed on matters that they should be able to discuss easily. This is especially disturbing when children ask questions to which they do not really know the answers but pretend that they do. For a brief time after the site opened, a short video about the creation of the site was shown in the park's visitor center. It still could be presented regularly since there it contains a good explanation of the process by which the site was created and its significance.

15. Young (1993: 10) observes that figurative monuments and sculptures serve "as a point of departure for political performances. It is as if the figurative sculpture were needed to engage viewers with likenesses of people, to evoke an empathic link between viewer and monument that might then be marshaled into particular meaning." Perhaps the absence of such figures or other objects that engage visitors emotionally at the site is important in explaining the reactions I have observed.

Chapter 6

1. See http://www.tonimorrisonsociety.org/bench.html for a description of the project and the twenty benches that exist to date.

2. One project that promises to vastly increase our knowledge of enslaved people is the Freedmen's Bureau Project, which is digitizing its records that were created immediately after the Civil War when four million enslaved people gained their freedom. The project, among other

goals, seeks to help descendants trace their ancestors through the Bureau's records and make them available online at http://www.discoverfreedmen.org/.

3. Baptist (2014) in his masterful study of the expansion of slavery into the Mississippi Delta area does not use the term "plantation" but instead calls them "slave labor camps"—entirely appropriate to emphasize, as he does, the experience of the enslaved people forced to work on them.

4. Although they are not sites of slavery as such, roads throughout the South are named after Confederate soldiers and heroes. For many African Americans these names are reminders that the Civil War was fought to maintain slavery in the region and led by the people after whom the roads are named. While calculating the precise number of miles named for Confederate figures is difficult, Darlin and Merrill (2015) suggest that it is in the thousands and that Jefferson Davis's name is on at least 468 miles of Southern roadways.

5. There has been a great deal of attention to the details of the lives of the enslaved at Monticello since the 1970s. Historians working there used Jefferson's extensive records to learn a great deal about them (http://www.monticello.org/site/plantation-and-slavery), much of which has also been published in a book that traces the lives of a group of descendants of those enslaved there, which provides rich details of their lives as free people (Stanton 2012). Since 1993 there have been extensive interviews with more than two hundred of their descendants (some of which are available on Monticello's excellent website), and Monticello has hosted reunions for the descendants. Monticello hosted a two-day conference "Telling the History of Slavery: Scholarship, Museum Interpretation, and the Public" in February 2013 that is available at http://www.monticello.org/site/multimedia/telling-history-slavery-symposium.

6. See Schwarz (2001) for a summary of the findings from the research about life at Mount Vernon.

7. Mount Vernon's website includes a short video, "Lives Bound Together," http://www.mountvernon.org/plan-your-visit/calendar/exhibitions/lives-bound-together-slavery-at-george-washingtons-mount-vernon/.

8. This burying ground was cleaned and a memorial stone placed there in 1929. In 1983, after a *Washington Post* article publicized its neglect, the area was cleaned again and a larger memorial installed. It is now the site of an annual memorial ceremony every October.

9. For a more complete description of the commission and its work to date, see http://www.richmondgov.com/CommissionSlaveTrail/.

10. In North Carolina, Stagville Plantation, (http://www.stagville.org) has not only restored a number of slave cabins but has also used available records to compile a 300-plus-page book with the names, descendants, and connections of the enslaved persons who lived and worked there (http://www.stagville.org/genealogy/). This is just one of many plantations where the records related to the enslaved were very detailed and are still available. For example, see Dunn (2014).

11. http://www.charleston-sc.gov/index.aspx?NID=160. Also see Yuhl (2013) who provides a background and more detail on this museum's history and evolution.

12. At Monticello, the reconstructed slave quarters were made of wood while at Mount Vernon they were brick. I assume these materials were used in the reconstruction because that is what was originally used.

13. http://www.boonehallplantation.com/.

14. "Magnolia Plantation & Gardens" video, http://magnoliaplantation.com/video_minutes.html.

15. For details of the tour, see Magnolia's website: http://www.magnoliaplantation.com/slaverytofreedom.html.

16. http://www.draytonhall.org/. The History Channel produced an hour-long show called *The Voices of Drayton Hall* that visitors can watch on a small DVD player while walking around

the plantation. It includes interviews with a number of African American descendants of the enslaved there talking about their connections to the site. The video is also for sale in the gift shop and at some online sites.

17. http://cdn.lib.unc.edu/commemorative-landscapes/media/monument/245_full.jpg.

18. "Slave memorial at Princes Hill Burial Ground Barrington, Rhode Island," https://en.wikipedia.org/wiki/File:Slave_memorial_at_Princes_Hill_Burial_Ground_Barrington,_Rhode_Island.jpg.

19. The city's website about the house makes no mention of slavery. However, the Wikipedia article on it does.

20. "The Slave Dwelling Project" website, http://slavedwellingproject.org/.

21. Wikipedia, s.v. "Huguenot Street Historic District," https://en.wikipedia.org/wiki/Huguenot_Street_Historic_District.

22. For a video showing McGill's visit, see "Where They Slept," at https://vimeo.com/143894765.

23. Isaac Royall Jr. was a Loyalist during the Revolutionary War; in 1775 the family fled to England, where he died of smallpox in 1781. Harvard Law School was established through a bequest from his estate. Royall's coat of arms, with its three stacked wheat sheaves, was the school's crest. It became a source of controversy in late 2015, and soon after Harvard voted to change the design of its crest ("Harvard 'Black Tape' Vandalism Brings Law School's Controversial Past to Fore," *Guardian*, November 21, 2005, http://www.theguardian.com/education/2015/nov/21/harvard-law-school-black-tape-vandalism-royall-must-fall-movement (Annear 2016).

24. The Royall House and Slave Quarters museum is run by the Royall House Association (http://www.royallhouse.org/).

25. See http://www.nyharborparks.org/visit/tour-this-hallowed-ground.html.

26. For more on Pinkster celebrations in New York, see White (1991: 95–106).

27. This is the memorial to the first Black regiment in the Union army that is portrayed in the film *Glory*. The guide on my tour spent about fifteen to twenty minutes talking about the bravery of the Black soldiers in the Fifty-Fourth and the sacrifices they made in South Carolina where many died.

28. Some slaving voyages set out from New York as late as the eve of the Civil War. Hodges (1999: 257) reports that there were at least fifty-seven slave ships from there between 1857 and 1860. Also see Farrow, Lang, and Frank (2005: 121–37).

29. This site presents the entire report by the Committee on Slavery and Justice at Brown: http://www.brown.edu/Research/Slavery_Justice/documents/SlaveryAndJustice.pdf and this one contains its curriculum recommendations for New England schools: http://www.choices.edu/curriculum-unit/forgotten-history-slave-trade-slavery-new-england/.

30. In 2015 the Episcopal diocese of Rhode Island, which "was steeped in the trans-Atlantic slave trade," announced that it would establish "a museum dedicated to telling that story" as part of a center for racial reconciliation and healing that would be housed in the two-hundred-year-old Cathedral of St. John in Providence (Seelye 2015 Smith 2014). The Museum opened in July 2017 (https://www.doorsopenri.org/2017/07/14/cathedral-of-st-john/).

31. http://www.brown.edu/initiatives/slavery-and-justice/dedication-slavery-memorial.

32. The eight-page booklet explains the Browns and the slave trade, but it costs $5 and I wonder how many visitors actually buy and read it.

33. This is typical on house tours, which are almost always object driven, and most guides like to use the objects as prompts to discuss a topic. At the Brown house, there was unease from the staff about changing the house tours to focus on slavery and the slave trade without objects that could serve as prompts for their discussion (Melish 2009: 109).

34. James's own mansion, not far away, was destroyed by a 1903 fire. It seems reasonable to think of most of the nonresponses to her invitation as signs of embarrassment or shame.

Chapter 7

1. At the historical sites of slavery that I have visited in both the North and South, I often have asked, "Where were the remains of the enslaved who died here buried?" Often the answer is "We really are not sure."

2. Website of the Periwinkle Humanities Initiative, https://www.periwinklehumanities.org/mission.

3. For the most part, the terms "burial ground" and "burying ground" are used interchangeably in books, articles, and reports I have found so I use them both here. A good example is found in the Sammons and Cunningham book, which sometimes uses them both on the same page (e.g., Sammons and Cunningham 2003: 60).

4. A moving video of the ceremony is available at http://www.africanburyinggroundnh.org/.

5. See the website of "God's Little Acre: America's Colonial African Cemetery" http://www.colonialcemetery.com/.

6. Website of "God's Little Acre: America's Colonial African Cemetery" (http://www.colonialcemetery.com/); see also Liz Gray, "God's Little Acre," Rhode Tour (http://rhodetour.org/items/show/40).

7. When the first archaeological team was fired following controversy at the African Burial Ground in New York, John Milner Associates were hired to complete the job there because of the way they had managed this dig.

8. For a more complete history of the site since 1755, see Fowler, Ruth, and Basalik (2013: 5–32).

9. The maps that were used were from the latter half of nineteenth century because no one turned up any from an earlier period despite the fact that the cemetery had been used since the middle of the eighteenth century. However, the original deed for the burial ground for the site had very precise measurements. The units used are different from those in use today, but they fit pretty well with what was shown in the later maps. The real question was whether any burials were outside the boundaries. In addition, the nineteenth-century houses that had been built with basements on part of the land would have disturbed burials outside the boundaries in any case (Peter DiCarlo, an architect living in Germantown, personal interview, November 2014).

10. These included the Pennsylvania State Historic Preservation Office, the Advisory Council on Historic Preservation, the Philadelphia Archaeological Forum, the Northwest Neighbors of Germantown, Avenging the Ancestors Coalition (ATAC), the Philadelphia Historical Commission, the Germantown Historical Society, the Preservation Alliance of Greater Philadelphia, Queen Lane Residents Council, Pulaski Town Community Association, Westside Neighborhood Council, Mount Moriah Baptist Church, Penn Knox Neighborhood Association, and the City of Philadelphia.

11. The quotes in this paragraph are from the agreement. "Programmatic Agreement Among the United States Department of Housing and Urban Development (HUD), the Philadelphia Housing Authority (PHA), the Pennsylvania State Historic Preservation Officer (SHPO), and the Advisory Council on Historic Preservation Regarding the Redevelopment of the Queen Lane Apartments in Philadelphia County, Pennsylvania" (ER #2011-0018-101), December, 16, 2013. Advisory Council on Historic Preservation website, http://www.achp.gov/docs/pa.hud.queen%20lane%20redevelopment%20project.pa.21feb14.pdf.

12. Also see http://bethelburyinggroundproject.com/2015/08/28/revised-timeline-for-bethel-burying-ground/.

13. See http://bethelburyinggroundproject.com.

14. A short video narrated by Doug Mooney, the lead archaeologist on the project, showing the site and explaining the findings is available at https://www.youtube.com/watch?v=UeA3JnwKzkE.

15. I attended all of the Friends of Bethel Burying Ground Coalition meetings and identified myself as a supporter of the group's demands, made substantive suggestions, and wore a "Friends of Bethel Burying Ground" button on different occasions. I also made it clear that I was doing research on the controversy.

Chapter 8

1. See the discussion in Chapter 3 of Henry Louis Gates Jr.'s interviews with famous white people who had no idea that their own ancestors were slave owners. Another example is the DeWolf family in Rhode Island and similar families who developed a narrative about their early ancestors that emphasized their role as merchants and businessmen rather than their slave trading and slave ownership.

2. I know of no systematic studies, yet I make this statement, after more than a decade of interest in the question, based on conversations I have had with hundreds of people, Black and white, books, and videos. In addition, almost every historian I have read expresses this point of view, as the many quotes I cite show. If I had to make an educated guess, it would be that today African Americans are more aware of Northern slavery than whites but that the proportion of each that is both aware of its existence and who know many details about it still is quite small.

3. Fath Davis Ruffins pointed out that when the Smithsonian's Museum of History and Technology opened in 1964, "slavery was left out of the discussion of the American nation because that was 'just a Southern problem'" (talk given at the Pennsylvania Convention Center, Philadelphia, to discuss the plans for the President's House site, June 5, 2006. It can be heard at http://media.ushistory.org/presidentshouse/ph060506ruffins.mp3).

4. What should be noted here is that for years what the data have shown is that in general Blacks will vote for white candidates, but whites are reluctant to vote for Black ones.

5. Georgetown University, located in Washington, D.C., which only ended slavery in 1862 during the Civil War, has been particularly forthright and open about its prior involvement in slavery. Jesuits, who founded and ran the school, sold 272 enslaved Blacks from its plantations in Maryland in 1839 to keep the university solvent and build its endowment. They were sent to New Orleans for sale and then to cotton plantations in Louisiana. The university formed a working group to study what happened to them and how to make amends. A genealogist identified a number of descendants of the enslaved. The university removed the names of two of Georgetown's presidents who had been involved in the sale from buildings and renamed a building after one of the enslaved who had been sold. Georgetown promised to give special consideration to descendants for admission as a form of reparation. The university also invited descendants to campus for a moving ceremony at which the Jesuits apologized for their actions (Swarns 2016; Zauzmer 2017).

6. For years before his book was completed or the miniseries produced, Haley gave inspiring public talks around the country about his research and how he did it, encouraging them to do the same (Delmont 2016).

7. In the late 1970s when *Roots* aired, there were still many people alive who had personally known older people in their youth who had once been enslaved.

8. The best known is the Shaw Memorial on the Boston Common honoring the Fifty-Fourth Regiment of Massachusetts, the first Black regiment, organized in the North, made famous in the film *Glory*, and led by Colonel Robert Gould Shaw, a wealthy white Bostonian.

9. Washington was concerned because Ona Judge had run away a few months earlier, and Hercules' son Richmond had been caught stealing money and the President feared both father and son were planning an escape.

10. Following the opening of the President's House/Slavery Memorial in December 2010, ATAC members and supporters gathered on the same date for the next three or four years to

mark their successful efforts to get the memorial site built and opened. As problems with the site's video monitors and leaking vitrine dragged on without solutions, the initial pride ATAC members felt with the achievement often turned to frustration and anger at the lack of progress in producing a solution to the unrepaired defects by the city or the architectural firm responsible for its construction.

Epilogue

1. I want to thank historian Richard Dunn for suggesting that I close with my reactions to this new national museum, comparing its treatment of enslavement to what older popular narratives communicated (or failed to communicate) about slavery.

2. Wilkins (2016) recounts the long, involved story of getting the museum approved in Congress and then built.

Works Cited

Achrati, Nora (2002). "500 Seek Slave Memorial at Liberty Bell." *Philadelphia Inquirer*, July 4.

Adams, Catherine, and Elizabeth H. Pleck (2010). *Love of Freedom: Black Women in Colonial and Revolutionary New England*. Oxford: Oxford University Press.

Adams, T. H. (1845). "Washington's Runaway Slave." *Granite Freeman* (Concord, NH), May 22.

Aden, Roger G. (2015). *Upon the Ruins of Liberty: Slavery, the President's House at Independence National Historical Park, and Public Memory*. Philadelphia: Temple University Press.

Alderman, Derek H., and Rachel M. Campbell (2008). "Symbolic Excavation and the Artifact Politics of Remembering Slavery in the American South: Observations from Walterboro, South Carolina." *Southeastern Geographer* 48 (3): 338–55.

Annear, Steve (2016). "Harvard Law School to Ditch Controversial Shield." *Boston Globe*, March 14.

Armstead, Myra B. Young, ed. (2003). *Mighty Change, Tall Within: Black Identity in the Hudson Valley*. Albany: State University of New York Press.

Armstrong, Karen (1996). *Jerusalem: One City, Three Faiths*. New York: Ballantine Books.

Assmann, Jan (1995). "Collective Memory and Cultural Identity." *New German Critique* 65 (Spring–Summer): 125–33.

Bailey, Ronald (1998). "'Those Valuable People, the Africans': The Economic Impact of the Slave(ry) Trade on Textile Industrialization in New England." In *The Meaning of Slavery in the North*, ed. David Roediger and Martin H. Blatt, 1–31. New York: Garland.

Bailyn, Bernard (2000). "Slavery and Population Growth in Colonial New England." In *Engines of Enterprise: An Economic History of New England*, ed. Peter Temin, 253–60. Cambridge, MA: Harvard University Press.

Baptist, Edward E. (2014). *The Half Has Never Been Told: Slavery and the Making of American Capitalism*. New York: Basic Books.

Beckert, Sven (2014). *Empire of Cotton: A Global History*. New York: Alfred A. Knopf.

Benvenisti, Meron (2000). *Sacred Landscape: The Buried History of the Holy Land Since 1948*. Berkeley: University of California Press.

Berlin, Ira (1998). *Many Thousands Gone: The First Two Centuries of Slavery in North America*. Cambridge, MA: Belknap Press of Harvard University Press.

—— (2003). *Generations of Captivity: A History of African-American Slaves*. Cambridge, MA: Belknap Press of Harvard University.

—— (2004). "American Slavery in History and Memory and the Search for Social Justice." *Journal of American History* 90 (4): 1251–68.

Berlin, Ira, and Leslie M. Harris (2005a). "Introduction: Uncovering, Discovering, and Recovering: Digging in New York's Slave Past Beyond the African Burial Ground." In *Slavery in New York*, ed. Ira Berlin and Leslie M. Harris, 1–27. New York: New Press.

——, eds. (2005b). *Slavery in New York*. New York: New Press.

Blackmon, Douglas A. (2009). *Slavery by Another Name: The Re-Enslavement of Black Americans from the Civil War to World War II.* New York: Anchor Books.

Blair, Carole, Greg Dickinson, and Brian L. Ott (2010). "Introduction: Rhetoric/Memory/Place." In *Places of Public Memory: The Rhetoric of Museums and Memorials.* Greg Dickinson, Carole Blair, and Brian L. Ott, 1–54. Tuscaloosa: University of Alabama Press.

Blakey, Michael L. (1994). "American Nationality and Ethnicity in the Depicted Past." In *The Politics of the Past*, ed. Peter Gathercole and David Lowenthal, 38–48. London: Routledge.

——— (1998). "The New York African Burial Ground Project: An Examination of Enslaved Lives, a Construction of Ancestral Ties." *Transforming Anthropology* 7 (1): 53–58.

——— (2001). "Bioarchaeology of the African Diaspora in the Americas: Its Origins and Scope." *Annual Review of Anthropology* 30:387–422.

Blight, David W. (2001). *Race and Reunion: The Civil War in American History.* Cambridge, MA: Belknap Press of Harvard University Press.

——— (2002). "Historians and 'Memory.'" *Common-Place* 2 (3). http://www.common-place -archives.org/vol-02/no-03/author/

Bodnar, John (1992). *Remaking America: Public Memory, Commemoration, and Patriotism in the Twentieth Century.* Princeton, NJ: Princeton University Press.

Bolling, Deborah (2004) "Slave Discovery." *Philadelphia City Paper*, July 8–14.

Brown University (2009). *Report of Commission on Memorials.* Providence, RI: Brown University.

Brown University Steering Committee on Slavery and Justice (2006). *Slavery and Justice.* Providence, RI: Brown University.

Buckalew, Terry (2012) "Weccacoe: Burying Ground, Garden, Park and Playground—A Historical Sketch and Timeline from 1800–2012." *genpa.org* http://genpa.org/sites/default/files/ BBG-HistoricalSketch.pdf

——— (2015). "The 'Hallowed Ground' Before Bethel Burying Ground." Bethel Burying Ground Project, February 1. http://bethelburyinggroundproject.com/2015/02/01/the -hallowed-ground-before-bethel-burying-ground/

Cantwell, Anne-Marie, and Diana diZerega Wall (2001). "'We Were Here': The African Presence in Colonial New York." In *Unearthing Gotham: The Archaeology of New York City*, 277–94. New Haven, CT: Yale University Press.

Chan, Alexandra A. (2007). *Slavery in the Age of Reason: Archaeology at a New England Farm.* Knoxville: University of Tennessee Press.

Clark-Pujara, Christy (2016). *Dark Work: The Business of Slavery in Rhode Island.* New York: New York University Press.

Coard, Michael (2009). "President's House Must Be Practical Too." *Philadelphia Inquirer*, August 31.

——— (2010). *Slavery Memorial/President's House.* Grand *Opening* Speech, December 15, 2010, Philadelphia.

——— (2012). "Apparently, No One at PHA Has Seen Poltergeist." *Philadelphia Magazine*, October 2.

——— (2017). "Officials Defend Jewish Cemetery but Defile Black One." *Philadelphia Tribune*, April 15.

Coates, Ta-Nehisi (2012). "Racism Against White People." *Atlantic*, July 6.

——— (2014). "The Case for Reparations." *Atlantic*, May 21.

Collins, Scott (2015). "Ben Affleck Apologizes in PBS 'Finding Your Roots' Slavery Uproar." *Los Angeles Times*, April 22.

Confino, Alon (1997). "Collective Memory and Cultural History: Problems and Method." *American Historical Review* 102 (5): 1386–1403.

——— (2011). "History and Memory." In *The Oxford History of Historical Writing*, vol. 5, *Historical Writing Since 1945*, ed. Axel Schneider and Daniel Woolf, 36–51. New York: Oxford University Press.

Connerton, Paul (1989). *How Societies Remember*. Cambridge: Cambridge University Press.
———— (2008). "Seven Types of Forgetting." *Memory Studies* 1 (1): 59–71.
———— (2009). *How Modernity Forgets*. Cambridge: Cambridge University Press.
Cosgrove, Denis E. (1998). *Social Formation and Symbolic Landscape*. Madison: University of Wisconsin Press.
Coski, John M. (2005). *The Confederate Battle Flag: America's Most Embattled Emblem*. Cambridge, MA: Belknap Press.
Coughtry, Jay (1981). *The Notorious Triangle: Rhode Island and the African Slave Trade*. Philadelphia: Temple University Press.
Cox, Karen L. (2003). "The Confederate Monument at Arlington: A Token of Reconciliation." In *Monuments to the Lost Cause: Women and the Landscapes of Southern Memory*, ed. Cynthia Mills and Pamela H. Simpson, 149–62. Knoxville: University of Tennessee Press.
Crane, Susan (1997). "Writing the Individual Back into Collective Memory." *American Historical Review* 102 (5): 1372–85.
Cranston, G. Timothy, with Neil Dunay (2014). *We Were Here Too: Selected Stories of Black History in North Kingstown*. North Kingstown, RI: G. Timothy Cranston and Neil Dunay.
Cruson, Daniel (2007). *The Slaves of Central Fairfield County: The Journey from Slave to Freeman in Nineteenth-Century Connecticut*. Charleston, SC: History Press.
Dandurant, Karen (2014). "African Burying Ground Ceremony Honors Portsmouth Legacy." *Seacoastonline.com*, August 19.
Darlin, Damon, and Jeremy B. Merrill (2015). "Honors for Confederates, for Thousands of Miles." *New York Times*, June 26.
Davis, David Brion (2006). *Inhuman Bondage: The Rise and Fall of Slavery in the New World*. New York: Oxford University Press.
Dayan, Daniel, and Elihu Katz (1992). *Media Events: The Live Broadcasting of History*. Cambridge, MA: Harvard University Press.
Delmont, Matthew F. (2016). *Making "Roots": A Nation Captivated*. Oakland: University of California Press.
Devine-Wright, Patrick, and Evanthia Lyons (1997). "Remembering Pasts and Representing Places: The Construction of National Identities in Ireland." *Journal of Environmental Psychology* 17 (1): 33–45.
Dew, Charles B. (2001). *Apostles of Disunion: Southern Secession Commissioners and the Causes of the Civil War*. Charlottesville: University Press of Virginia.
DeWolf, Thomas Norman (2008). *Inheriting the Trade: A Northern Family Confronts Its Legacy as the Largest Slave-Trading Dynasty in U.S. History*. Boston: Beacon Press.
di Bonaventura, Allegra (2013). *For Adam's Sake: A Family Saga in Colonial New England*. New York: Liveright.
Dinkins, David (1994). "Preface." In *Reclaiming Our Past, Honoring Our Ancestors: New York's 18th Century African Burial Ground and the Memorial Competition*, ed. Edward Kaufman. New York: African Burial Ground Competition Coalition.
Douglas, Mary (1986). *How Institutions Think*. Syracuse, NY: Syracuse University Press.
DuBois, W. E. B. ([1899] 1967). *The Philadelphia Negro: A Social Study*. New York: Schocken Books.
Dunay, Neil (2014). "Captives at Cocumscussoc: From Bondage to Freedom." In *We Were Here Too: Selected Stories of Black History in North Kingstown*, by G. Timothy Cranston with Neil Dunay, 62–93. North Kingstown, RI: G. Timothy Cranston and Neil Dunay.
Dunbar, Erica Armstrong (2017). *Never Caught: The Washingtons' Relentless Pursuit of Their Runaway Slave, Ona Judge*. New York: Atria Books/37 Ink.
Dunn, Richard S. (2014). *A Tale of Two Planatations: Slave Life and Labor in Jamaica and Virginia*. Cambridge, MA: Harvard University Press.

Durkheim, Emile ([1915] 1995). *The Elementary Forms of Religious Life.* New York: Free Press.

Earle, Alice Morse (1898). *In Old Narragansett.* New York: Charles Scribner's Sons.

——— (1900). *Home Life in Colonial Days.* New York: Macmillan.

Eichstedt, Jennifer L., and Stephen Small (2002). *Representations of Slavery: Race and Ideology in Southern Plantation Museums.* Washington, DC: Smithsonian Books.

Ellsworth, Scott (1982). *Death in a Promised Land: The Tulsa Race Riot of 1921.* Baton Rouge: Louisiana State University Press.

Faden, Regina (2012). "Museums and the Story of Slavery: The Challenge of Language." In *Politics of Memory: Making Slavery Visible in the Public Space,* ed. Ana Lucia Araujo, 252–66. New York: Routledge.

Fanelli, Doris Devine (2004). *President's House Civic Engagement Forum, October 30, 2004, Report.* http://www.nps.gov/inde/upload/Forumgrantreport.pdf.

Farrell, Joelle (2008). "More Than 200 Gather to Honor Washington's Slaves." *Philadelphia Inquirer,* July 4.

Farrow, Anne, Joel Lang, and Jenifer Frank (2005). *Complicity: How the North Promoted, Prolonged, and Profited from Slavery.* New York: Ballantine Books.

Feagin, Joe R. (2013). *The White Racial Frame: Centuries of Racial Framing and Counter-Framing.* New York: Routledge.

Fernandez, Manny, and Christine Hauser (2015). "Texas Mother Teaches Textbook Company a Lesson on Accuracy." *New York Times,* October 5.

Finkenbine, Roy E. (2007). "Belinda's Petition: Reparations for Slavery in Revolutionary Massachusetts." *William and Mary Quarterly* 64 (1): 95–104.

Fitts, Robert K. (1996). "The Landscapes of Northern Bondage." *Historical Archaeology* 30 (2): 54–73.

——— (1998). *Inventing New England's Slave Paradise: Master/Slave Relations in Eighteenth-Century Narragansett, Rhode Island.* New York: Garland.

Fitzgerald, Frances (1979). *America Revised: History Schoolbooks in the Twentieth Century.* New York: Vintage Books.

Flam, Faye (2001). "Formerly on Ice, Past Unearthed: The Icehouse Found in Philadelphia Gives a Glimpse into Colonial History." *Philadelphia Inquirer,* February 23.

Fogu, Claudio, and Wulf Kansteiner (2006). "The Politics of Memory and the Poetics of History." In *The Politics of Memory in Postwar Europe,* ed. Richard Ned Lebow, Wulf Kansteiner, and Claudio Fogu, 284–310. Durham, NC: Duke University Press.

Foner, Eric (2015). *Gateway to Freedom: The Hidden History of the Underground Railroad.* New York: W. W. Norton.

Fowler, Rachael E., Philip Ruth, and Kenneth J. Basalik (2013). *Phase I Archaeological Survey, Queen Lane Apartments Project.* Lansdale, PA: Cultural Heritage Research Services, for Shoemaker/Synterra.

Francis, Megan Ming (2014). *Civil Rights and the Making of the Modern American State.* New York: Cambridge University Press.

Franklin, John Hope, and Scott Ellsworth (2001). "History Knows No Fences: An Overview." In *Tulsa Race Riot: A Report by the Oklahoma Commission to Study the Tulsa Race Riot of 1921,* 21–36. Oklahoma City: Oklahoma State Government.

Fuentes, Marisa J., and Deborah Gray White, eds. (2016). *Scarlet and Black: Slavery and Dispossession in Rutgers History.* New Brunswick, NJ: Rutgers University Press.

Galland, China (2007). *Love Cemetery: Unburying the Secret History of Slaves.* New York: HarperOne.

Geertz, Clifford (1973). "Thick Description: Toward an Interpretive Theory of Culture," in *The Interpretation of Cultures.* New York: Basic Books, pp. 3–30.

Gerzina, Gretchen Holbrook (2008). *Mr. and Mrs. Prince: How an Extraordinary Eighteenth-Century Family Moved out of Slavery and into Legend.* New York: Amistad.

Gigantino, James J. (2015). *The Ragged Road to Abolition: Slavery and Freedom in New Jersey, 1775–1865*. Philadelphia: University of Pennsylvania Press.

Gluckman, Max (1954). *Rituals of Rebellion in South-East Africa*. Manchester: Manchester University Press.

Gould, Stephen Jay (1981). *The Mismeasure of Man*. New York: W. W. Norton.

Greene, Lorenzo Johnston ([1942] 1969). *The Negro in Colonial New England*. New York: Atheneum.

Greenspan, Elizabeth (2013). *Battle for Ground Zero: Inside the Political Struggle to Rebuild the World Trade Center*. New York: Palgrave Macmillan.

Griswold, Mac (2013). *The Manor: Three Centuries of a Slave Plantation on Long Island*. New York: Farrar, Straus and Giroux.

Grondahl, Paul (2015). "Remains of Schuyler Slaves to Be Reburied." *Albany Times Union*, September 30.

Groth, Michael E. (2003). "Laboring for Freedom in Dutchess County," in *Mighty Change, Tall Within: Black Identity in the Hudson Valley*. Myra B. Young Armstead. Albany: State University of New York Press, pp. 58–79.

Groth, Michael E. (2017). *Slavery and Freedom in the Mid-Hudson Valley*. Albany: SUNY Press.

Halbwachs, Maurice (1995 [1950]). *La memoire collective*. Paris: Albin Michel.

Hanlon, Christopher (January 24, 2013) "Disunion: Puritans vs. Cavaliers." *New York Times*. http://opinionator.blogs.nytimes.com/2013/01/24/puritans-vs-cavaliers/?_r = 0.

Hardesty, Jared Ross (2016). *Unfreedom: Slavery and Dependence in Eighteenth-Century Boston*. New York: NYU Press.

Harper, Douglas (2003), Slavery in the North. http://slavenorth.com/

Harrington, Spencer P. M. (2003). "Bones & Bureaucrats: New York's Great Cemetery Imbroglio." *Archaeology*(March/April): 29–38.

Harris, Leslie M. (2003). *In the Shadow of Slavery: African-Americans in New York City 1626–1863*. Chicago: University of Chicago Press.

Hayes, Katherine Howlett (2013). *Slavery Before Race: Europeans, Africans and Indians at Long Island's Sylvester Manor Plantation, 1651–1884*. New York: NYU Press.

Hightower, Robert (2007). "President's House Slave Quarters Covered to Preserve Dig Find." *Philadelphia Tribune*, August 3.

——— (2009). "Heated Debate on President's House Work." *Philadelphia Tribune*, May 10.

Hill, Michael (2016). "Presumed Slave Remains Await Reburial, 11 Years After Discovery of Unmarked Grave Near Albany." *Daily Freeman* (Kingston, NY), May 12.

Hobsbawm, Eric, and Terence Ranger, eds. (1983). *The Invention of Tradition*. Cambridge: Cambridge University Press.

Hodges, Graham Russell (1996). *The Black Loyalist Directory: African Americans in Exile After the American Revolution*. New York: Garland.

——— (1999). *Root and Branch: African Americans in New York and East Jersey, 1613–1863*. Chapel Hill: University of North Carolina Press.

Hoffler, Janae (2006). "Groups Working to Settle Dispute." *Philadelphia Tribune*, September 19.

Holt, Sharon Ann (2003). "Race in the Park." *Common-Place* 3 (4).

Horowitz, Helen Lefkowitz (1994). *The Power and the Passion of M. Carey Thomas*. New York: Alfred A. Knopf.

Horton, James Oliver, and Lois E. Horton (1997). *In Hope of Liberty: Culture, Community, and Protest Among Northern Free Blacks, 1700–1860*. New York: Oxford University Press.

Horwitz, Tony (1999). *Confederates in the Attic: Dispatches from the Unfinished Civil War*. New York: Vintage Books.

Hurmence, Belinda, ed. (1984). *My Folks Don't Want Me to Talk About Slavery: Twenty-One Oral Histories of Former North Carolina Slaves*. Winston-Salem, NC: John F. Blair.

Irons, Meghan E. (2013). "Governor Maggie Hassan Signs Bill into Law that Frees 14 African Slaves." Boston.com, June 7.

Johnson, Cynthia Mestad (2014). *James DeWolf and the Rhode Island Slave Trade.* Charleston, SC: History Press.

Johnson, Hannibal B. (2012). "Reparations and the 1921 Tulsa Race Riot: Righting the Wrongs of History." http://www.hannibalbjohnson.com/reparations-and-the-1921-tulsa-race-riot-righting-the-wrongs-of-history/

Johnson, Lyndon Baines (1976). "Running Against the Twelfth Man of History." *New York Times.* December 26.

Kachun, Mitch (2011). "Celebrating Freedom: Juneteenth and the Emancipation Festival Tradition." In *Remixing the Civil War: Meditations on the Sesquicentennial*, ed. Thomas J. Brown, 71–91. Baltimore: Johns Hopkins University Press.

Katz, Sarah R. (2006). "Redesigning Civic Memory: The African Burial Ground in Lower Manhattan." Master's thesis, University of Pennsylvania.

Katznelson, Ira (2005). *When Affirmative Action Was White: An Untold History of Racial Inequality in Twentieth-Century America.* New York: W. W. Norton.

Kelman, Ari (2013). *A Misplaced Massacre: Struggling over the Memory of Sand Creek.* Cambridge, MA: Harvard University Press.

Kilgannon, Corey (2003). "Public Lives: Unearthing the Past, Then Burying It with Respect." *New York Times*, October 2.

Kutz, David (1994). *The African Burial Ground: An American Discovery.* Videocassette. Four-part documentary produced by Kutz Television for U.S. General Services Administration. Narrated by Ossie Davis and Ruby Dee. Longtail Distribution.net.

LaBan, Craig (2010a) "A Birthday Shock from Washington's Chef." *Philadelphia Inquirer*, February 22.

——— (2010b) "Hercules: Master of Cuisine, Slave of Washington." *Philadelphia Inquirer*, February 21.

LaRoche, Cheryl J. (2007a). "Public History at Sites of Protest: Citizenship on the President's House Viewing Platform." *Cross Ties* [Mid-Atlantic Regional Center for the Humanities newsletter] 2 (3): 1–3.

——— (2007b) "Walk with the Ancestors." *Philadelphia Inquirer*, July 4.

LaRoche, Cheryl J., and Michael L. Blakey (1997). "Seizing Intellectual Power: The Dialogue at the New York African Burial Ground." *Historical Archaeology* 31 (3): 84–106.

Lawler, Edward Jr. (2002a). "George Washington's Philadelphia Slave Quarters." *Center for History and the New Media*, December 2. http://www.ushistory.org/presidentshouse/news/hnn120202.htm.

——— (2002b). "The President's House in Philadelphia: The Rediscovery of a Lost Landmark." *Pennsylvania Magazine of History and Biography* 126 (1): 5–95.

——— (2005). "The President's House Revisited." *Pennsylvania Magazine of History and Biography* 129 (4): 371–410.

——— (n.d.) "A Brief History of the President's House in Philadelphia." No longer available at http://www.ushistory.org/presidentshouse/history/briefhistory.htm

Leahy, Kristin (2003). "Invisible Hands: Slaves and Servants of the Chew Family." http://www.cliveden.org/wp-content/uploads/2013/09/Invisible-Hands-Slaves-and-Servants.pdf

Lebow, Richard Ned (2006). "The Memory of Politics in Postwar Europe." In *The Politics of Memory in Postwar Europe*, ed. Richard Ned Lebow, Wulf Kansteiner, and Claudio Fogu, 1–39. Durham, NC: Duke University Press.

Lee, Felicia R. (2008). "Bench of Memory at Slavery's Gateway." *New York Times*, July 28.

Lee, Nathaniel (2014). "Queen Lane Implosion Brings Nostalgia." *Philadelphia Tribune*, September 15.

Lepore, Jill (2005a). *New York Burning: Liberty, Slavery, and Conspiracy in Eighteenth-Century Manhattan*. New York: Alfred A. Knopf.

——— (2005b). "The Tightening Vise: Slavery and Freedom in British New York." In *Slavery in New York*, ed. Ira Berlin and Leslie M. Harris, 57–90. New York: New Press.

Levine, David (2017). "African American History: A Past Rooted in the Hudson Valley." *Westchester Magazine*, February.

LeVine, Robert A. (1984). "Properties of Culture: An Ethnographic View." In *Culture Theory: Essays on Mind, Self, and Emotion*, ed. Richard A. Schweder and Robert A. LeVine, 67–87. Cambridge: Cambridge University Press.

Levinson, Sanford (1998). *Written in Stone: Public Monuments in Changing Societies*. Durham, NC: Duke University Press.

Lewis, Bernard (1975). *History: Remembered, Recovered, Invented*. Princeton, NJ: Princeton University Press. Reprint, New York: Simon and Schuster, 1987.

Lin, Rachel Chernos (2002). "The Rhode Island Slave-Traders: Butchers, Bakers, and Candlestick-Makers." *Slavery and Abolition* 23 (1): 21–38.

Lind, Jennifer (2008). *Sorry States: Apologies in International Affairs*. Ithaca, NY: Cornell University Press.

Linenthal, Edward Tabor (1993). *Sacred Ground: Americans and Their Battlefields*. Urbana: University of Illinois Press.

Litwack, Charles (1961). *North of Liberty, 1790–1860*. Chicago: University of Chicago Press.

Lovejoy, Paul E. (2010). "The African Background of Venture Smith." In *Venture Smith and the Business of Slavery and Freedom*, ed. James Brewer Stewart, 35–55. Amherst: University of Massachusetts Press.

Lowenthal, David (1998). "Fabricating Heritage." *History and Memory* 10 (1): 5–24.

Lubrano, Alfred (2014). "Blighted 16-story Queen Lane Apts. Imploded in Germantown." *Philadelphia Inquirer*, September 15.

Luo, Michael (2003). "In Manhattan, Another Burial for 400 Colonial-Era Blacks." *New York Times*, October 2.

Macalaster, Gretyl (2013). "More Than 230 Years Later, Portsmouth Slaves Granted Freedom." *New Hampshire Union Leader*, June 10.

Madigan, Tim (2001). *The Burning: Massacre, Destruction, and the Tulsa Race Riot of 1921*. New York: Thomas Dunne Books.

Main, Jackson Turner (1985). *Society and Economy in Colonial Connecticut*. Princeton, NJ: Princeton University Press.

Malcolm, Joyce Lee (2009). *Peter's War: A New England Slave Boy and the American Revolution*. New Haven, CT: Yale University Press.

Manegold, C. S. (2010). *Ten Hills Farm: The Forgotten History of Slavery in the North*. Princeton, NJ: Princeton University Press.

Mayes, Eric (2009). "How to Tell the Story?" *Philadelphia Tribune*, November 21.

McDermott, Deborah (2014). "African Burying Ground Construction Involves Careful Consideration." *Seascoastonline.com*, August 19.

McDuffie, Trenae V. (2013). "Black Human Remains Buried Under Playground." *Philadelphia Tribune*, July 29.

McElya, Micki (2003). "Commemorating the Color Line: The National Mammy Monument Controversy in the 1920s." In *Monuments to the Lost Cause: Women, Art, and the Landscapes of Southern Memory*, ed. Cynthia Mills and Pamela H. Simpson, 203–33. Knoxville: University of Tennessee Press.

——— (2007). *Clinging to Mammy: The Faithful Slave in Twentieth-Century America*. Cambridge, MA: Harvard University Press.

McGill, Joseph (2014). "Miseducation of a Nation." October 27. http://slavedwellingproject.org/the-miseducation-of-a-nation/

——— (2015a). "Slavery in New York." August 30. http://slavedwellingproject.org/2015/08/

——— (2015b). "They Lived Where They Worked." November 16. http://slavedwellingproject .org/they-lived-where-they-worked/

——— (n.d.) "Slaves in the Attic." http://comingtothetable.org/stories/stories-action/slaves -attic/

McManus, Edgar J. (1973). *Black Bondage in the North.* Syracuse, NY: Syracuse University Press.

——— (2001). *A History of Negro Slavery in New York.* Syracuse, NY: Syracuse University Press.

McPherson, James M. (1988). *Battle Cry of Freedom: The Civil War Era.* New York: Oxford University Press.

——— (1997). *For Cause and Comrades: Why Men Fought in the Civil War.* New York: Oxford University Press.

——— (1999). "Was Blood Thicker Than Water? Ethnic and Civic Nationalism in the American Civil War." *Proceedings of the American Philosophical Society* 143 (1): 102–8.

Melish, Joanne Pope (1998). *Disowning Slavery: Gradual Emancipation and "Race" in New England, 1780–1860.* Ithaca, NY: Cornell University Press.

——— (2009). "Recovering (from) Slavery: Four Struggles to Tell the Truth." In *Slavery and Public History,* ed. James Oliver Horton and Lois E. Horton, 103–34. Chapel Hill: University of North Carolina Press.

Middleton, David, and Derek Edwards (1990). "Introduction." In *Collective Remembering,* ed. David Middleton and Derek Edwards, 1–22. London: Sage.

Miles, Tira (2017). *The Dawn of Detroit: A Chronical of Slavery and Freedom in the City of the Straits.* New York: New Press.

Miller, Larry (2010). "The Wait for 'President's House' Finally Over." *Philadelphia Tribune,* December 16.

Minardi, Margot (2010). *Making Slavery History: Abolitionism and the Politics of Memory in Massachusetts.* New York: Oxford University Press.

——— (2012). "Making Slavery Visible (Again): The Nineteenth-Century Roots of a Revisionist Recovery in New England." In *Politics of Memory: Making Slavery Visible in the Public Space,* ed. Ana Lucia Araujo, 92–105. New York: Routledge.

Mires, Charlene (2002). *Independence Hall in American Memory.* Philadelphia: University of Pennsylvania Press.

——— (2009). "Invisible House, Invisible Slavery: Struggles of Public History at Independence National Historical Park." In *Culture and Belonging in Divided Societies: Contestation and Symbolic Landscapes,* ed. Marc Howard Ross, 216–37. Philadelphia: University of Pennsylvania Press.

Mooney, Douglas, and Kimberly Morrell (2013). *Phase IB Archaeological Investigations of the Mother Bethel Burying Ground, 1810–Circa 1864.* Burlington, NJ: Prepared by URS for Pennsylvania Horticultural Society.

Moore, Acel (2002a). "Park Service's Promise on the Slave Flap Is Doubted." *Philadelphia Inquirer,* November 3.

——— (2002b) "Unearth Bitter History of Washington's Slaves." *Philadelphia Inquirer,* April 2.

Morrison, Toni (1989). "A Bench by the Road." *World: Journal of the Unitarian Universalist Association* 3 (1): 4–5, 37–41.

Mosbrucker, Kristen (2012). "Three Possible Grave Sites Discovered at Potter's Field Site in Germantown." *Newsworks.org,* July 13.

Muhammad, Jehron (2014). "Coalition Fights for Historic Burial Ground." *Final Call,* March 13. http://www.finalcall.com/artman/publish/National_News_2/article_101279.shtml.

Nash, Gary B. (1988). *Forging Freedom: The Formation of Philadelphia's Black Community, 1720– 1840.* Cambridge, MA: Harvard University Press.

——— (2004). "For Whom Will the Liberty Bell Toll? From Controversy to Collaboration." *George Wright Forum* 21 (1): 39–52.

———— (2010). *The Liberty Bell.* New Haven, CT: Yale University Press.

Nash, Gary B., and Jean R. Soderlund (1991). *Freedom by Degrees: Emancipation in Pennsylvania and Its Aftermath.* New York: Oxford University Press.

Nell, William C. ([1855] 1968). *The Colored Patriots of the American Revolution.* New York: Arno Press and New York Times.

Nora, Pierre (1989). "Between Memory and History: *Les Lieux de Mémoire.*" *Representations* 26 (Spring): 7–24.

Norton, Anne (2004). *95 Theses on Politics, Culture, and Method.* New Haven, CT: Yale University Press.

O'Brien, Jean M. (2010). *Firsting and Lasting: Writing Indians Out of Existence in New England.* Minneapolis: University of Minnesota Press.

O'Brien, William (1960). "Did the Jennison Case Outlaw Slavery in Massachusetts?" *William and Mary Quarterly* 17 (2): 219–41.

Ogline, Jill (2004). " 'Creating Dissonance for the Visitor': The Heart of the Liberty Bell Controversy." *Public Historian* 26 (3): 49–57.

O'Grady, Joseph (1981). *Pulaski Town: The Evolution of a Black Community.* Philadelphia: Urban Studies and Community Service Center, La Salle College.

Oklahoma Commission to Study the the Tulsa Race Riot of 1921 (2001). *Tulsa Race Riot: A Report.* Oklahoma City: Oklahoma State Government. http://www.okhistory.org/research/forms/freport.pdf

Olick, Jeffrey K. (1999). "Collective Memory: The Two Cultures." *Sociological Theory* 17 (3): 333–48.

Olick, Jeffrey K., and Joyce Robbins (1998). "Social Memory Studies: From 'Collective Memory' to the Historical Sociology of Mnemonic Practices." *Annual Review of Sociology* 24:105–40.

Olick, Jeffrey K., Vered Vinitzky-Seroussi, and Daniel Levy (2011). Introduction to *The Collective Memory Reader,* ed. Jeffrey K. Olick, Vered Vinitzky-Seroussi, and Daniel Levy, 3–62. Oxford: Oxford University Press.

O'Toole, Marjory Gomez (2016). *If Jane Should Want to Be Sold: Stories of Enslavement, Indenture, and Freedom in Little Compton, Rhode Island.* Little Compton, RI: Little Compton Historical Society.

Ottley, Roi, and William J. Weatherby, eds. (1967). *The Negro in New York: An Informal Social History.* New York: New York Public Library; Dobbs Ferry, NY: Oceana.

Paynter, Robert (1994). "Afro-Americans in the Massachusetts Historical Landscape." In *The Politics of the Past,* ed. Peter Gathercole and David Lowenthal, 49–62. London: Routledge.

Phillips, Karin (2008). "Photos Show President's House Site on Independence Mall in a Different Light." *KYW Newsradio,* April 27.

Piersen, William D. (1988). *Black Yankees: The Development of an Afro-American Subculture in Eighteenth-Century New England.* Amherst, MA: University of Massachusetts Press.

Pusey, Grace (2015). "Early Bryn Mawr Black History, 1719–1824." http://blackatbrynmawr.brynmawr.edu/2015/06/09/harriton/.

Quinn, Amy Z. (2013a). "Dissension Arises Among Germantown Neighbors at Potter's Field Meeting." *Newsworks.org,* May 23.

———— (2013b). "No Human Remains Found at Potter's Field Site, Final PHA Decision Pending." *Newsworks.org,* March 20.

Rabinowitz, Richard (2016). *Curating America: Journeys Through Storyscapes of the American Past.* Chapel Hill: University of North Carolina Press.

Ragovin, Helene (2002). "The Untold Story of the Royall House Slaves." *Tufts Journal,* August 20. http://tuftsjournal.tufts.edu/archive/2002/august/calendar/royall2.shtml

Ranger, Terence (1997). "The Invention of Tradition in Colonial Africa." In *Perspectives on Africa: A Reader in Culture, History, and Representation,* ed. Roy Richard Grinker and Christopher B. Steiner, 597–612. Oxford: Blackwell.

Rappleye, Charles (2006). *Sons of Providence: The Brown Brothers, the Slave Trade and the American Revolution.* New York: Simon and Schuster.

Remnick, Noah (2017). "Yale Will Drop John Calhoun's Name from College." *New York Times,* February 11.

Rieff, David (2016). *In Praise of Forgetting: Historical Memory and Its Ironies.* New Haven, CT: Yale University Press.

Robinson, Richard E., prod.-dir. (1988). *Ground Truth: Archaeology in the City.* Silverwood Films.

Rockmore, Ellen Bresler (2015). "How Texas Teaches History." *New York Times,* October 21.

Rollason, David (2016). *The Power of Place: Rulers and Their Palaces, Landscapes, Cities, and Holy Places.* Princeton, NJ: Princeton University Press.

Rosenzweig, Roy, and David Thelen (1998). *The Presence of the Past: Popular Uses of History in American Life.* New York: Columbia University Press.

Ross, Marc Howard (2002). "The Political Psychology of Competing Narratives: September 11 and Beyond." In *Understanding September 11,* ed. Craig Calhoun, Paul Price, and Ashley Timmer, 303–20. New York: New Press.

—— (2007). *Cultural Contestation in Ethnic Conflict.* Cambridge: Cambridge University Press.

—— (2009a). "Cultural Contestation and the Symbolic Landscape: Politics by Other Means?" In *Culture and Belonging in Divided Societies: Contestation and Symbolic Landscapes,* ed. Marc Howard Ross, 1–24. Philadelphia: University of Pennsylvania.

—— (2009b). "Culture in Comparative Political Analysis." In *Comparative Politics: Rationality, Culture, and Structure,* ed. Mark Irving Lichbach and Alan S. Zuckerman, 134–61. 2nd ed. Cambridge: Cambridge University Press.

Rowan, Tommy (2017). "1882: Grave Robbers Sold Black Bodies to Medical College." *Philadelphia Inquirer,* February 26.

Russ, Valerie (2014). "Bethel Burying Ground Meeting Draws Large Crowd." *Philadelphia Inquirer,* May 6.

Saffron, Inga (2006a). "A Historic Site That Has Defied Designers: President's House Memorial." *Philadelphia Inquirer,* September 8.

—— (2006b). "Try This in One High-Profile Memorial: Honor America's First White House, Acknowledge the Stain of Slavery." *Philadelphia Inquirer,* August 24.

Salisbury, Stephan (2002a). "Panel Calls for Slave Commemoration." *Philadelphia Inquirer,* July 10.

—— (2002b). "Proposed Wording on Slave Quarters Draws Fire." *Philadelphia Inquirer,* October 31.

—— (2002c). "Slavery Story to Be Part of Bell Site." *Philadelphia Inquirer,* August 11.

—— (2003a). "Bell's Move Resonates Harmony, Decorum." *Philadelphia Inquirer,* October 10.

—— (2003b). "Design of Liberty Bell Site Criticized." *Philadelphia Inquirer,* January 16.

—— (2003c). "On Moving Day for Bell, Dissent Will be Ringing In." *Philadelphia Inquirer,* September 10.

—— (2004a). "Forum Furthers Memorial to Slaves." *Philadelphia Inquirer,* November 7.

—— (2004b). "Slave Discovery Roils Mall Issue." *Philadelphia Inquirer,* July 4.

—— (2005). "Committee Is Put in Place to Guide Slavery Memorial." *Philadelphia Inquirer,* September 23.

—— (2007a). "Designer Chosen for National Monument." *Philadelphia Inquirer,* February 28.

—— (2007b). "Washington's Slaves Finally Get Full Phila. Burial." *Philadelphia Inquirer,* July 3.

—— (2008a). "City Honors Washington's Slave and 'Power of Archaeology.'" *Philadelphia Inquirer,* February 26.

—— (2008b). "Long-Buried Stories of Slavery Now Heard." *Philadelphia Inquirer,* July 3.

—— (2008c). "Remaking History." *Philadelphia Inquirer*, June 30.

—— (2009a). "Despite Criticism, President's House Project Advances." *Philadelphia Inquirer*, October 10.

—— (2009b). "President's House Design Criticized." *Philadelphia Inquirer*, August 20.

—— (2009c). "Progress Lagging on the President's House Project." *Philadelphia Inquirer*, November 23.

—— (2009d). "2/3 of President's House Contracts to Minorities, Women." *Philadelphia Inquirer*, August 22.

—— (2010a). "Critics Denounce Plans for President's House." *Philadelphia Inquirer*, May 10.

—— (2010b). "President's House—with Memorial to Enslaved Africans—Opens on Independence Mall." *Philadelphia Inquirer*, December 16.

—— (2011). "Glitches Bedevil President's House." *Philadelphia Inquirer*, September 25.

—— (2012a). "Faulty Video Screen at President's House Being Replaced." *Philadelphia Inquirer*, February 29.

—— (2012b). "Problems Still Plague Philadelphia's President's House Memorial." *Philadelphia Inquirer*, August 19.

—— (2013a). "Archaeological Survey of Unmarked Mother Bethel Cemetery Begins This Week." *Philadelphia Inquirer*, May 20.

—— (2013b). "New Group to Challenge Mother Bethel Graveyard Plan." *Philadelphia Inquirer*, December 6.

—— (2013c). "Old Mother Bethel Grave Site Could Hold Thousands." *Philadelphia Inquirer*, July 26.

—— (2013d). "Pastor to Back Preservation of Historic Cemetery." *Philadelphia Inquirer*, May 29.

—— (2014a). "Inadequate Maintenance May Threaten Bethel Burial Ground." *Philadelphia Inquirer*, March 3.

—— (2014b). "New Group Seeks City Action on Burial Ground." *Philadelphia Inquirer*, February 20.

—— (2014c). "President's House Still a Soggy Mess." *Philadelphia Inquirer*, May 23.

—— (2015). "City About to Turn Over the President's House." *Philadelphia Inquirer*, August 18.

—— (2016). "Civil War Museum Transfers Collection to Gettysburg with Constitution Center Exhibit Planned." *Philadelphia Inquirer*, May 4.

Salisbury, Stephan, and Inga Saffron (2002). "Echoes of Slavery at the Liberty Bell Site." *Philadelphia Inquirer*, March 24.

Sammons, Mark J., and Valerie Cunningham (2004). *Black Portsmouth: Three Centuries of African-American Heritage*. Durham: University of New Hampshire Press.

Savage, Kirk (1997). *Standing Soldiers, Kneeling Slaves: Race, War, and Monument in Nineteenth-Century America*. Princeton, NJ: Princeton University Press.

Sawyer, Sean (2005). "Slavery and Servitude at the Pieter Claesen Wyckoff House." In *Slavery in New York*, ed. Ira Berlin and Leslie M. Harris, 54–55. New York: New Press.

Schudson, Michael (1989). "The Present in the Past Versus the Past in the Present." *Communication* 11:105–13.

Schuessler, Jennifer (2015). "Confronting Slavery at Long Island's Oldest Estates." *New York Times*, August 12.

—— (2017). "Princeton Digs Deep int Its Fraught Racial History. *New York Times*, November 6.

Schwartz, Barry (1991). "Social Change and Collective Memory: The Democratization of George Washington." *American Sociological Review* 56 (2): 221–36.

—— (1997). "Collective Memory and History: How Lincoln Became a Symbol of Racial Equality." *Sociological Quarterly* 38 (3): 469–96.

———— (2000). *Abraham Lincoln and the Forge of National Memory.* Chicago: University of Chicago Press.

Schwarz, Philip J., ed. (2001). *Slavery at the Home of George Washington.* Mount Vernon, VA: Mount Vernon Ladies' Association.

Seelye, Katharine Q. (2015). "Rhode Island Church Taking Unusual Step to Illuminate Its Slavery Role." *New York Times*, August 23.

Seitz, Phillip (2014). *Slavery in Philadelphia: A History of Resistance, Denial and Wealth.* Philadelphia: History for Healing.

Shackel, Paul A. (2003). *Memory in Black and White: Race, Commemoration, and the Post-Bellum Landscape.* Walnut Creek, CA: Altamira Press.

Sheldon, George (1893). "Negro Slavery in Old Deerfield." *New England Magazine* 8:49–60.

———— (1895–96). *A History of Deerfield, Massachusetts: The Times When and the People by Whom It Was Settled, Unsettled, and Resettled.* 2 vols. Deerfield, MA: Pocumtuck Valley Memorial Association.

Shipman, Bob (2009). "President's House Commemorative Site Information Meeting for Construction Opportunities Was the Proposed Agenda." Philly1.com, May 7.

Simmons, Ruth (2007). "Hidden in Plain Sight: Slavery and Justice in Rhode Island." In *The Eagle*, 52–62. Cambridge: St John's College, Cambridge University.

Slavery's Buried Past (1996). Videocassette. Bill Kurtis, executive producer; Molly Bedell, producer; David Kutz, director, New York footage. Chicago: Kurtis Productions and Chicago Production Center/WTTW. Originally broadcast December 18, 1996, as a segment of the PBS series *The New Explorers.*

Slobodzian, Joseph A. (2005). "Independence Hall Slavery Memorial Gets Federal Funding." *Philadelphia Inquirer*, September 6.

Smith, Jennifer (2015). "Event Notes Boston's History of Slavery." *Boston Globe*, August 23,

Smith, Martin H. (1905). "Reminiscences of Old Negro Slave Days: The Story of Old 'Ti,' a Connecticut Slave in Revolutionary Times" and "Old Slave Days in Connecticut." *Connecticut Magazine* 9:145–53 and 753–63.

———— (1906). "Old Slave Days in Connecticut." *Connecticut Magazine* 10:113–28 and 319–31.

Smith, Michelle R. (2014). "Showing North's Role in Slavery." *Philadelphia Inquirer*, November 28.

Smith, Venture (1798). *A Narrative of the Life and Adventures of Venture, a Native of Africa: But Resident Above Sixty Years in the United States of America.* New London, CT: C. Holt, at the Bee-Office.

Stackhouse, Eugene Glenn (2003). "Germantown's Potter's Field." *Germantown Crier* 53 (1): 25–27.

Stanton, Lucia (2012). *"Those Who Labor for My Happiness": Slavery at Thomas Jefferson's Monticello.* Charlottesville: University of Virginia Press and the Thomas Jefferson Institute.

Staples, Brent (1999). "Unearthing a Riot." *New York Times Magazine*, December 19.

———— (2001). "To Be a Slave in Brooklyn." *New York Times*, June 24.

———— (2005). "A Convenient Amnesia About Slavery." *New York Times*, December 15.

Stewart, James Brewer, ed. (2010). *Venture Smith and the Business of Slavery and Freedom.* Amherst: University of Massachusetts Press.

Strausbaugh, Linda, Joshua Suhl, Craig O'Connor, and Heather Nelson (2010). "The Genomics Perspective on Venture Smith: Genetics, Ancestry, and the Meaning of Family." In *Venture Smith and the Business of Slavery and Freedom*, ed. James Brewer Stewart, 207–30. Amherst: University of Massachusetts Press.

Sugrue, Thomas J. (2008). *Sweet Land of Liberty: The Struggle for Civil Rights in the North.* New York: Random House.

Swarns, Rachel L. (2016). "272 Slaves Were Sold to Save Georgetown: What Does It Owe Their Descendants?" *New York Times*, April 16.

Sweet, John Wood (2003). *Bodies Politic: Negotiating Race in the American North, 1730–1830.* Baltimore: Johns Hopkins University.

Takezawa, Yasuko I. (1995). *Breaking the Silence: Redress and Japanese American Ethnicity.* Ithaca, NY: Cornell University Press.

Taylor, Kate (2011). "The Thorny Path to a National Black Museum." *New York Times,* January 22.

Teicher, Stacy A., and Walter H. Robinson (2003). "The Other Side of Liberty." *Christian Science Monitor,* July 3.

Tomek, Beverly C. (2011). *Colonization and Its Discontents: Emancipation, Emigration, and Antislavery in Antebellum Pennsylvania.* New York: New York University Press.

Trouillot, Michel-Rolph (1995). *Silencing the Past: Power and the Production of History.* Boston: Beacon Press.

Verba, Sidney (1961). *Small Groups and Political Behavior: A Study of Leadership.* Princeton, NJ: Princeton University Press.

Vivian, Bradford (2010). *Public Forgetting: The Rhetoric and Politics of Beginning Again.* University Park: Pennsylvania State University Press.

Vlach, John Michael (2005). "Slave Housing in New York's Countryside." In *Slavery in New York,* ed. Ira Berlin and Leslie M. Harris, 72–73. New York: New Press.

Volkan, Vamik D. (1988). *The Need to Have Enemies and Allies: From Clinical Practice to International Relationships.* Northvale, NJ: Jason Aronson.

——— (1997). *Bloodlines: From Ethnic Pride to Ethnic Terrorism.* New York: Farrar, Straus and Giroux.

Waldstreicher, David (2004). *Runaway America: Benjamin Franklin, Slavery and the American Revolution.* New York: Hill and Wang.

Warner, W. Lloyd (1959). *The Living and the Dead: A Study of the Symbolic Life of Americans.* New Haven, CT: Yale University Press.

Warren, Wendy (2016). *New England Bound: Slavery and Colonization in Early America.* New York: Liveright Publishing.

Warrington, Karen (2007). "Commentary: Tell Slaves' Story Truthfully." *Philadelphia Inquirer,* December 14.

Washington, Linn, Jr. (2002). "Park Service Burying a Shameful Fact." *Philadelphia Tribune,* April 2.

——— (2010). "Facing Facts from Timbuktu to Center City." *Philadelphia Tribune,* May 11.

Waters, Kenny (2006) "Finding Black Contractors." *Philadelphia Tribune,* July 8.

Weller Robb, and Grossman, Gary, executive producers (1999). *The Night Tulsa Burned.* Documentary produced by Weller/Grossman Productions for the History Channel's *In Search of History* series.

Wertsch, James V., and Henry L. Roediger III (2008). "Collective Memory: Conceptual Foundations and Theoretical Approaches." *Memory* 16 (3): 318–26.

White, Shane (1991). *Somewhat More Independent: The End of Slavery in New York City, 1770–1810.* Athens: University of Georgia Press.

——— (1995). "Slavery in New York State in the Early Republic." *Australasian Journal of American Studies* 14 (2): 1–29.

Wilder, Craig Steven (2013). *Ebony and Ivy: Race, Slavery, and the Troubled History of America's Universities.* New York: Bloomsbury Press.

Wilkins, Robert L. (2016). *Long Road to Hard Truth: The 100-Year Mission to Create the National Museum of African American History and Culture.* Washington, DC: Proud Legacy Publishing.

Wilson, Kendall (2003). "Park Project Will Recognize U.S. Slave Era." *Philadelphia Tribune,* January 17.

Winter, Jay, and Emmanuel Sivan (1999). "Setting the Framework." In *War and Remembrance in the Twentieth Century*, ed. Jay Winter and Emmanuel Sivan, 6–39. Cambridge: Cambridge University Press.

Wright, Roberta Hughes, and Wilbur B. Hughes III (1996). *Lay Down Body: Living History in African American Cemeteries*. Detroit: Visible Ink Press.

Yamin, Rebecca (2008). *Digging in the City of Brotherly Love: Stories from Philadelphia Architecture*. New Haven, CT: Yale University Press.

Young, James E. (1993). *The Texture of Memory: Holocaust Memorials and Meaning*. New Haven, CT: Yale University Press.

Yuhl, Stephanie E. (2013). "Hidden in Plain Sight: Centering the Domestic Slave Trade in American Public History." *Journal of Southern History* 79 (3): 593–624.

Zauzmer, Julie (2017). "Grappling with Its History of Slavery, Georgetown Gathers Descendants for a Day of Repentance." *Washington Post*, April 18.

Zernike, Kate (2001). "Slave Traders in Yale's Past Fuel Debate on Restitution." *New York Times*, August 13.

Zerubavel, Eviatar (2006). *The Elephant in the Room: Silence and Denial in Everyday Life*. Oxford: Oxford University Press.

Zerubavel, Yael (1995). *Recovered Roots: Collective Memory and the Making of Israeli National Tradition*. Chicago: University of Chicago Press.

Zilversmit, Arthur (1967). *The First Emancipation: The Abolition of Slavery in the North*. Chicago: University of Chicago Press.

Index

Acknowledgments

Many people helped me in this project in many ways, and in some cases I regret that I do not know their names, so I can only thank them indirectly. I want to especially mention Michael Coard and the members of Avenging the Ancestors Coalition (ATAC) for both the help and friendship they offered. I also want to thank the many people who spent time with me explaining their perspective on the President's House/Slavery Memorial conflict and the other conflicts I write about here: including Clay Armbrister, Terry Buckalew, Joe Certaine, Peter DiCarlo, John Dowell, Lauren Dougherty, Doris Fanelli, Michelle Flamer, Lisa Hopkins, Germaine Ingram, Emanuel Kelly, Emma Lapsansky-Werner, Ed Lawler, Donald Leland, Jed Levin, Ron McCoy, Joseph McGill, Roz McPherson, Randall Miller, Cynthia MacLeod, Louis Massiah, Joe Nicholson, Richard Rabinowitz, Sacaree Rhodes, Stephan Salisbury, Karen Warrington, and David Young. Among those people who read some or all of the manuscript at various stages, I wish to thank are David Karen, Michael Rock, Randall Miller, and Mark Wolfgram provided detailed comments on the entire manuscript. In addition, Ed Linenthal, Bob Washington, Sharon Ullman, Michael Zuckerman, David Waldstreicher, Joanne Melish, and Terry Buckalew provided helpful ideas after reading some or all of the manuscript. I owe special thanks to Pamela Haag for particularly careful and thoughtful editing as well as myriad useful suggestions. At the University of Pennsylvania Press, I want to especially thank editor-in-chief Peter Agree for his strong support and many thoughtful ideas and suggestions that significantly improved the organization and arguments I offer here, from the time he first heard about this project through its completion. As always, Noreen O'Connor-Abel did a superb job in guiding the book through the production stage, offering many carefully considered, thoughtful, and detailed editorial suggestions.

I also want to add a special shout-out to Natalie Mankoff, our charming granddaughter, who asked me a lot of questions about the book a few months before she turned seven. When I told her, I had a completed first draft and was going to edit and rewrite many things in the next round, she solemnly explained to me, "You know, Gramps, I know that editing and rewriting anything several times *always* makes it better." How sweet and how true coming from a person of any age.

Last, as always, I want to thank the love of my life, Katherine Conner, who not only read early drafts of the chapters, but also patiently heard me go on endlessly about what I was reading and thinking about as this project progressed. She also accompanied me on every road trip we took for this research and shared her thoughts and reactions to each site we visited helping me articulate my own ideas much more clearly than I would have otherwise. I am very lucky.